AF592943

PRESS RELEASE

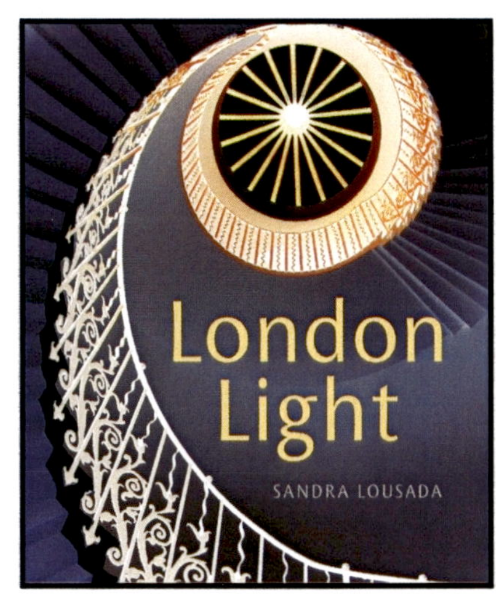

LONDON LIGHT

by

Sandra Lousada

London Light is Sandra's love letter to London – a celebration of a great city.

Over the course of a long career Sandra Lousada has worked as a theatre photographer, a portrait photographer and in the worlds of fashion, beauty and advertising, becoming internationally renowned in all those areas.

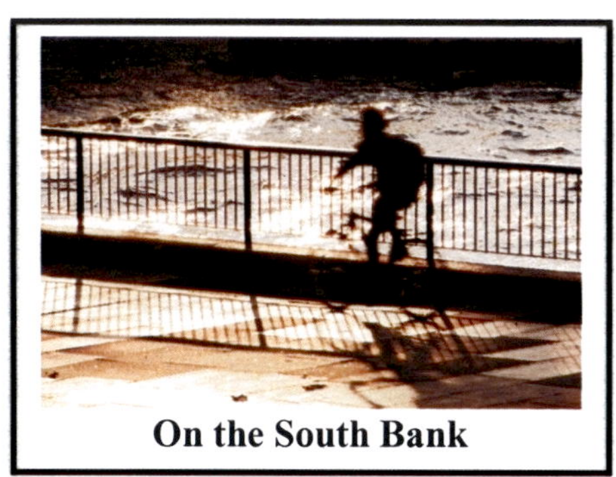

On the South Bank

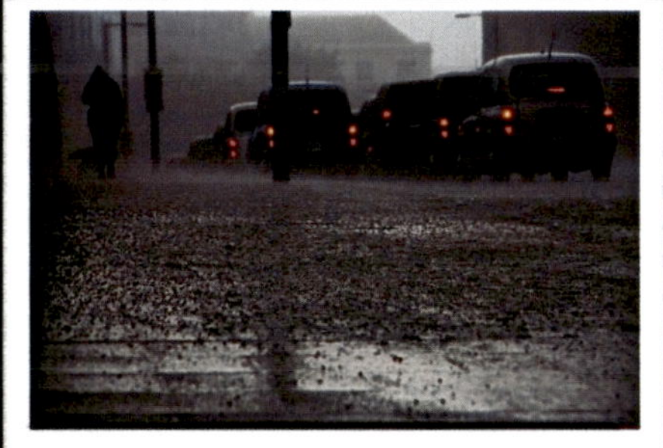

Taxis on Bishop's Bridge Road, queuing for Paddington Station

In her sixties she became fascinated by the new medium of digital photography and the way it could enable her to capture light, movement and colour; and she found a new subject in London, the city she has lived in and loved all her life. Her inspired photographs open our eyes to London as we have never seen it before.

£25 Hardback
Publication date: 2nd September 2010

For further information, please contact:
Emma O'Bryen, Frances Lincoln Publicity
Tel: 020 7619 0098
E: eobr@blueyonder.co.uk

FRANCES LINCOLN LIMITED
PUBLISHERS
4 Torriano Mews Torriano Avenue
London NW5 2RZ
Telephone: 020 7284 4009 Fax: 020 7485 0490
email: reception@frances-lincoln.com
www.franceslincoln.com

London Light

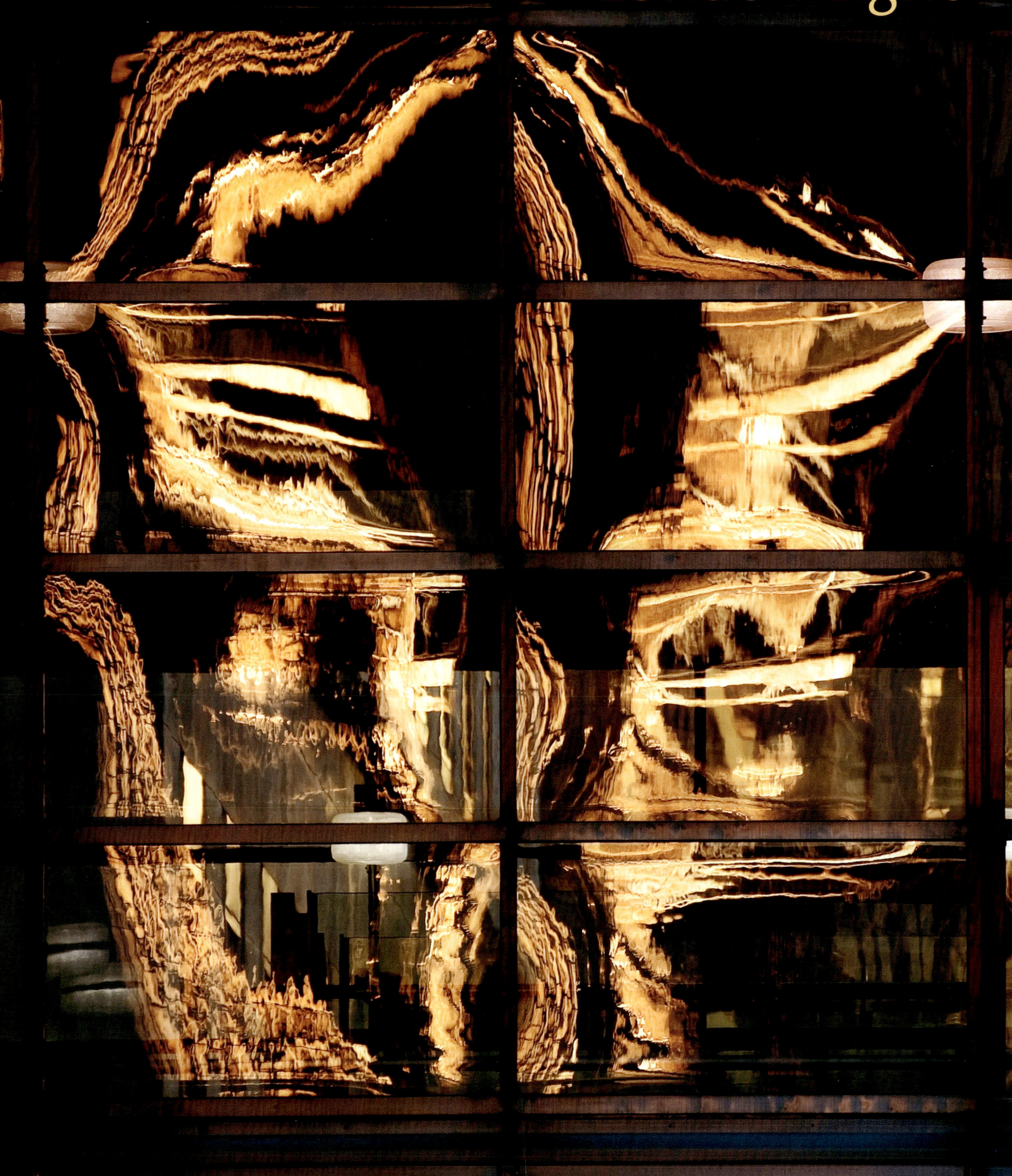

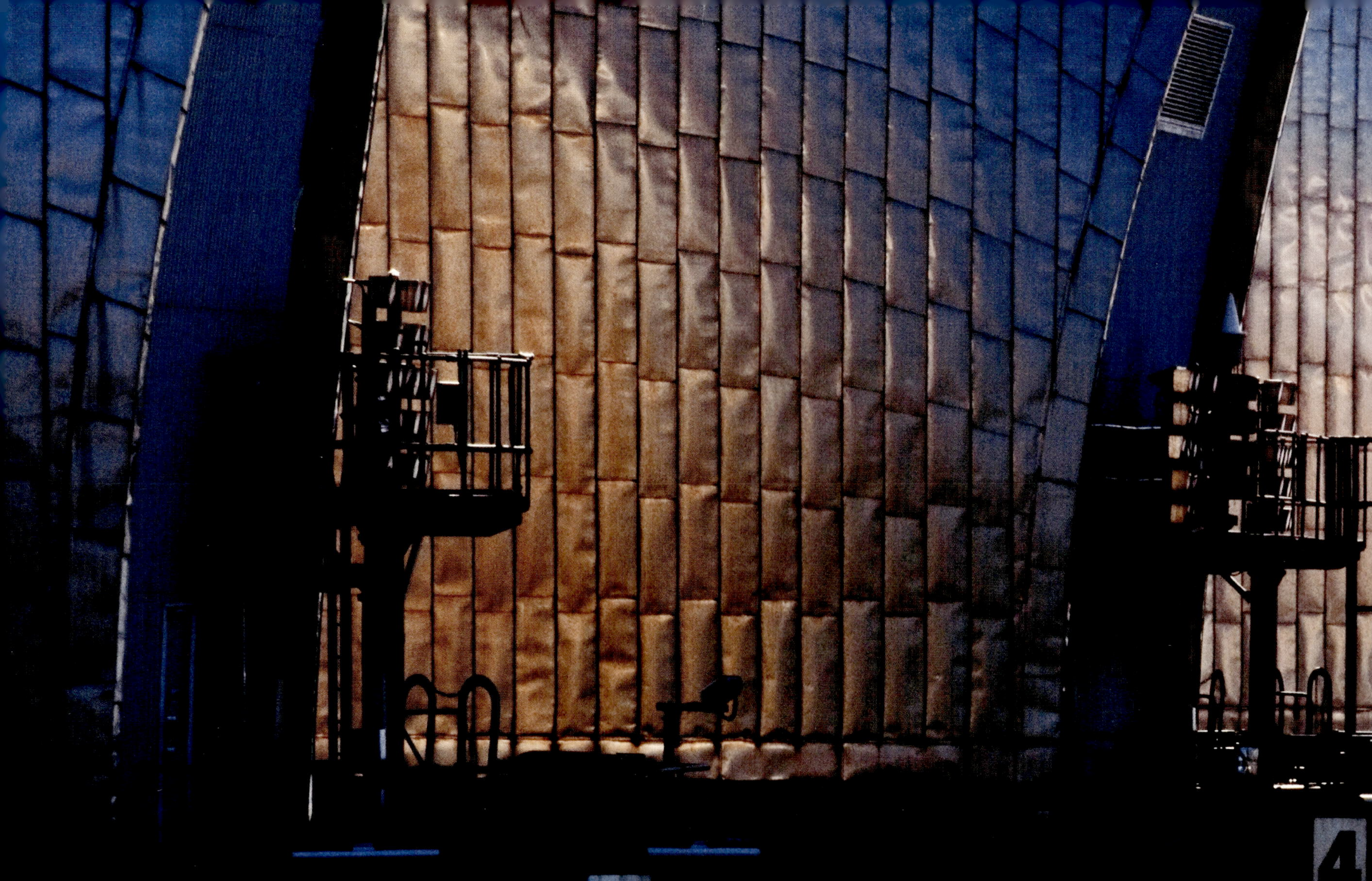
3
4

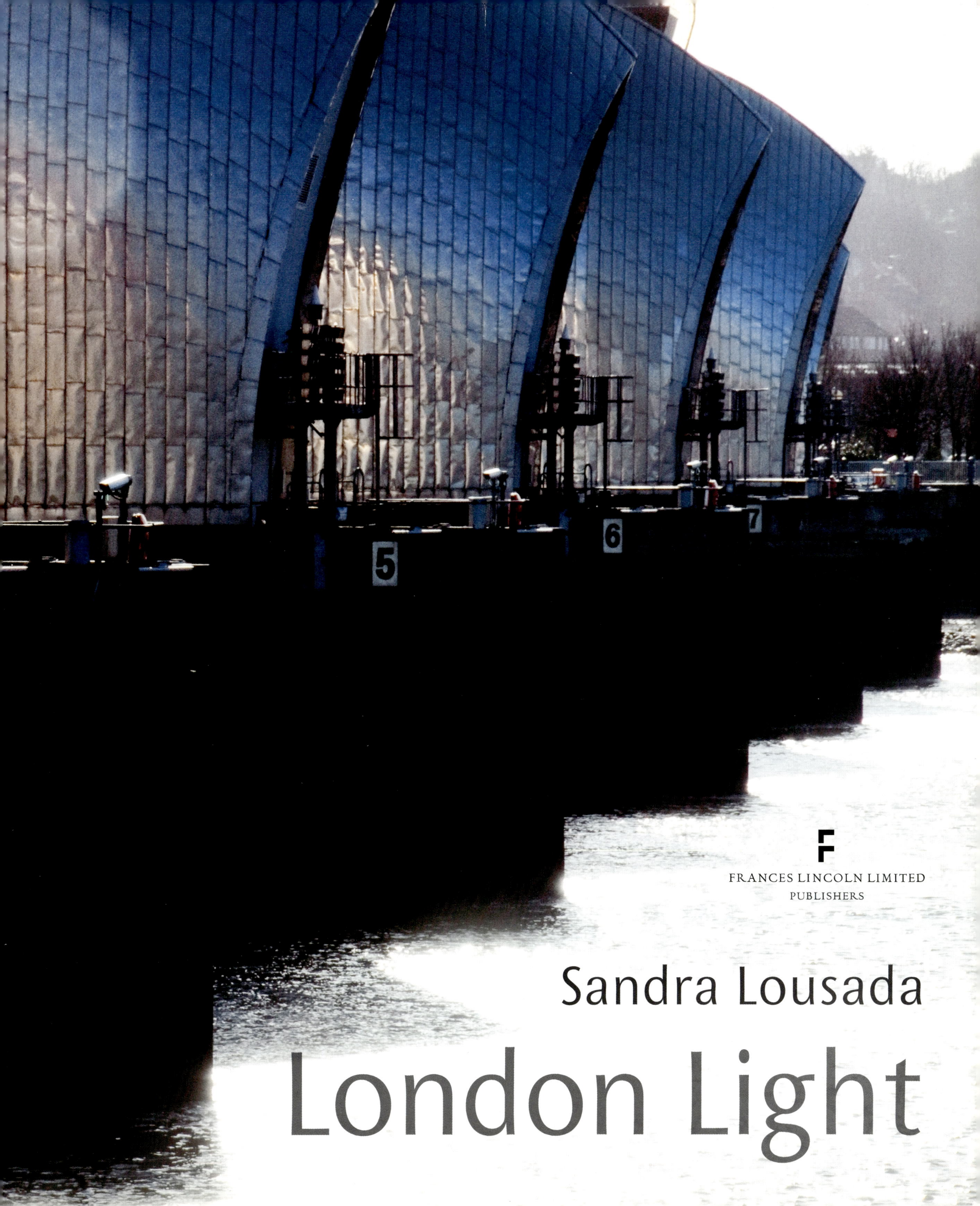

F
FRANCES LINCOLN LIMITED
PUBLISHERS

Sandra Lousada

London Light

This book is for Brian, who encouraged me to explore.

Frances Lincoln Ltd
4 Torriano Mews
Torriano Avenue
London NW5 2RZ
www.franceslincoln.com

First Frances Lincoln edition 2010

A catalogue record for this book is available from the British Library.

ISBN 978-0-7112-3066-8

Printed and bound in China

9 8 7 6 5 4 3 2 1

Half-title page Sunset reflected through windows on Canary Wharf's South Colonnade
Title page The Thames Barrier
Right Paddington Basin at night

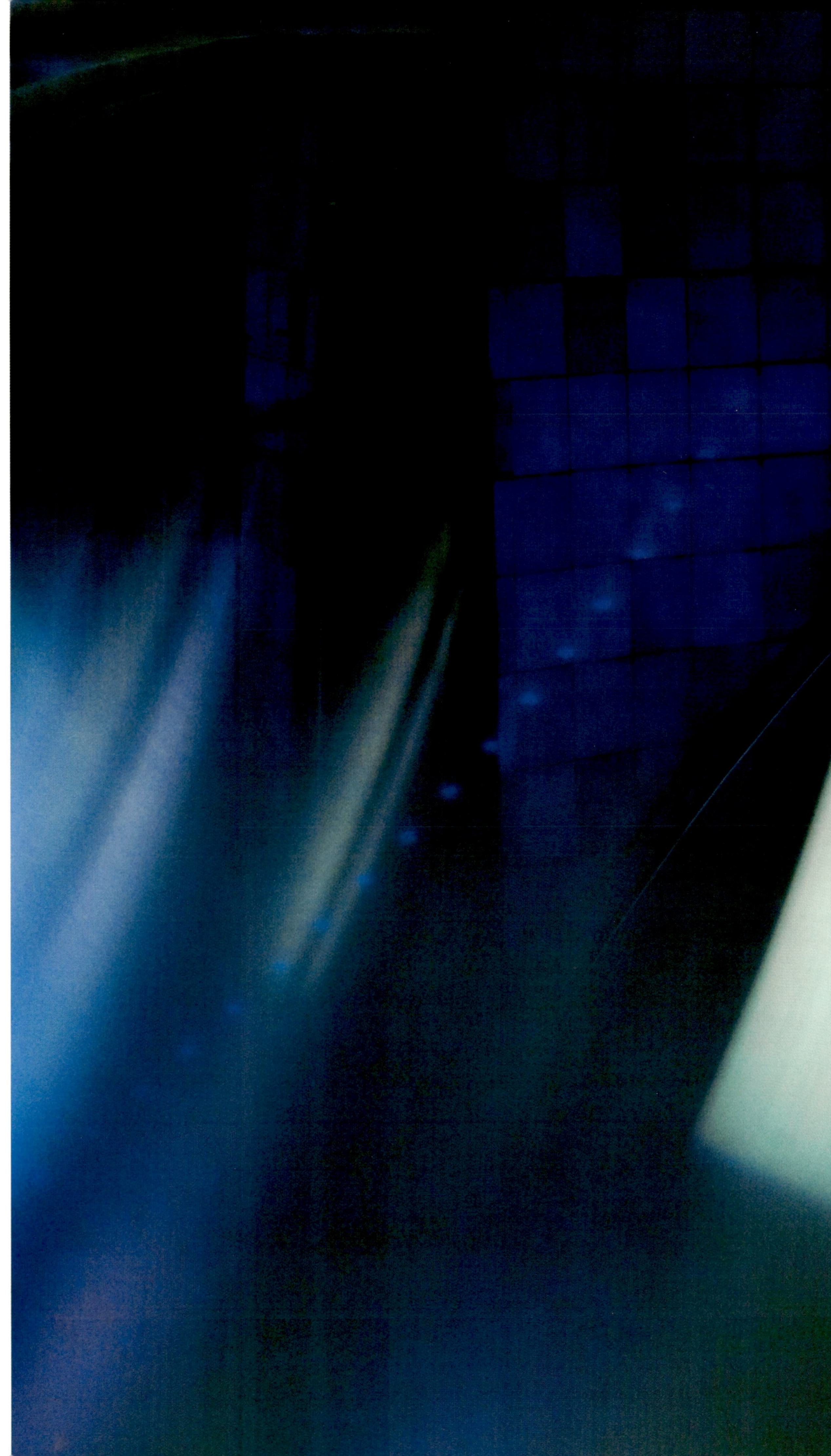

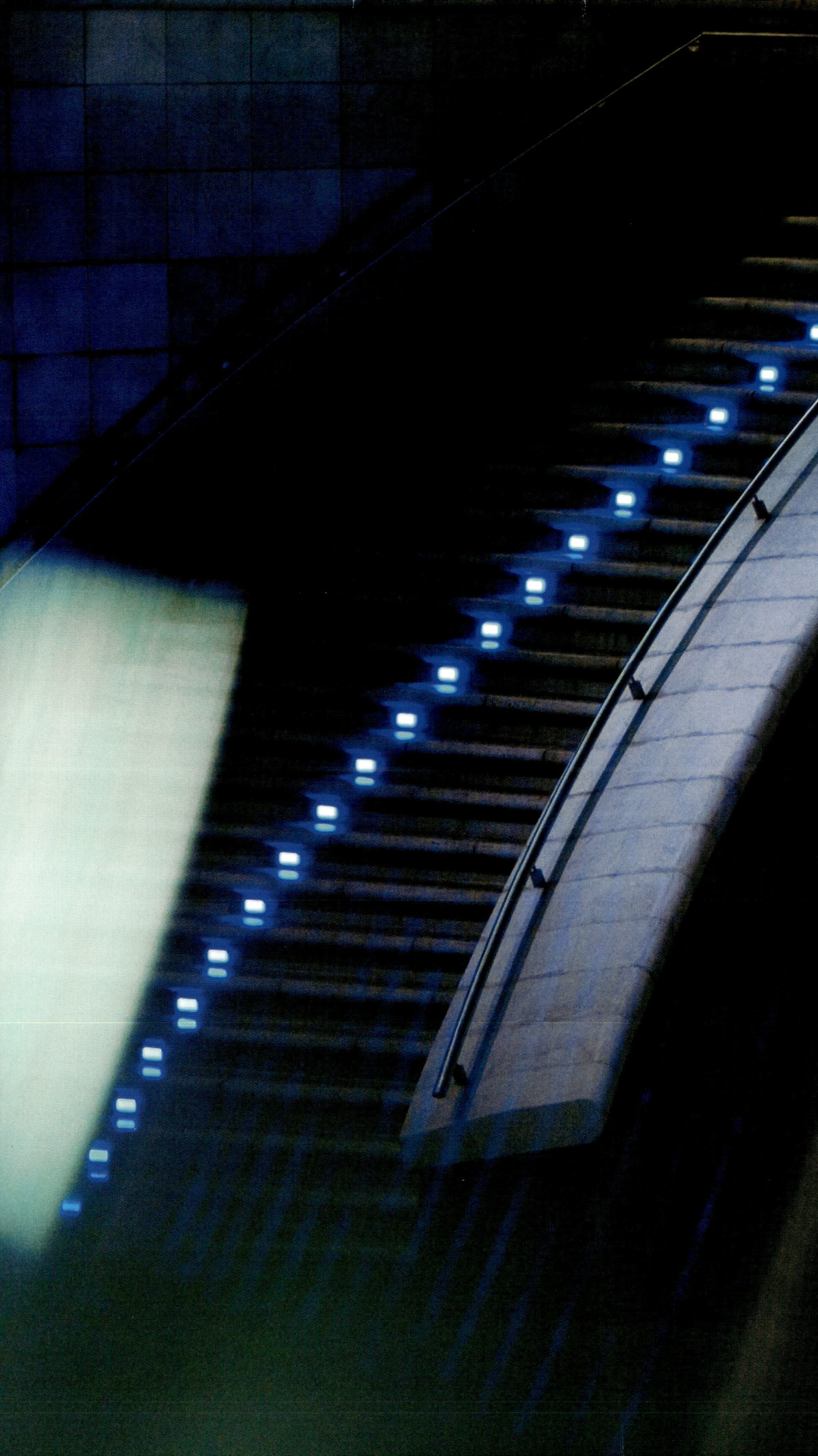

Contents

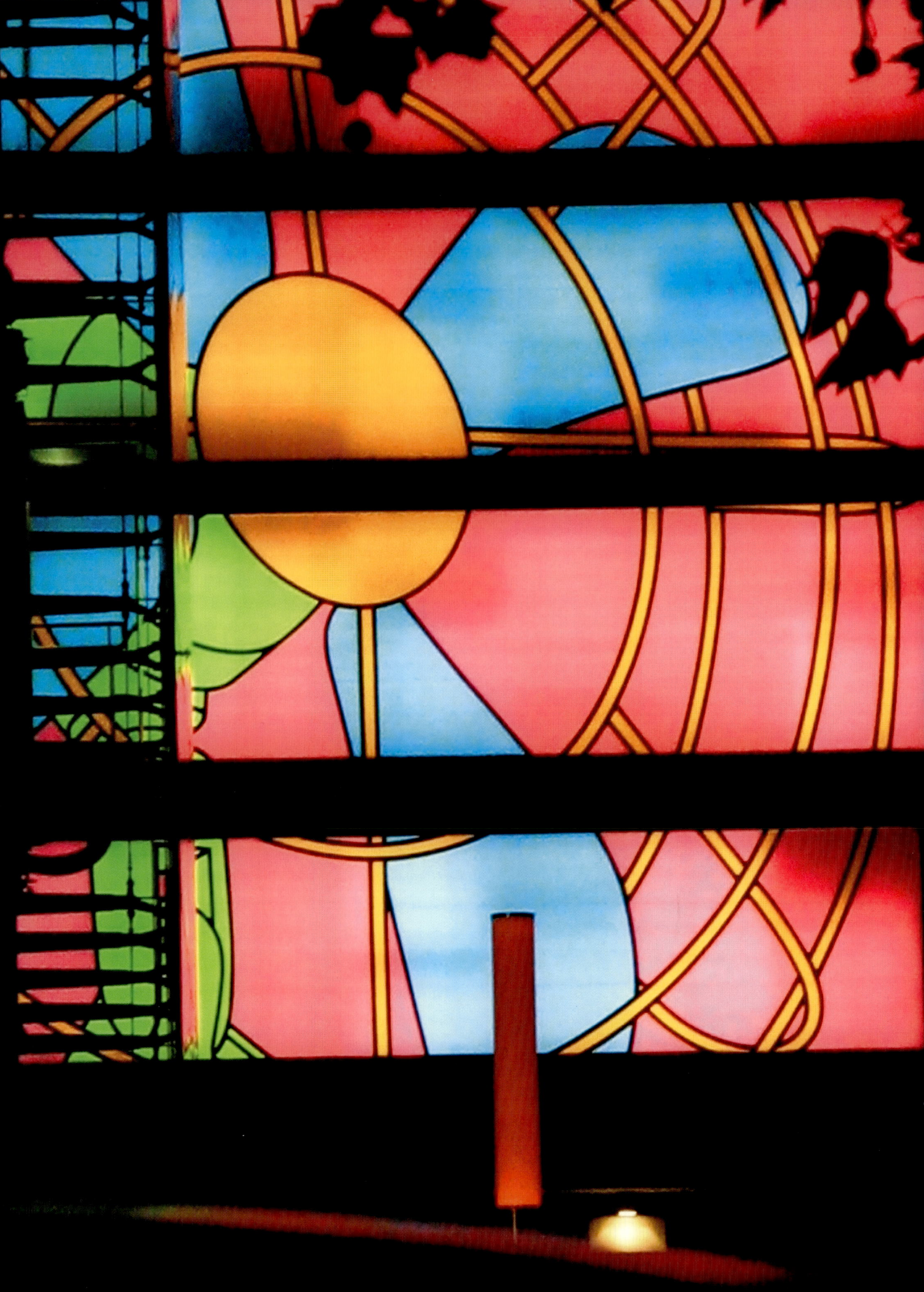

London Light

I began to take these photographs of London when I embarked on a postgraduate course in 2004 at St Martin's School of Art. My main intention was to give myself a concentrated period of time to learn to work with a digital camera. Until then I had always worked on 35mm and medium-format film cameras and I was curious to explore the differences between using film and digital. But I was also hoping for the space to start photographing London the way I saw it when I was moving around the city. This was a project that had been in my mind for some time.

London is a city I know well. I was born in London and I have lived here, and loved living here, all my life. With this project I was trying to find a way to express what I felt and saw as I drove, walked or cycled around the city. It changes all the time with the seasons and the time of day: at sunrise and in the evening, in artificial as well as natural light. Reflections have always interested me, as has the way big modern grey monster buildings become completely transformed by artificial lighting in the dark, or sometimes by hard sunlight and turbulent skies. Nothing stays still. Every day the scene changes, made more dramatic by the weather, and I love not knowing what is coming next.

These photographs were largely taken in the middle of London, from the Thames Barrier to Chelsea, mostly around the river. 'Light and water' was the brief I gave myself, to try and keep my brain and eye on one track. I started with photographs of the buildings and places I like to take my grandchildren to see on night-time drives through the city when it's lit up, looking beautiful and strangely different from daytime; or at Christmas with the garlands of white, blue or multicoloured lights that are everywhere; sometimes in the wind and rain, and once or twice in a fog.

The house I grew up in was by the Thames at Chiswick, and that was where I first became aware of light and water – the two, in the beginning, barely divisible. I spent a lot of time on the river (and quite often fell in it). Flawless blue skies and eternal sunshine have never held my interest, but I will go a long way to find thundery clouds and the intense sunlight after a storm where everything is glistening from the rain.

Later, when I began work as a photographer, I spent a great deal of time looking at the way things were lit. The lighting was a vital element in every photograph, to the extent that I found it almost impossible to take a portrait of someone if I hadn't got the light right. I never used the same lighting on two consecutive or similar jobs and I would always use daylight if possible. I still think that working with available light is nearly always more interesting than anything you can do with artificial light.

Movement too has often been important in my photographs and in this series I have explored it to the limit. I didn't set out deliberately to move the camera, or to make the photographs abstract. In the beginning it was as much as anything the rough winter weather buffeting the hand-held camera that made them what they were.

In 2005 my husband, Brian, died and, looking back, I can see how clearly these photographs were influenced by losing him. And even more, in some miraculous way, by the journey of our life together, a sort of merging of my vision and our different passions, his for transport and architecture, mine for photography.

In the winter months that followed his death I couldn't sleep, so I would drive around London in the middle of the night, quite often in strong winds and rain. Every so often something would catch my eye and I'd get out of the car and struggle to see what I had noticed and try to work out how to record it. Often, to start with, I found myself photographing a bus or a series of traffic lights or a train on a bridge in the rain, probably because I was so used to following a new tram or bus route while Brian tried them out. My children called these my crying pictures. It took me a long time to turn my eyes to the other subjects that were all around me.

Mural on the Euston Road

I was working mostly with a 70–200mm zoom and a Nikon D200, and then graduated to a Nikon D300; no tripod (to leave myself a quick escape route if I felt threatened or about to be accosted by a policeman), long exposures, up to one second or more. The wind shook the lens and the rain soaked the camera, so the elements and the movement of the lenses during the exposure formed the end result. Nothing new in that, other photographers before me have used effects of this kind, but this was the first time I had tried it. I could see by checking the screen (the best thing about digital) whether what I was trying to capture was coming through, and slowly I began to take pictures that reflected what I was feeling at that moment. It didn't always work and quite a few times I came home with nothing worth keeping. But now and then there was a good one and that gave me the courage to continue until I had a series of photographs that were starting to work together.

Keeping on with a project that is not going well is hell. It takes immense effort and hard work to pull oneself through the barrier of bad pictures: a sort of photographer's block. Learning that how you are feeling can be such an influence on how you see things is chastening. Even tougher is the realization that you can make a really bad job of something wonderful simply by not concentrating one hundred per cent on what's in front of you.

Working like this was the complete opposite of the methodical concentration I had needed when working on an advertising campaign, to make sure I had covered all the points in my brief. There was, of course, a professional satisfaction in being able to do that well and with enjoyment, but eventually I reached my limit. I began to feel like an automaton without a vision, especially when digital arrived and art directors had even more immediate hands-on control over my photographs. I felt I had become just a technician, and one who had gone rather past her sell-by date.

Now I had to shed the accumulated knowledge of all those years of careful advance planning and learn again just to go for whatever I saw, taking a chance and not minding feeling insecure, even nervous, putting myself on the line just as I had at twenty-one when I first began to earn my living as a photographer. In those days I had very little technical know-how and everything was done on a wing and a prayer. It was much the same at the beginning of this project.

I learnt again to react fast to what suddenly appeared out of the blue in front of me. Stopping to use a Polaroid would have meant that I missed almost every shot I wanted to take. At the beginning, more often than not, I did miss them. Trying to look into the subject of the moment with more depth took some time. What was it that had caught my eye? I didn't plan anything about the way they would look, or the style. I just went out with the subject in my mind, in a rather numb daze, to try to divert my thoughts and loneliness away from the negative of loss into something positive.

I have never been the kind of photographer who is ruled by the need for pin-sharp pictures. For this project I have mostly worked on long lenses with a low f/stop. I found I could push myself farther faster because I could see so quickly what I'd captured. The thrill of coming home with a good image was all the more intense for seeing it so quickly.

After all my years of photographing people in studios and on location, I am now working mostly out of doors, carrying a small amount of inconspicuous equipment, completely on my own. No more the big gang of assistants, stylists, models, clients. It's a new experience, quite lonely sometimes, but very satisfying to know that you and only you are the person responsible for your image.

The photographs in this book are completely and utterly different from anything I have ever done before. I had no idea that this would be so when I started. There is nothing about them that would tell you what sort of pictures I took during the decades when I was doing commercial and editorial work. My technical knowledge was gained over the years by trial and error and learning to be methodical in my approach.

But – and I now know it's a very large but – after a while this sort of work conditions your eye and way of thinking and, more importantly, looking. I have taken a long time to regain my instincts of the moment, to learn to grab what I'm looking at and not stop myself taking the picture because something isn't quite perfect, to find a way to make it work. What I look for is energy, light and movement, captured just as it is and, if possible, without any alteration.

Of course, with the advent of digital it is easy to alter anything. But I feel that in today's search for computerized perfection, a lot of photographs have lost their way and become static, over-controlled and dead. Because we have so many tools at our disposal, there is a tendency to smooth out all the life and energy. Maybe this is just a fashion of the moment. I hope so. I too have fallen into this trap, and probably will again, but the photographs in this series have not been digitally altered – they have simply been adjusted to make as good a print as possible, just as I would have done with a film. Otherwise, they are as they were shot, no manipulation in the way of taking things out or putting them in. Sometimes I have increased the contrast a bit, and the saturation, but nothing else.

I still love to take pictures, whatever medium I use. All that matters is getting a good photograph. For me digital has one major advantage over film: its ability to show you then and there what you've just taken. And, of course, no budget is required for film and processing. When I was about two-thirds of the way through this project, I realized I would never have been able to do it with film; the cost would have been astronomical. But that will not stop me working on film in the future if it is the more suitable medium for what I am trying to do.

But whatever you use, the biggest thrill of all is to know that once in a while you have captured what you saw and felt in front of you, at one moment in time. The camera, the medium, the print quality are all important to the final picture, but they can't, on their own, make a good photograph. For that, the good image has to be there in the beginning.

Sandra Lousada, March 2010

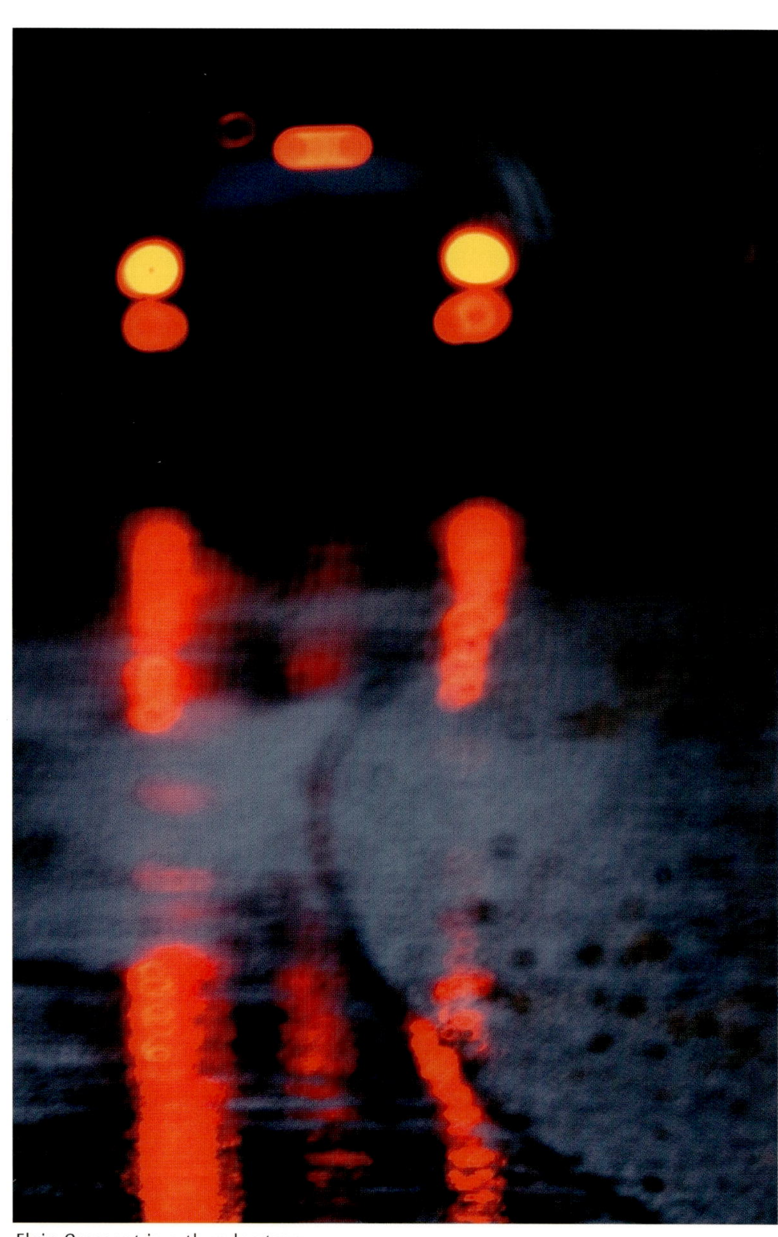

Elgin Crescent in a thunderstorm
Above Car lights reflected

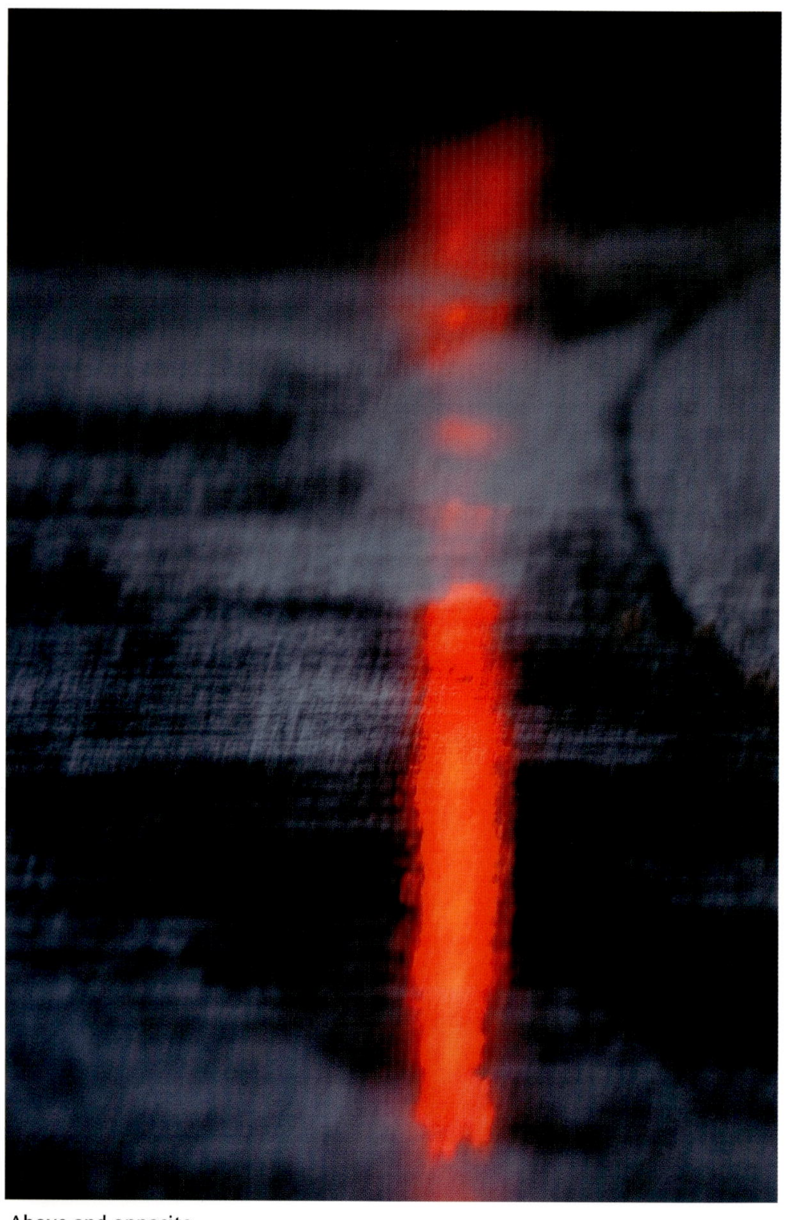

Above and opposite
Traffic light reflections

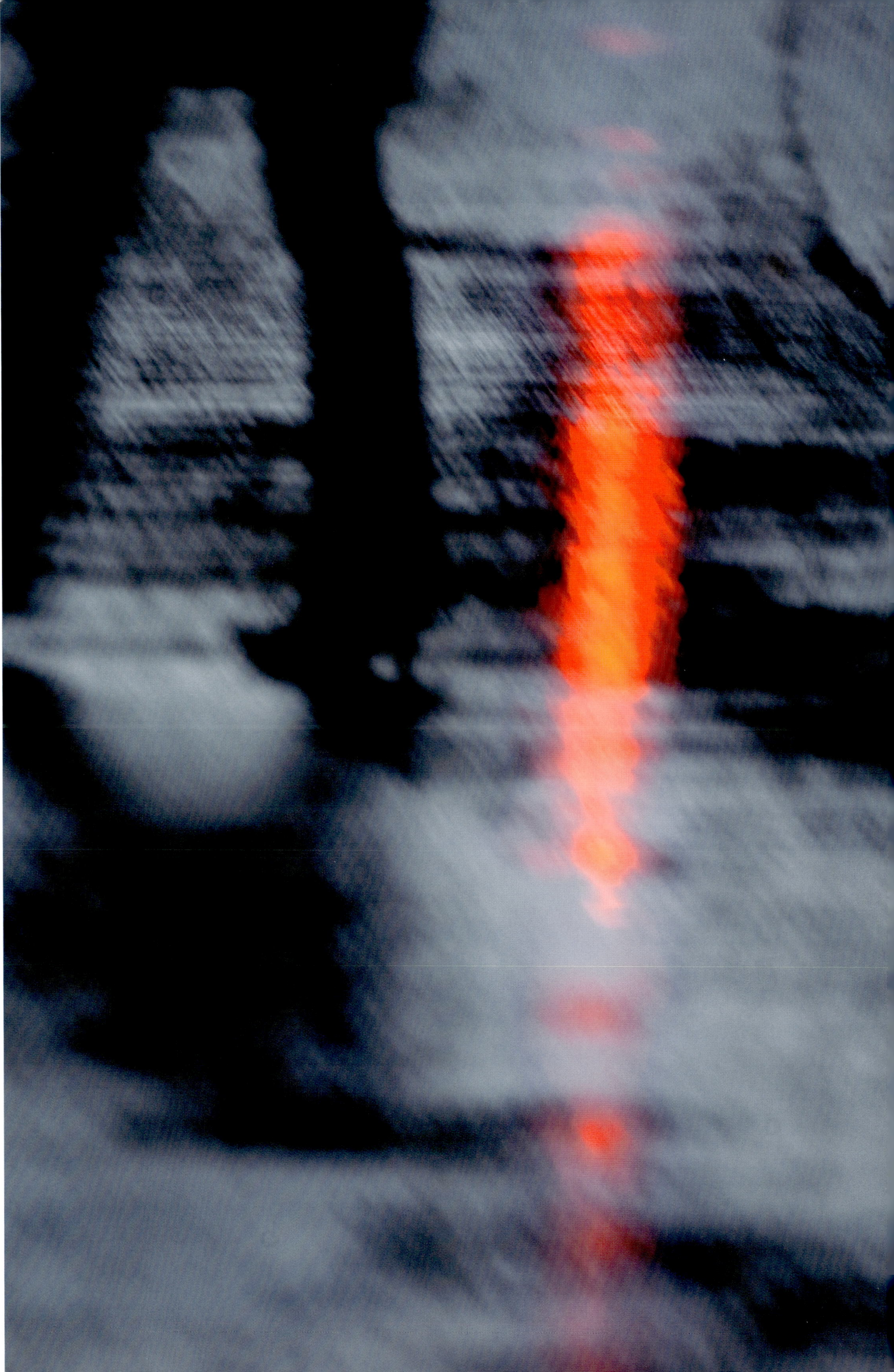

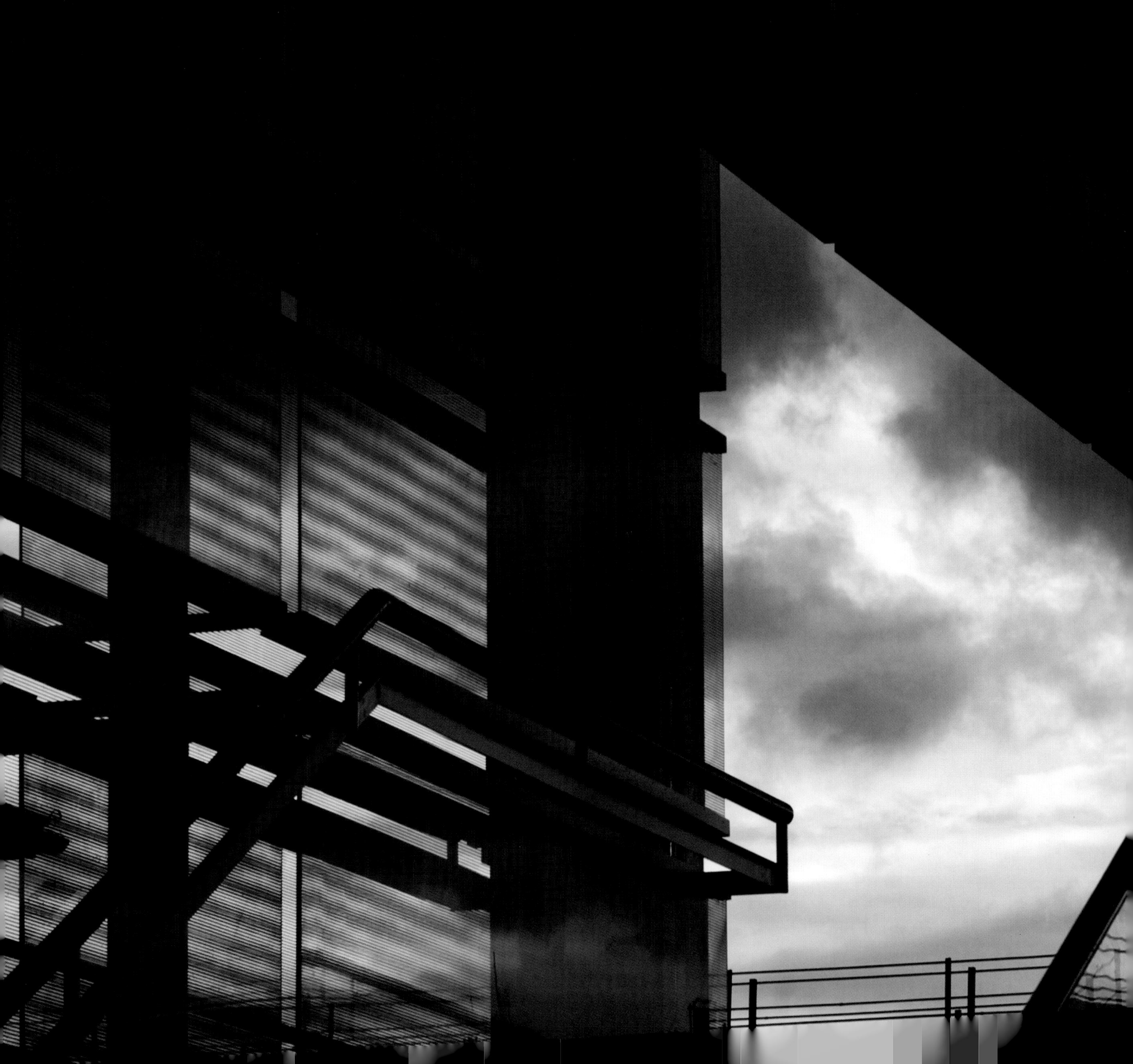

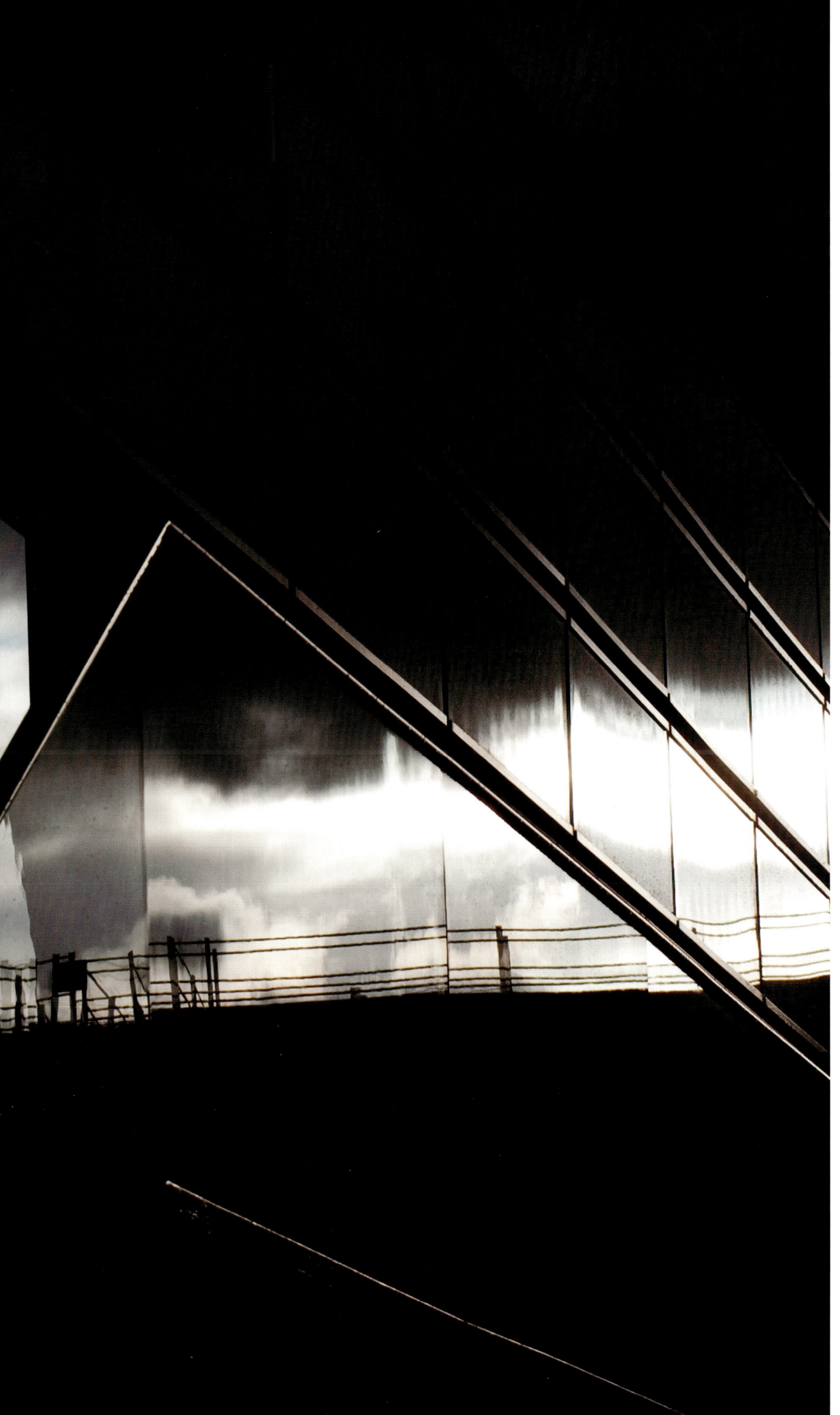

Paddington Basin footbridge
and an office block

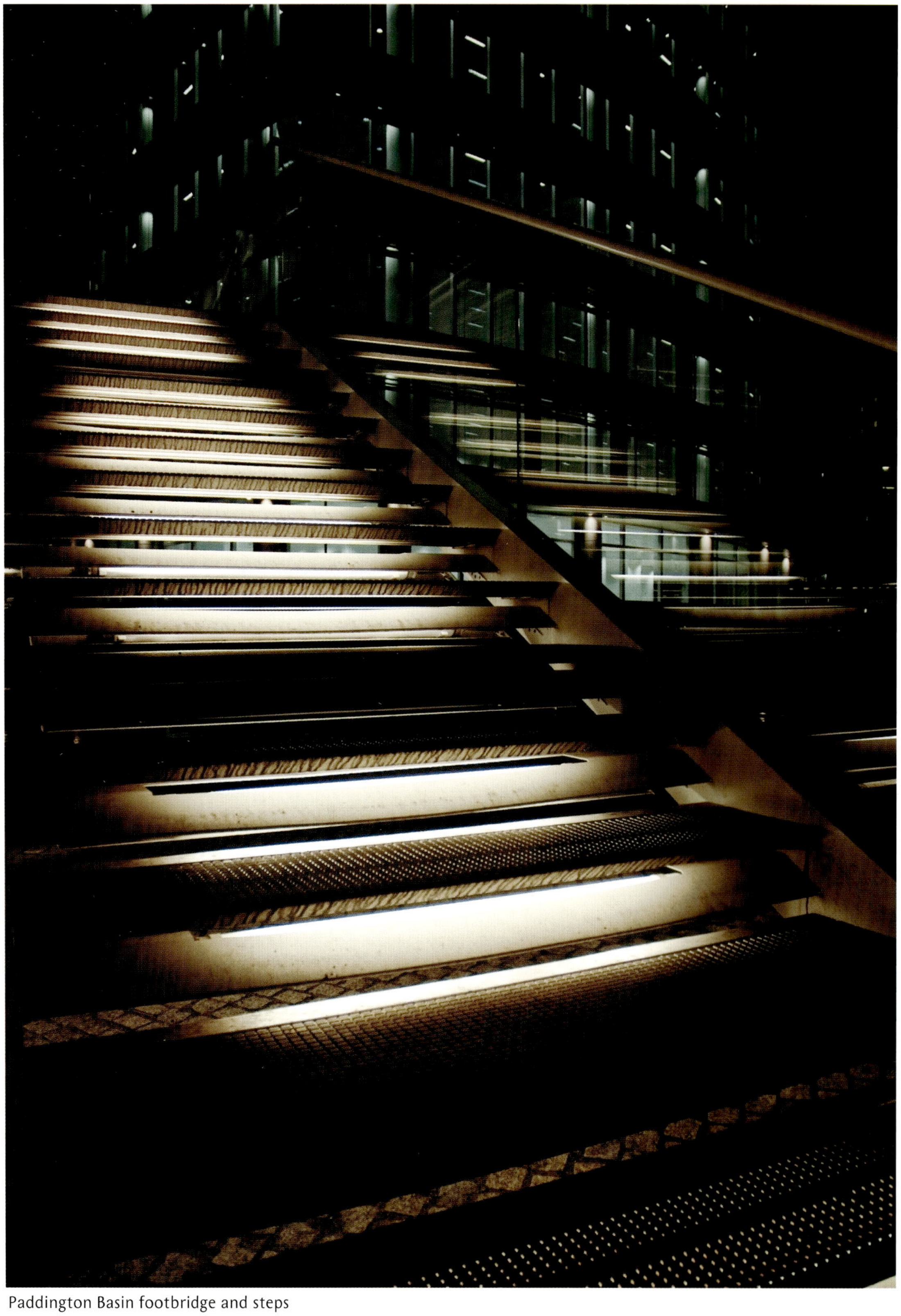

Paddington Basin footbridge and steps

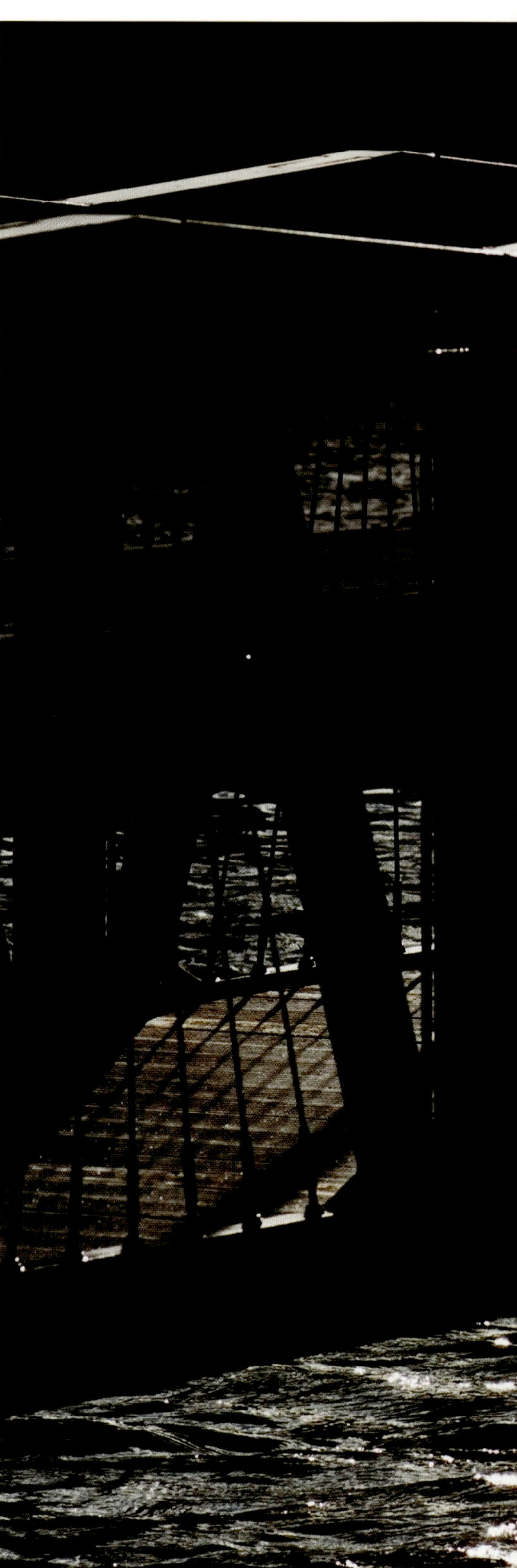

Paddington Basin Rolling Bridge

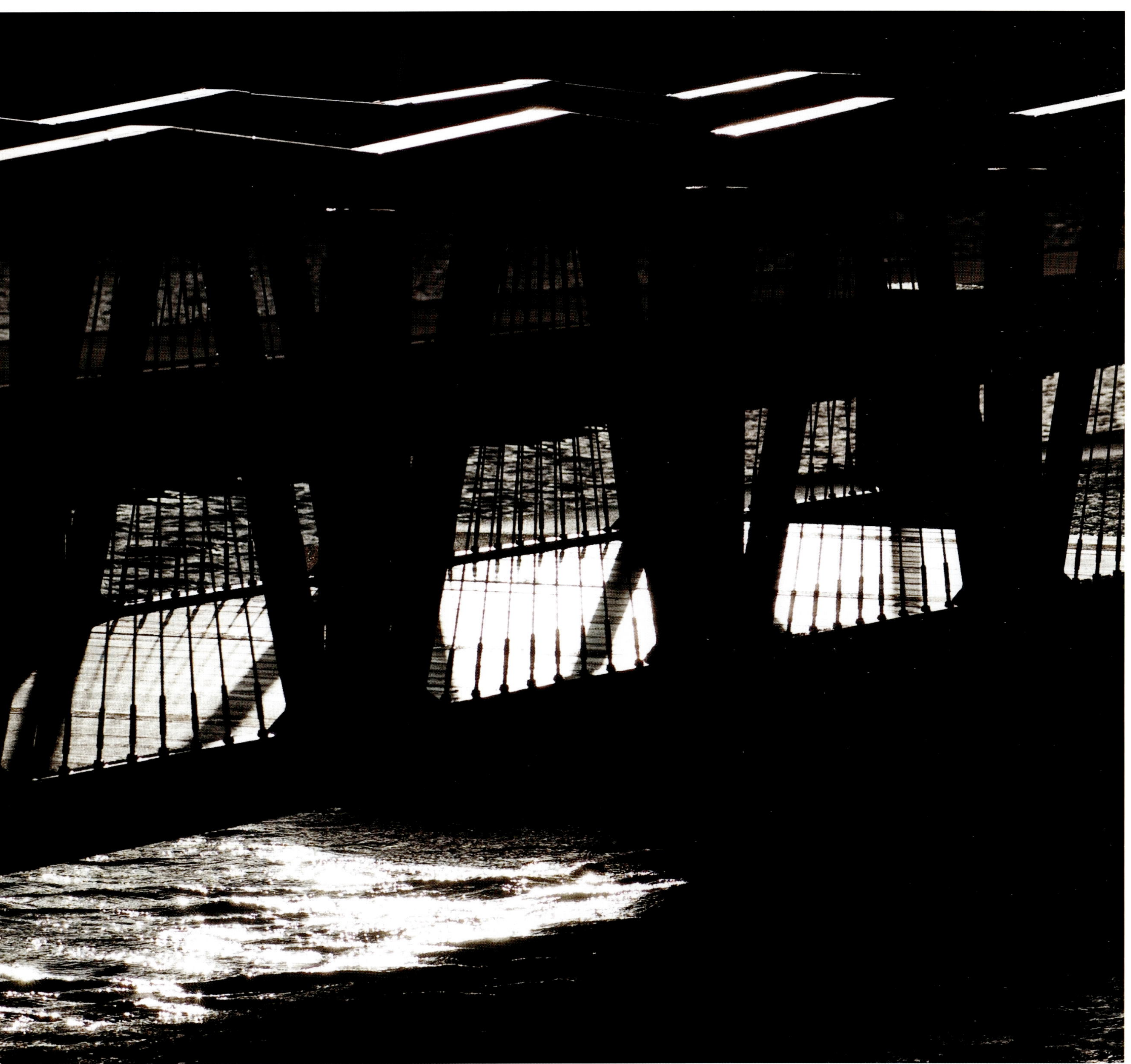

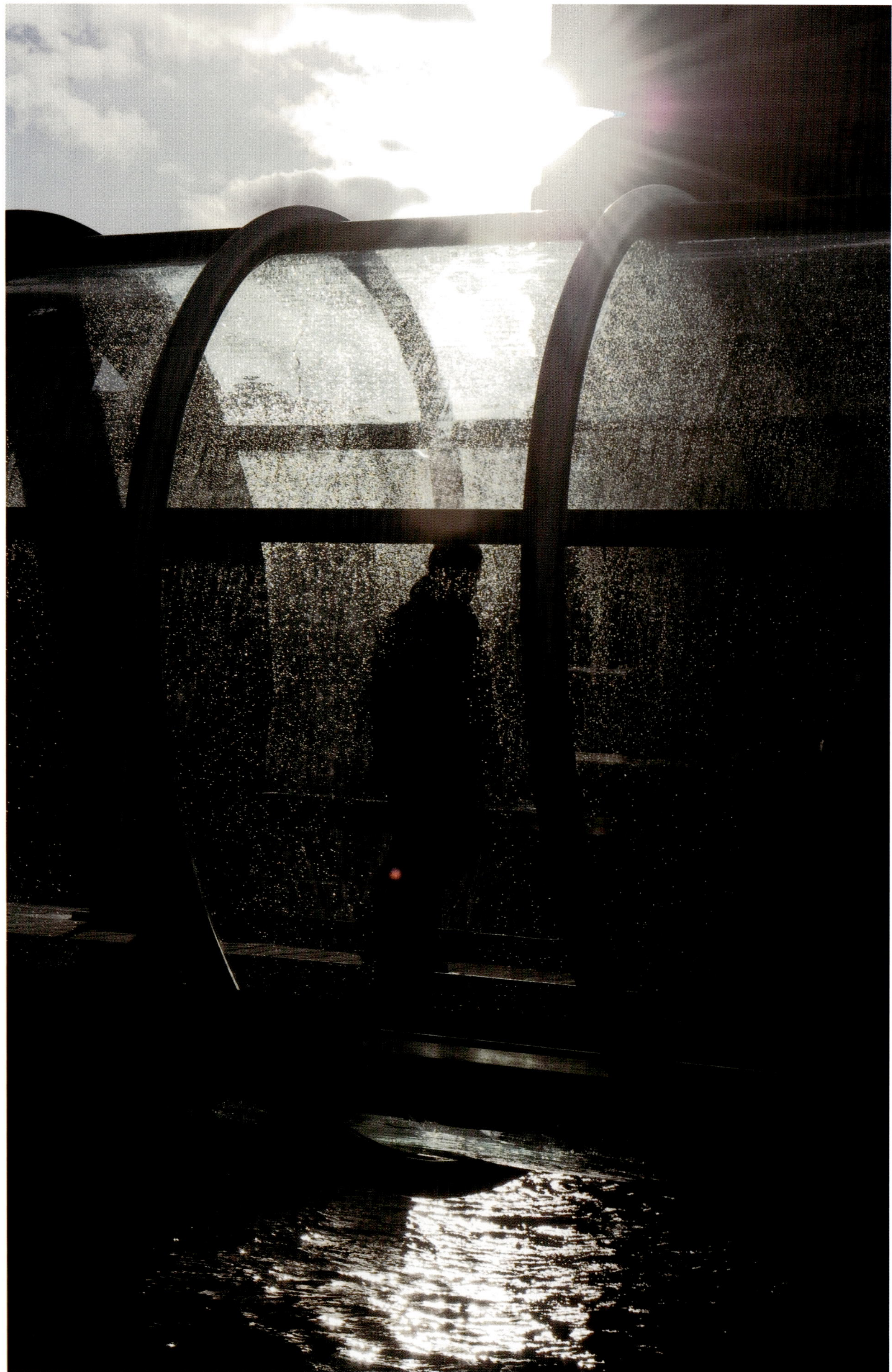

Paddington Basin Helix Bridge

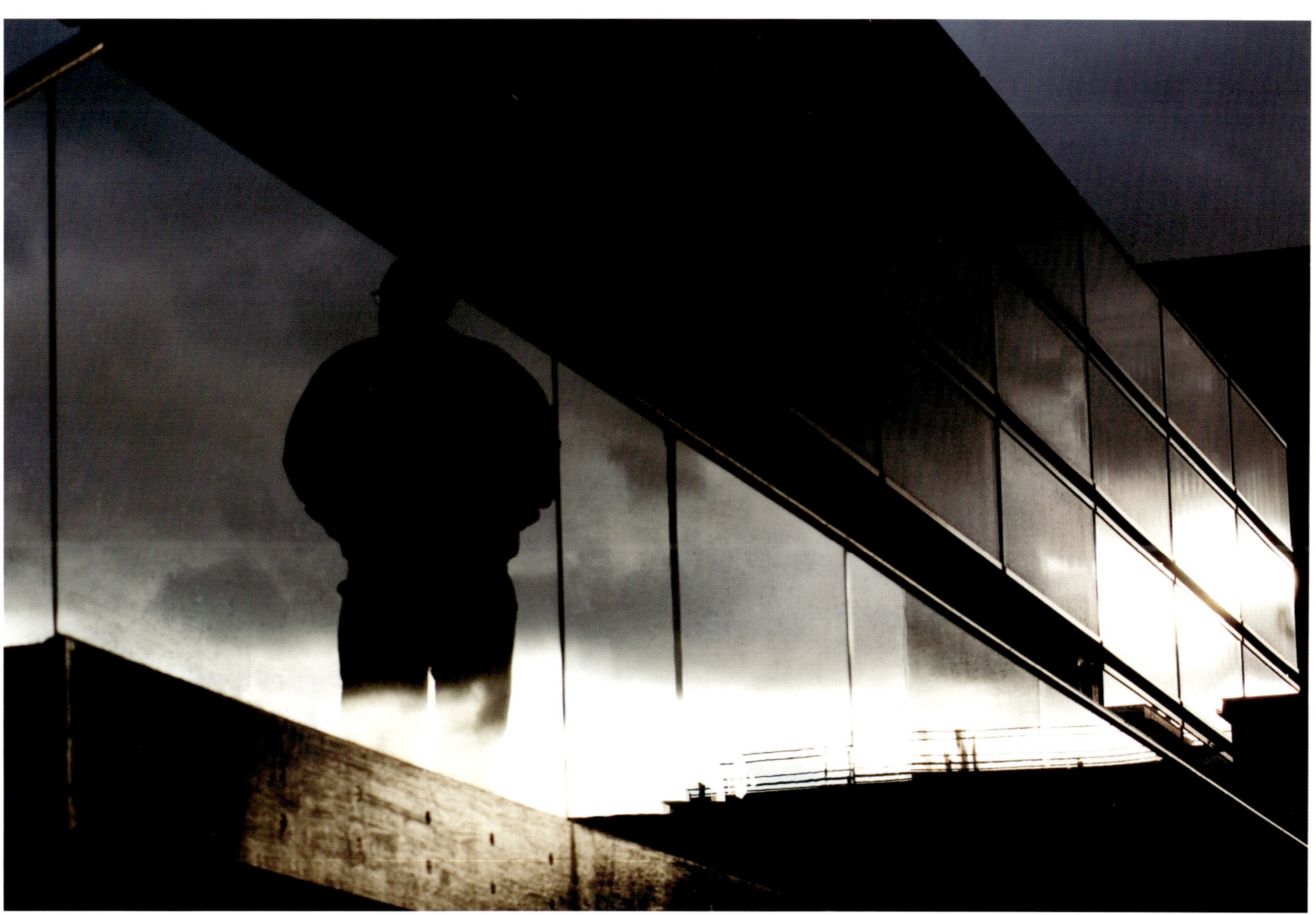

Crossing the Paddington Basin footbridge as a storm approaches

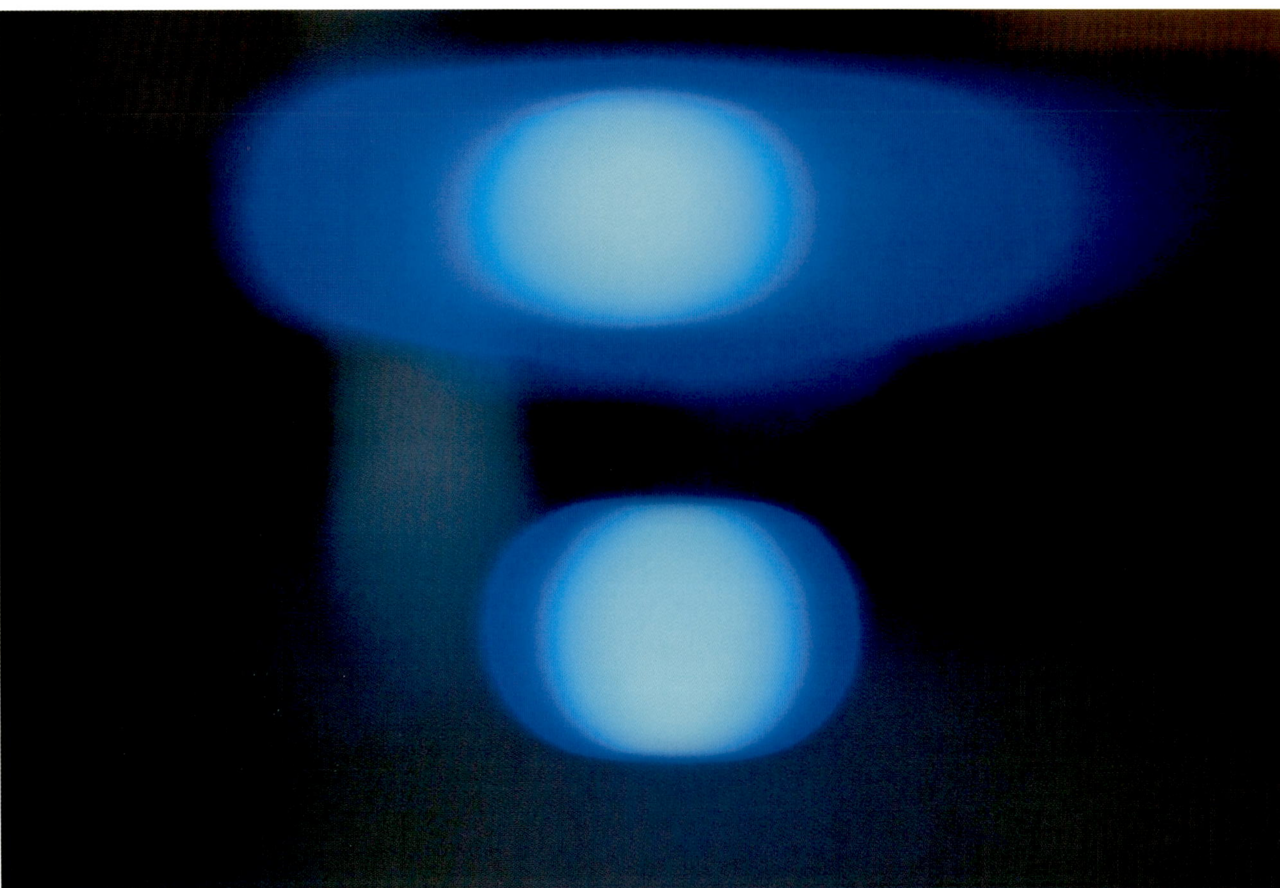

Above Blue lights on the Paddington Basin footbridge
Opposite Building security lights reflected in Paddington Basin

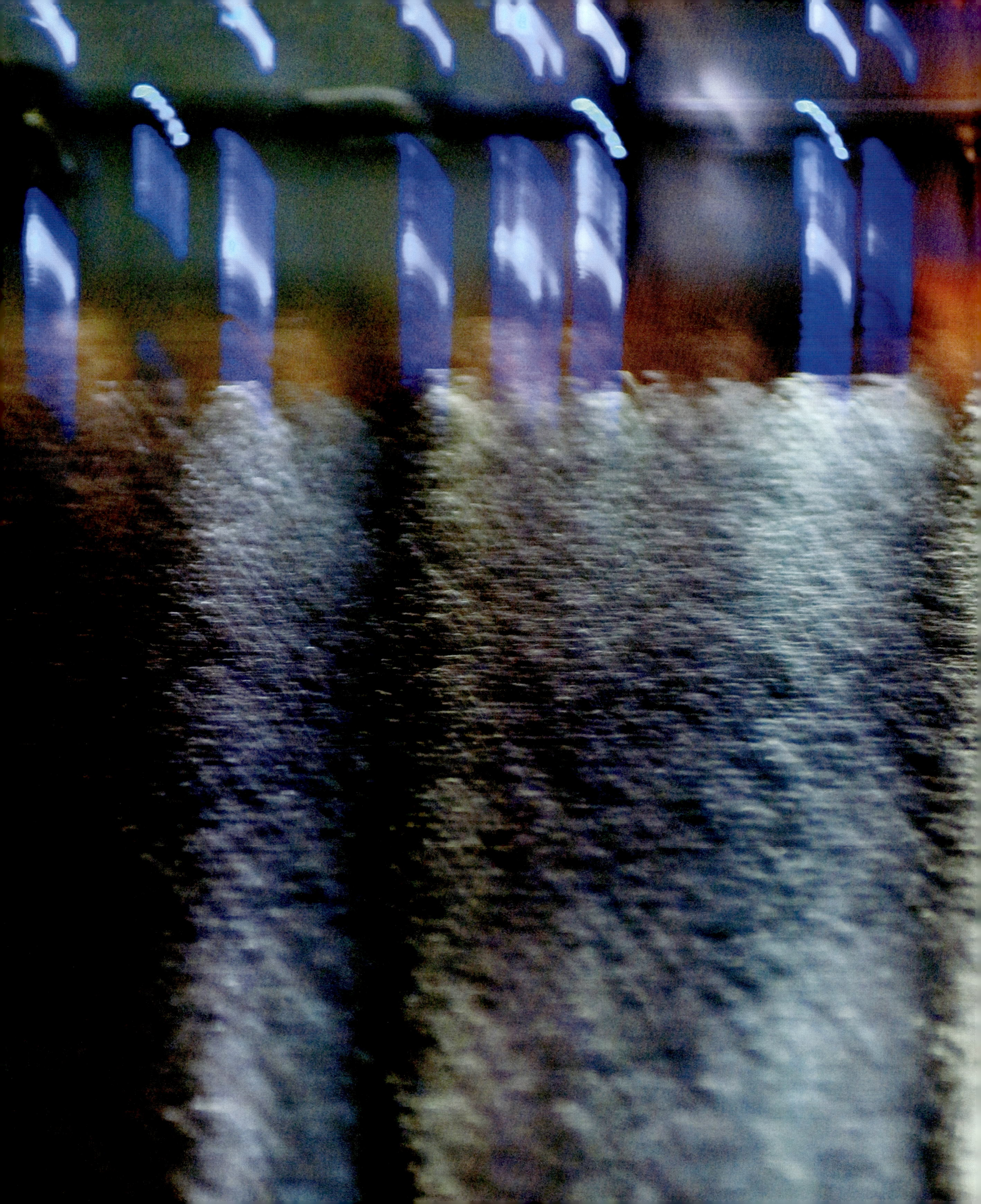

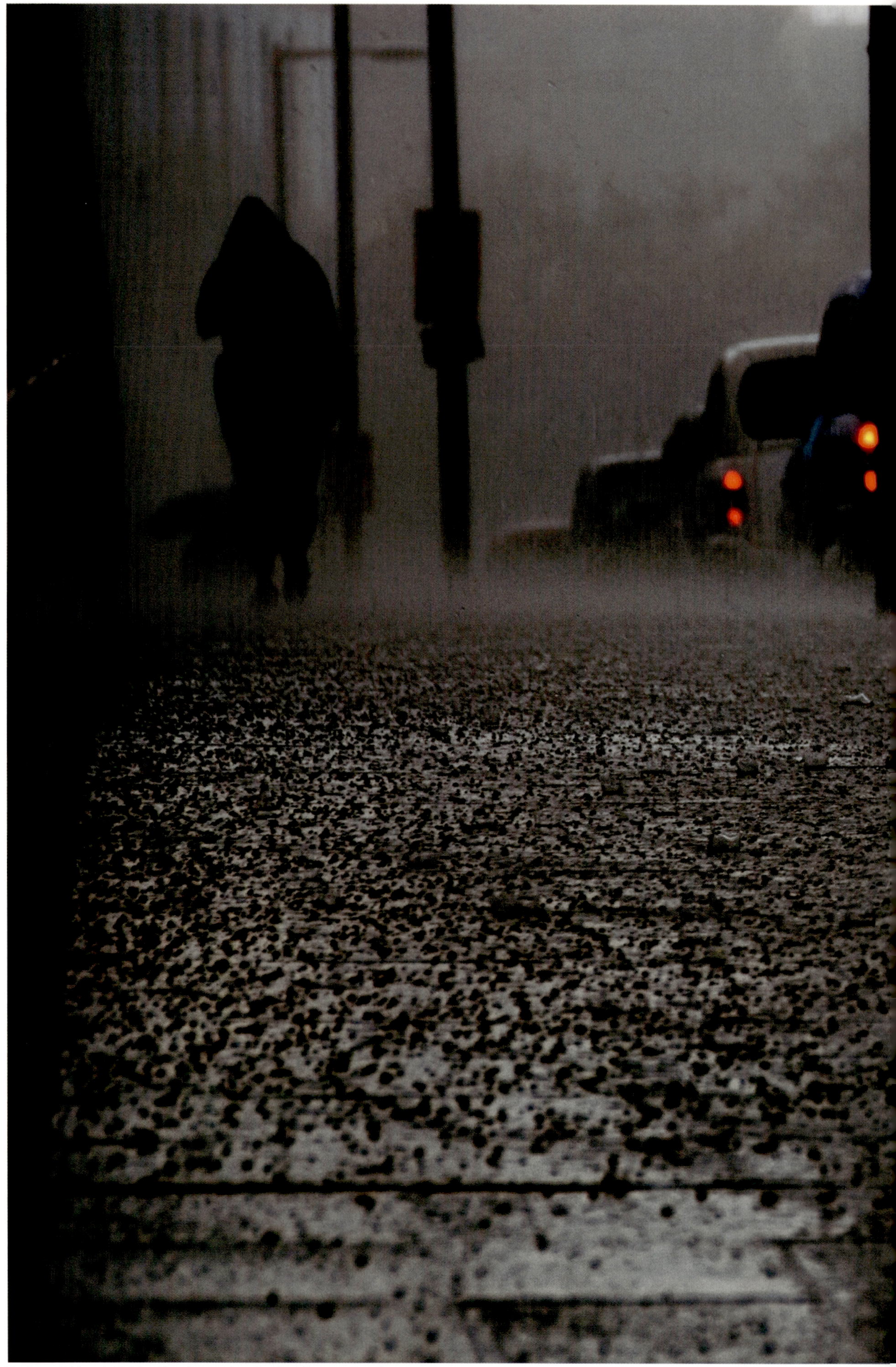

Taxis on Bishop's Bridge Road, queuing for Paddington Station

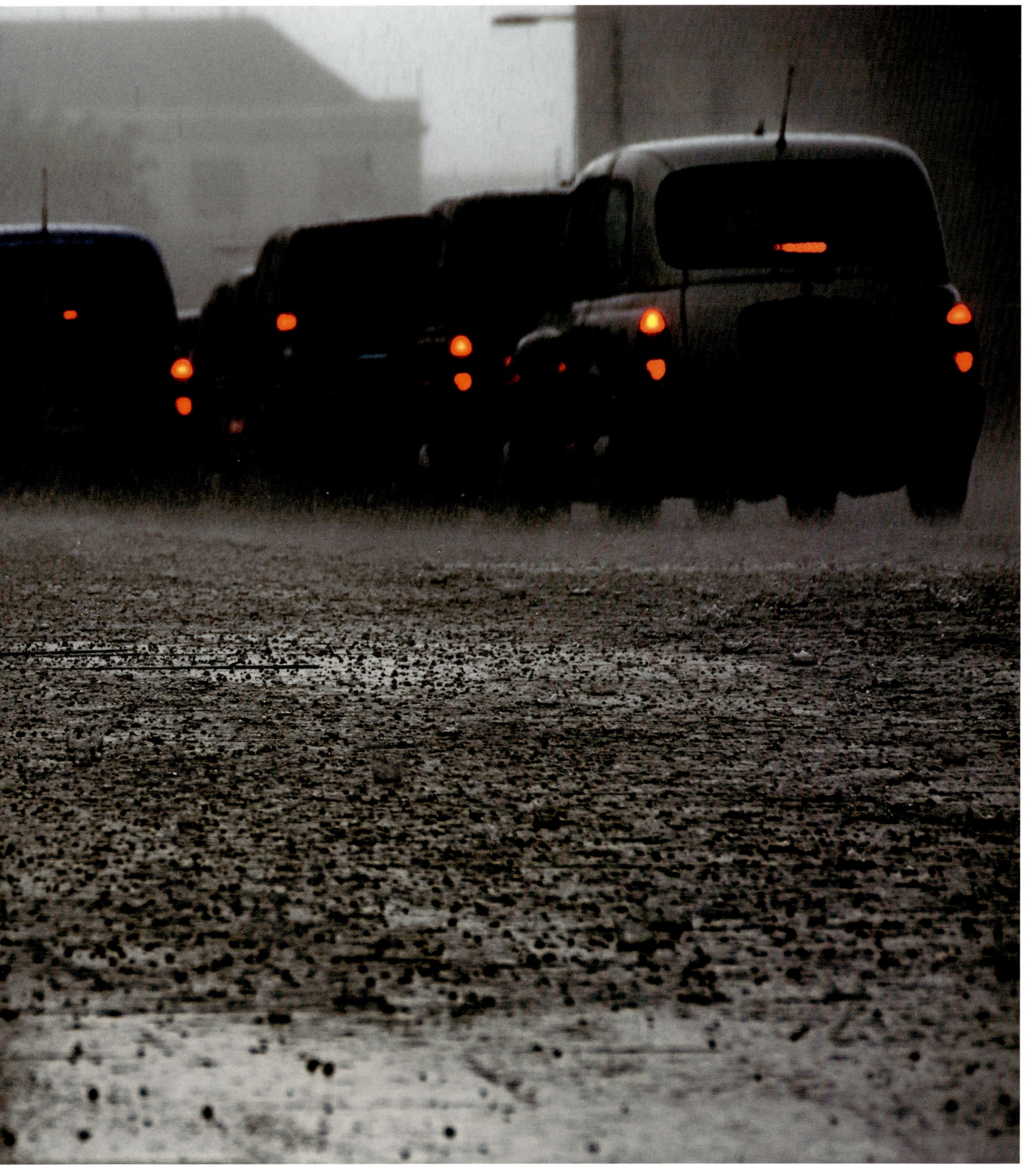

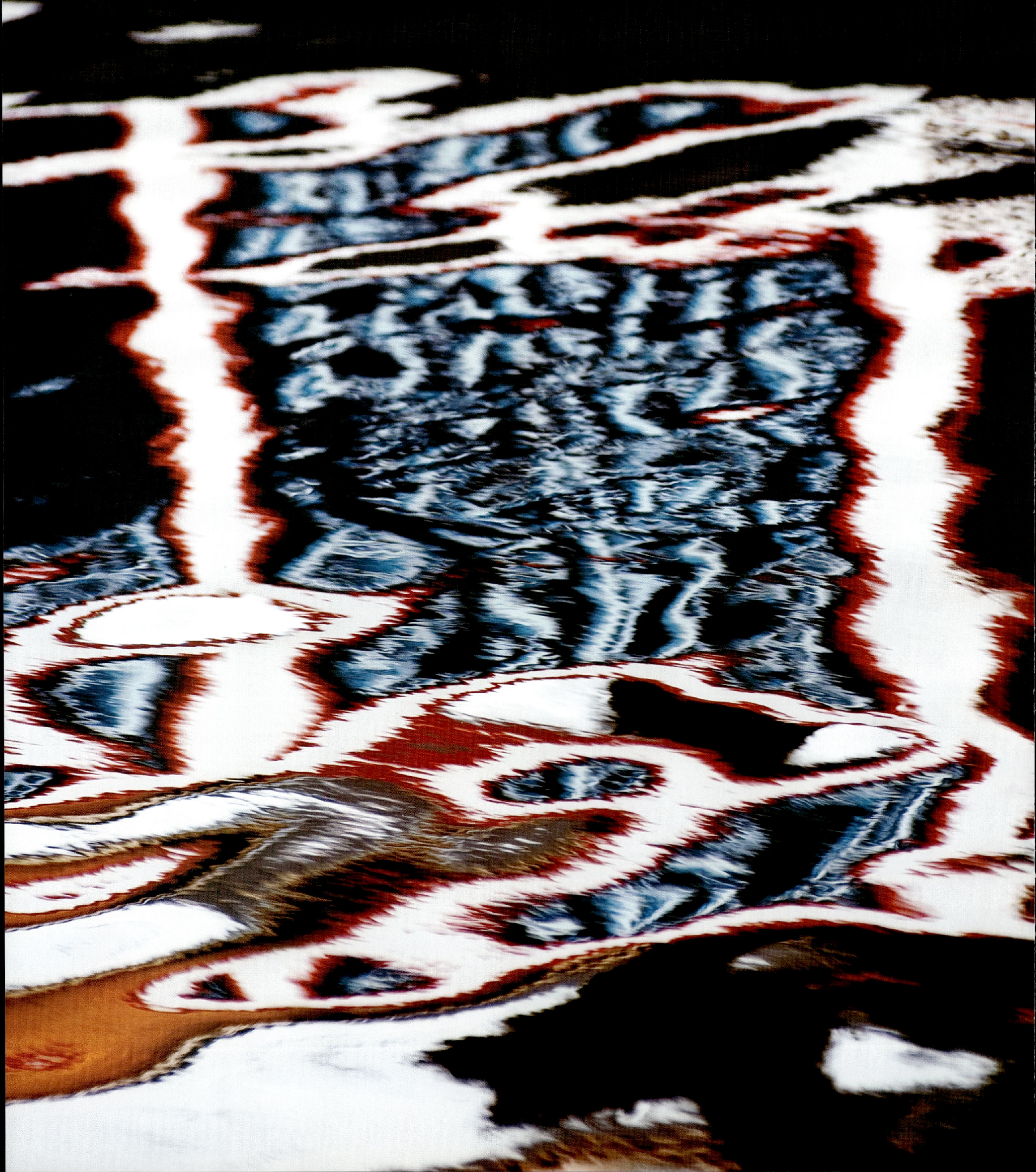

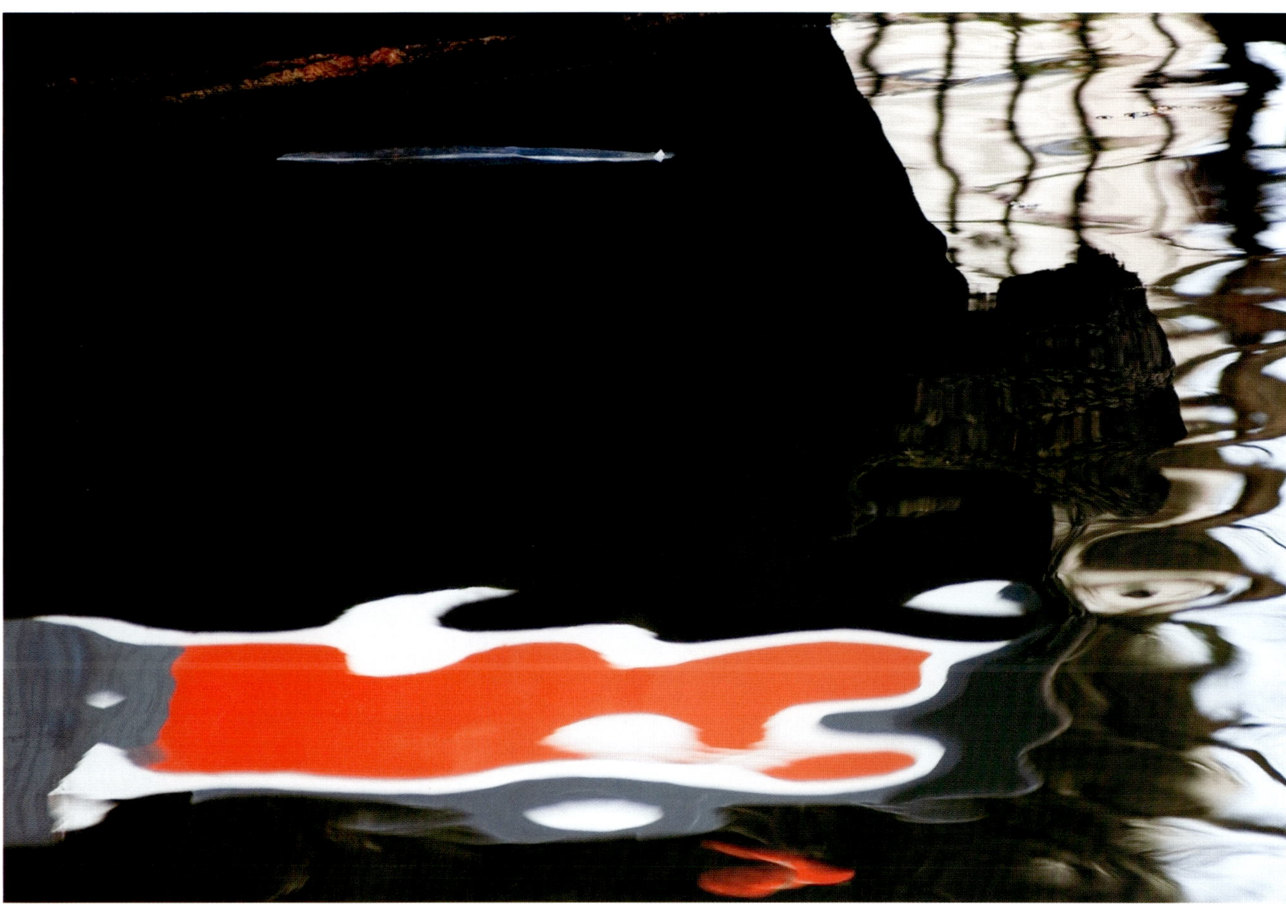

Above and opposite
Reflections in the Regent's Canal at Little Venice

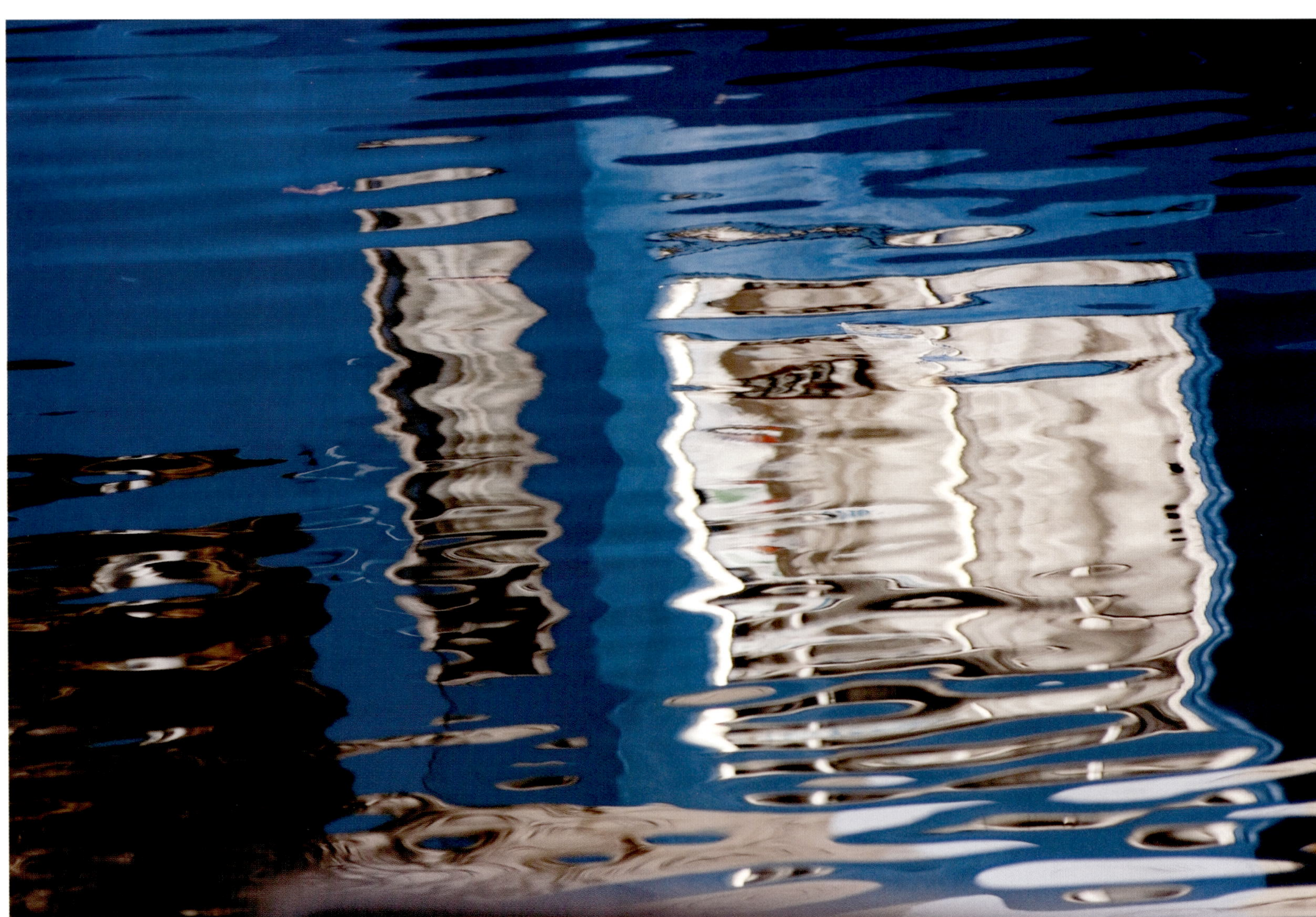

Above and opposite
Reflections in the Regent's Canal at Little Venice

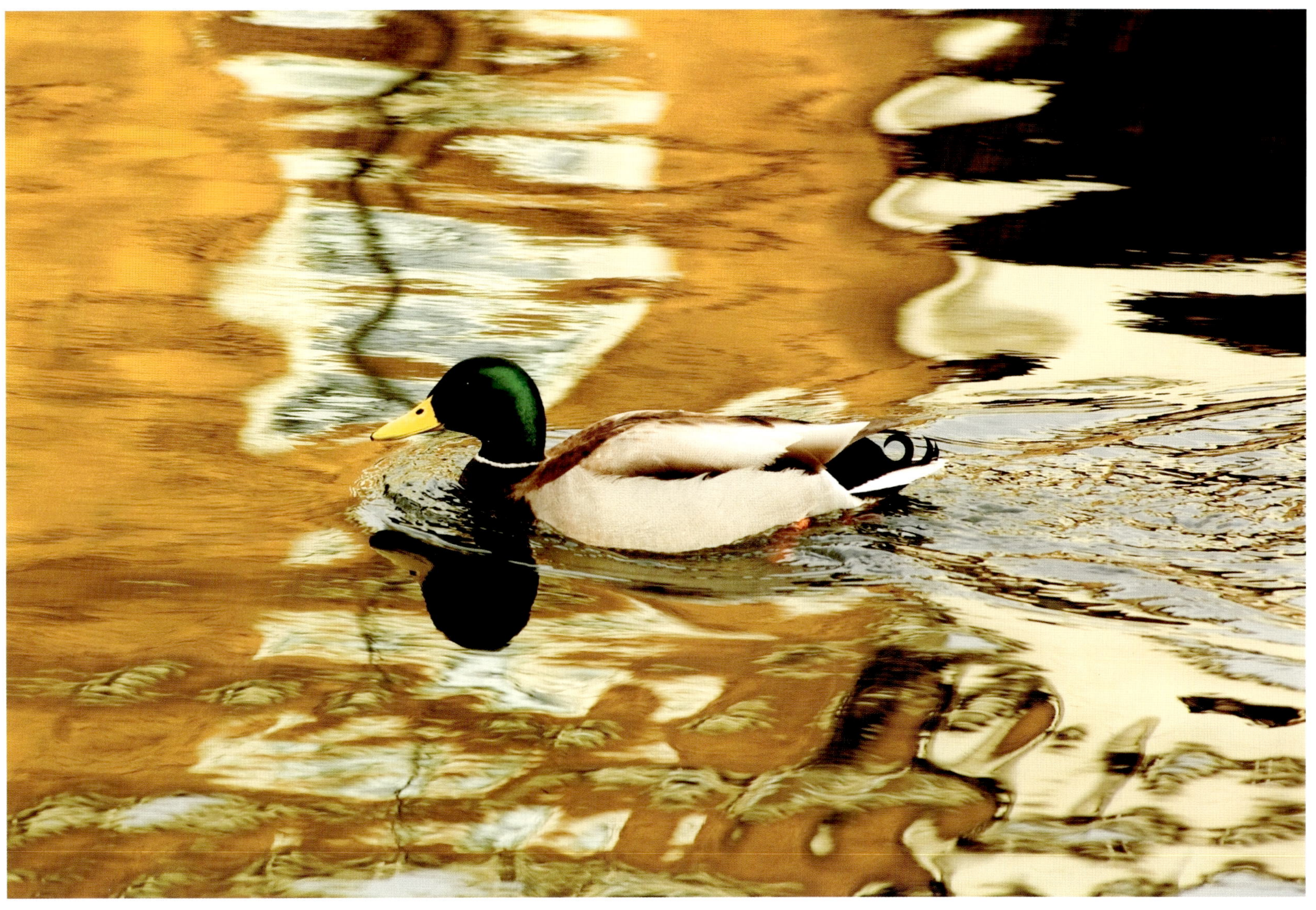

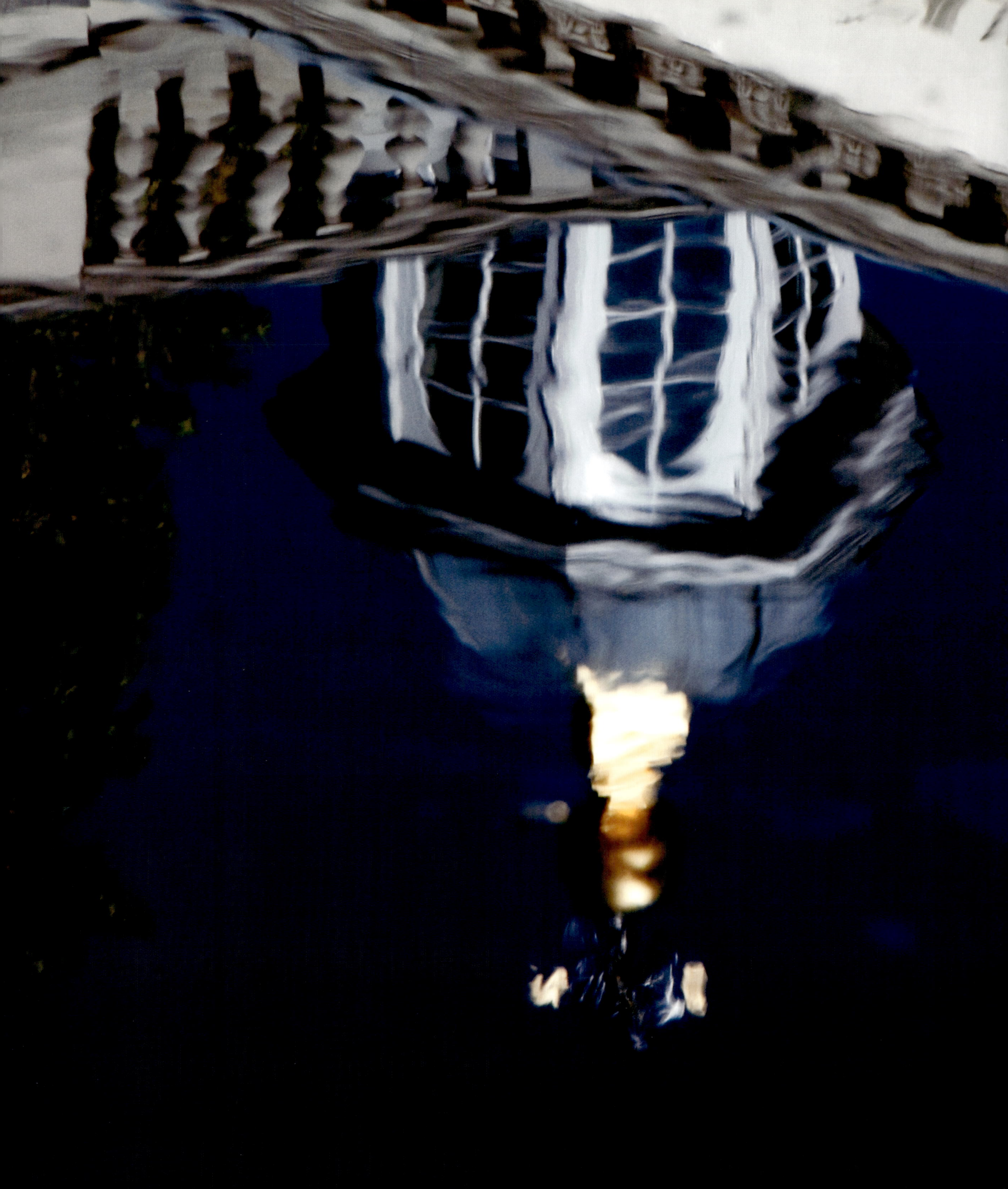

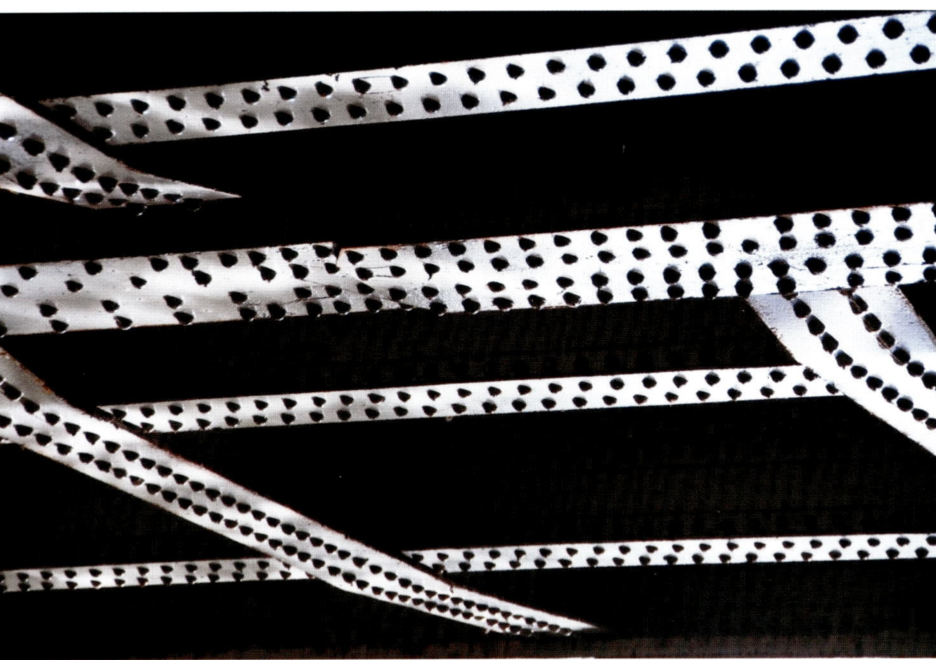

Above The metalwork of a bridge over Regent's Canal, glowing in reflected sunlight
Left Reflection in the Regent's Canal near Regent's Park, of a house newly built after a design by John Nash

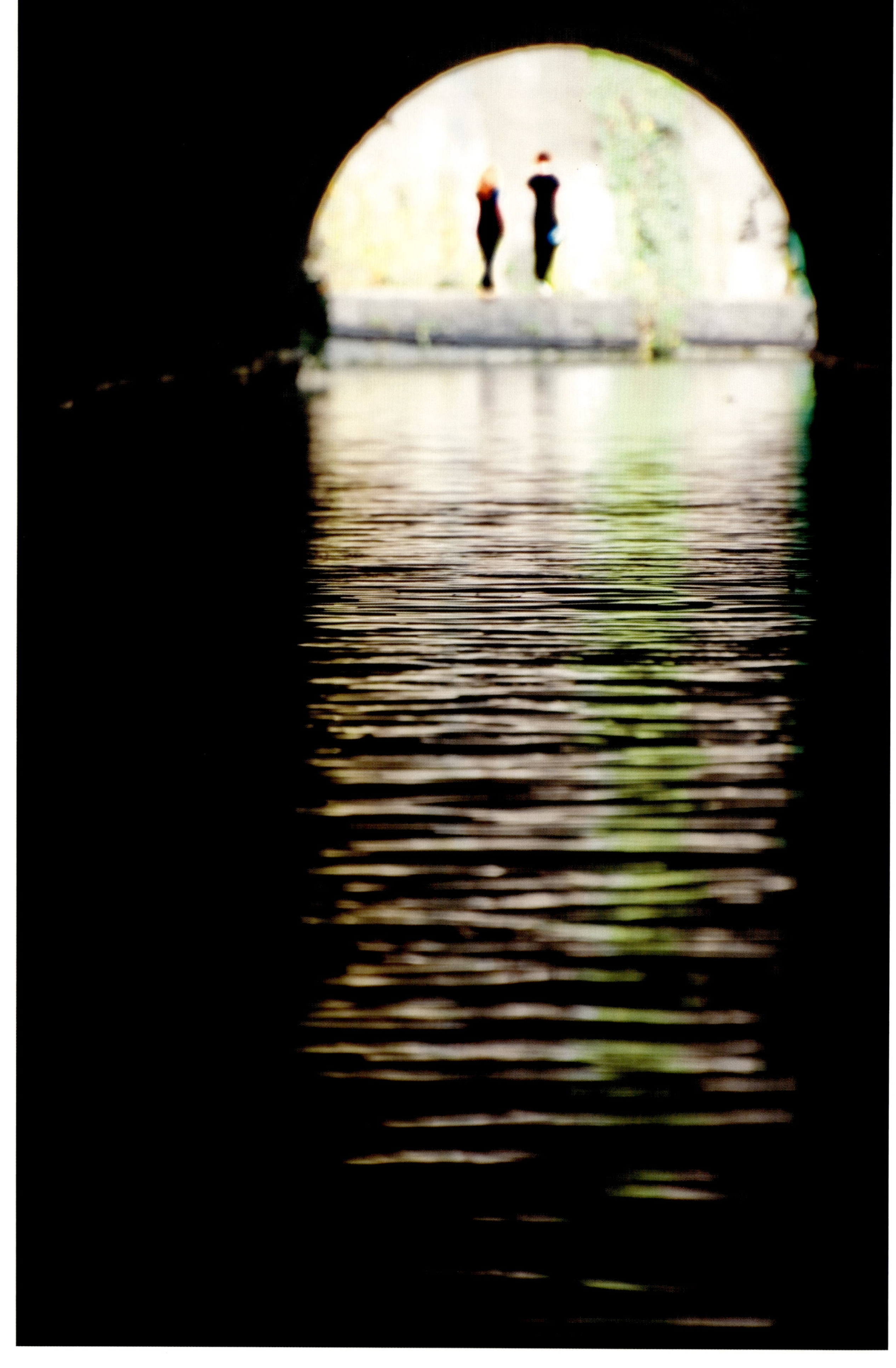

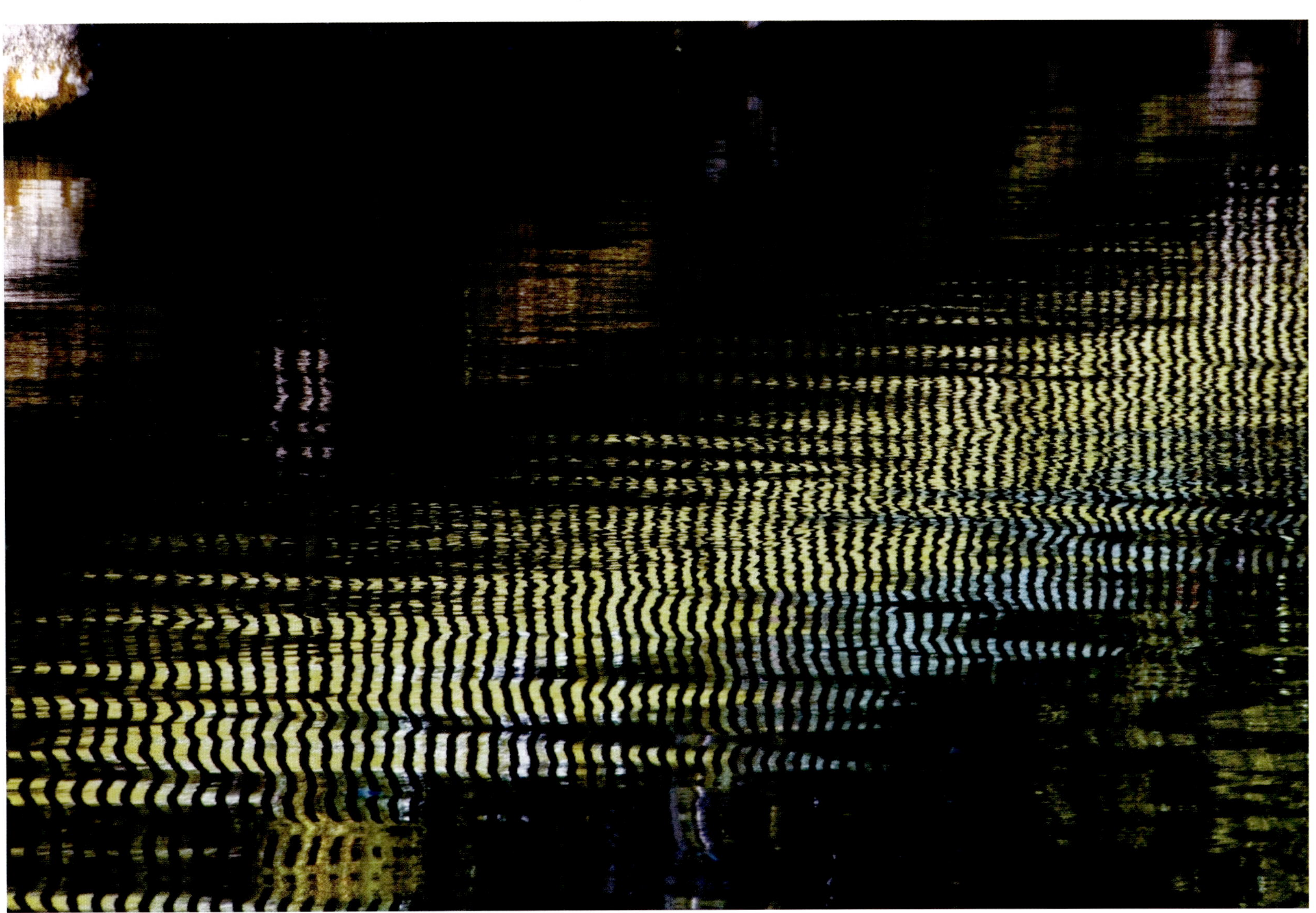

Above Railings reflected in the Regent's Canal
Left Tunnel under the Regent's Canal at Lisson Grove

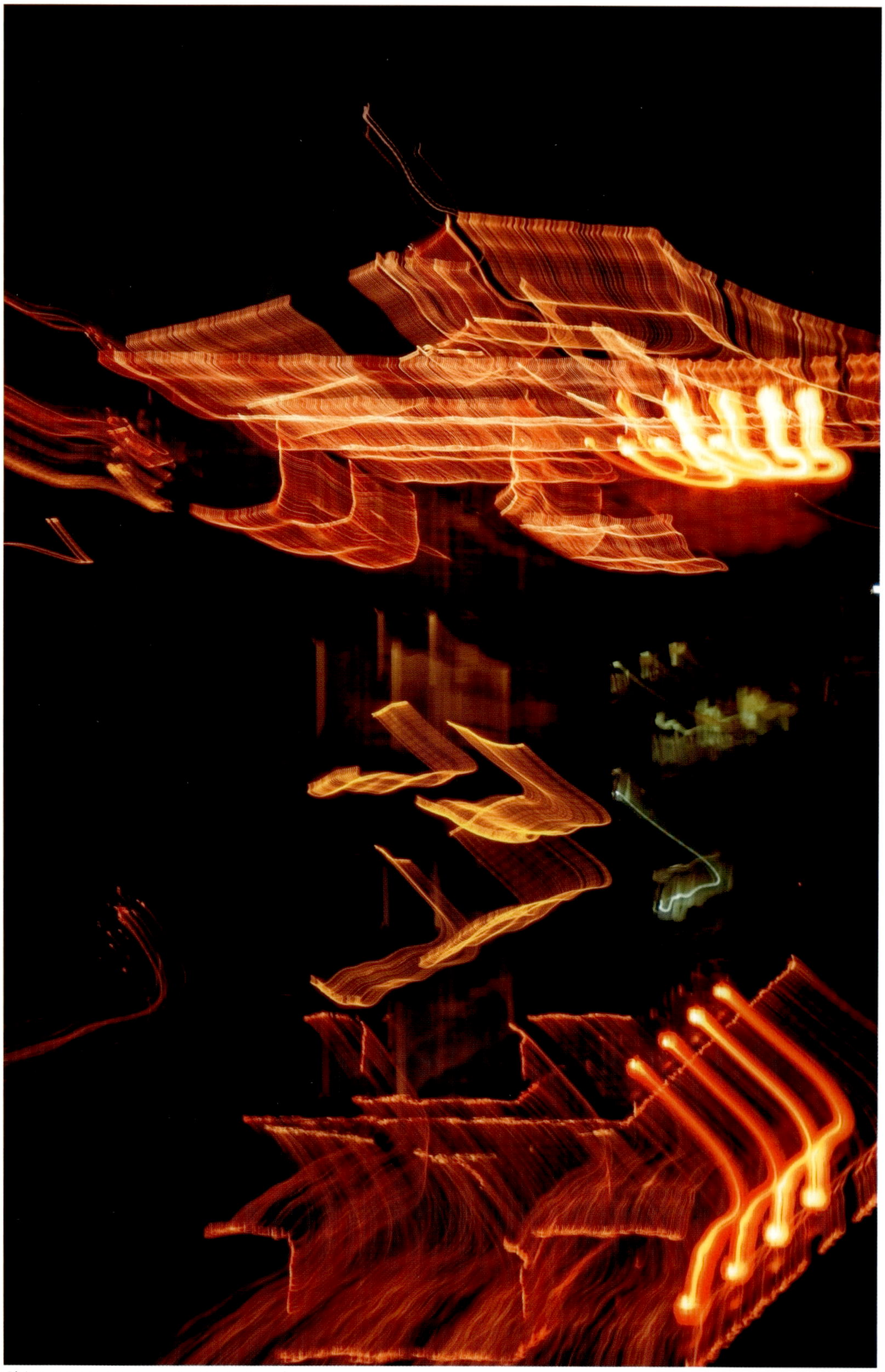

Chinese restaurant on Regent's Canal,
near Regent's Park

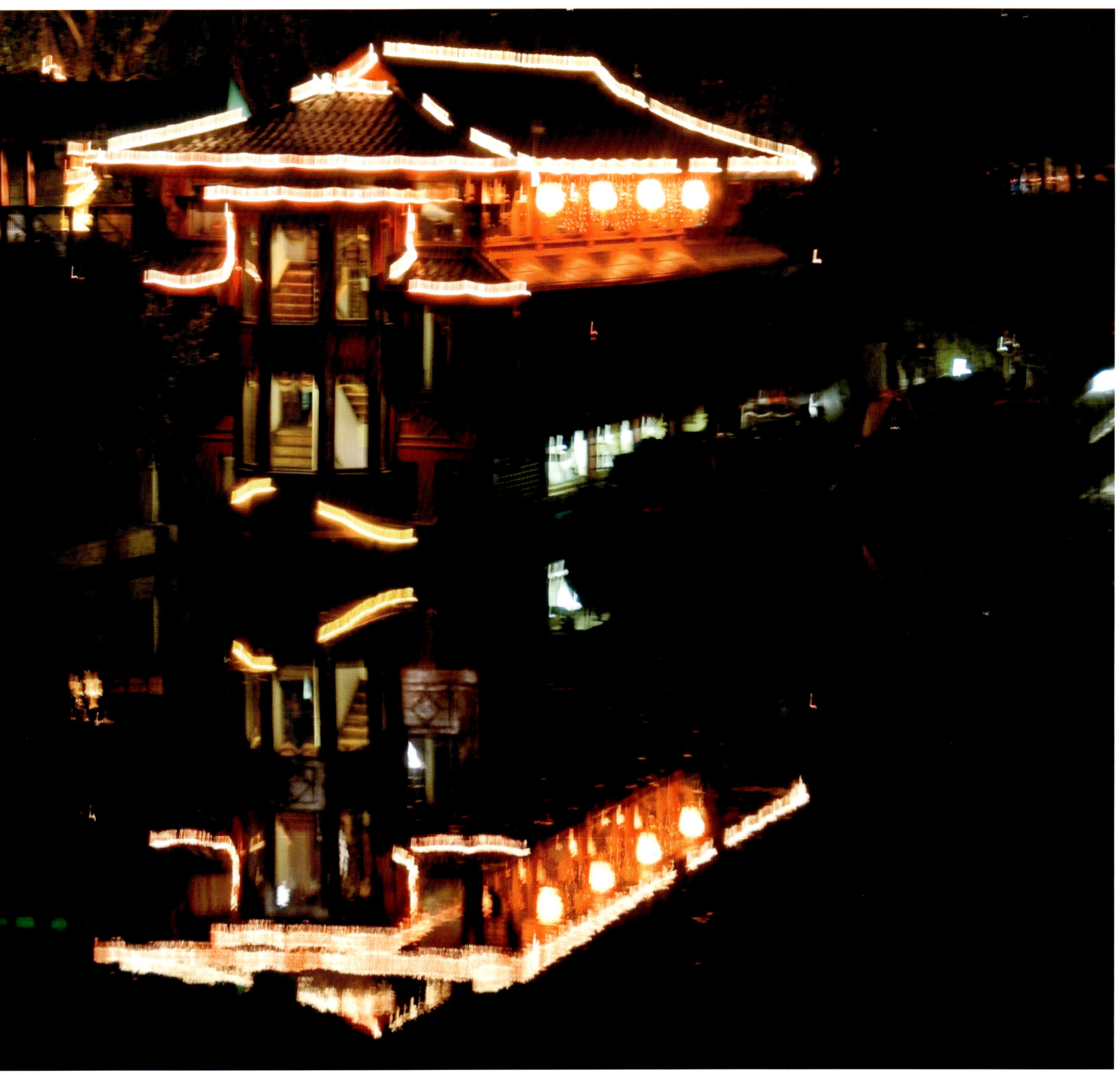

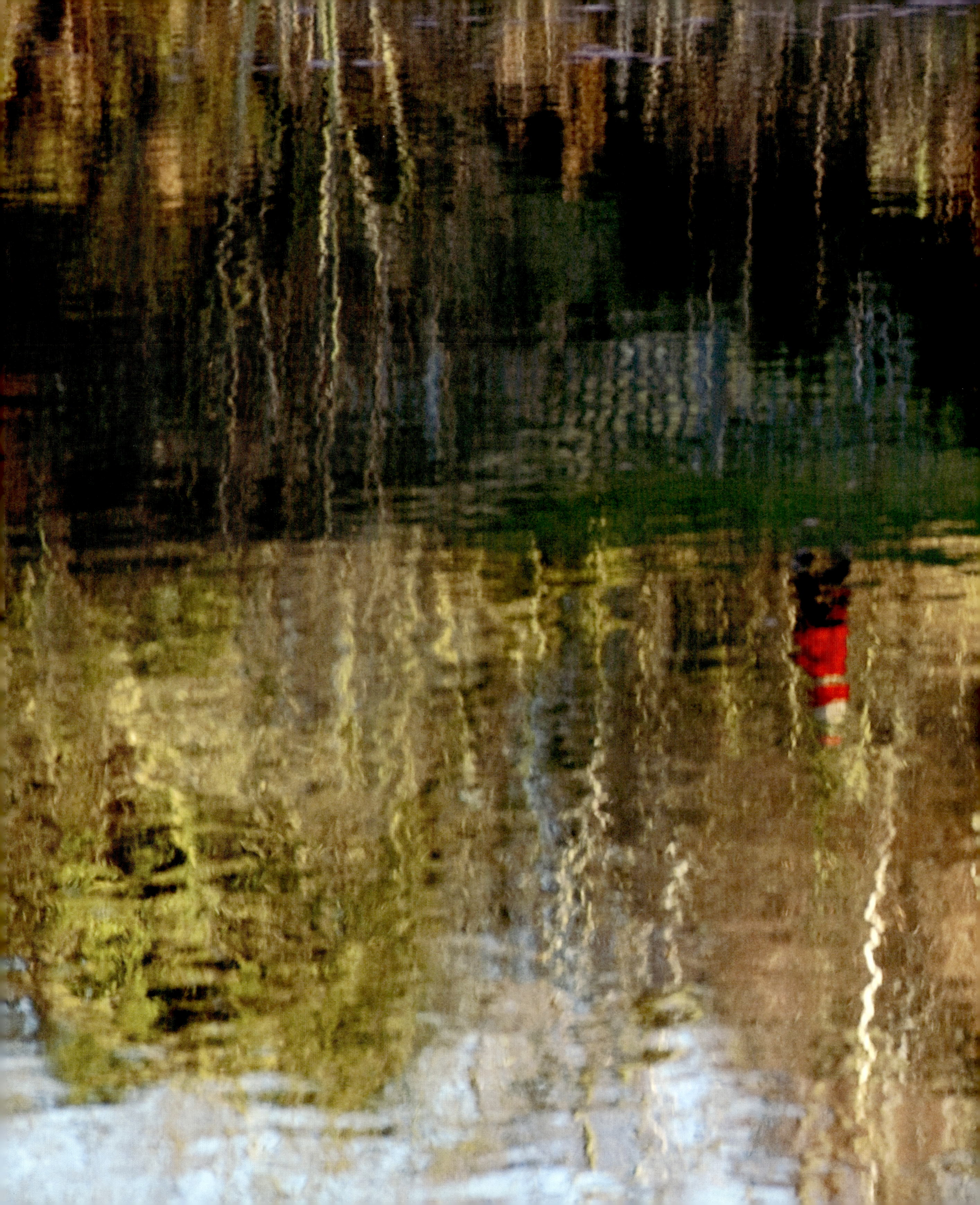

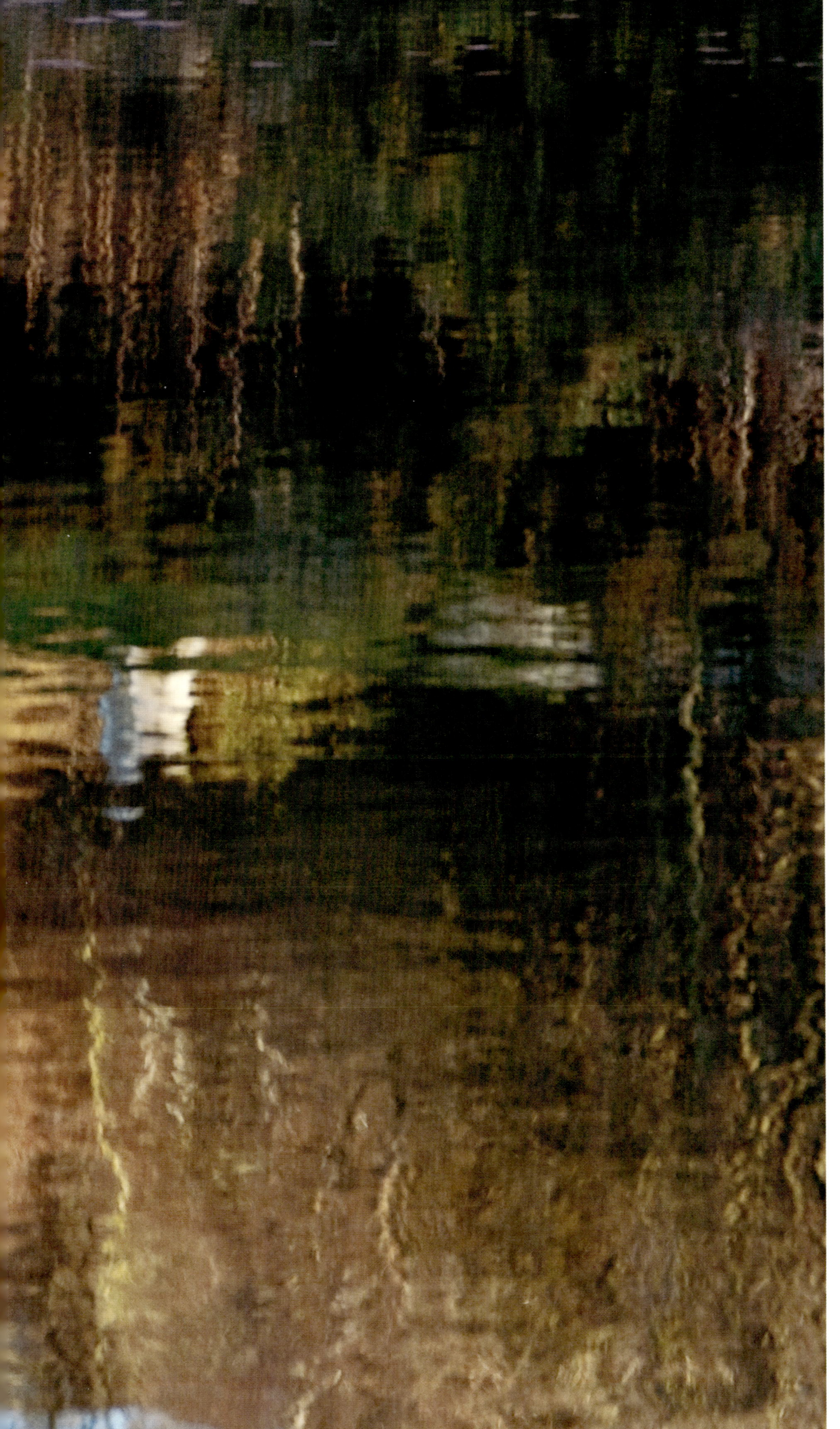

Reflections in Viaduct Pond,
on Hampstead Heath

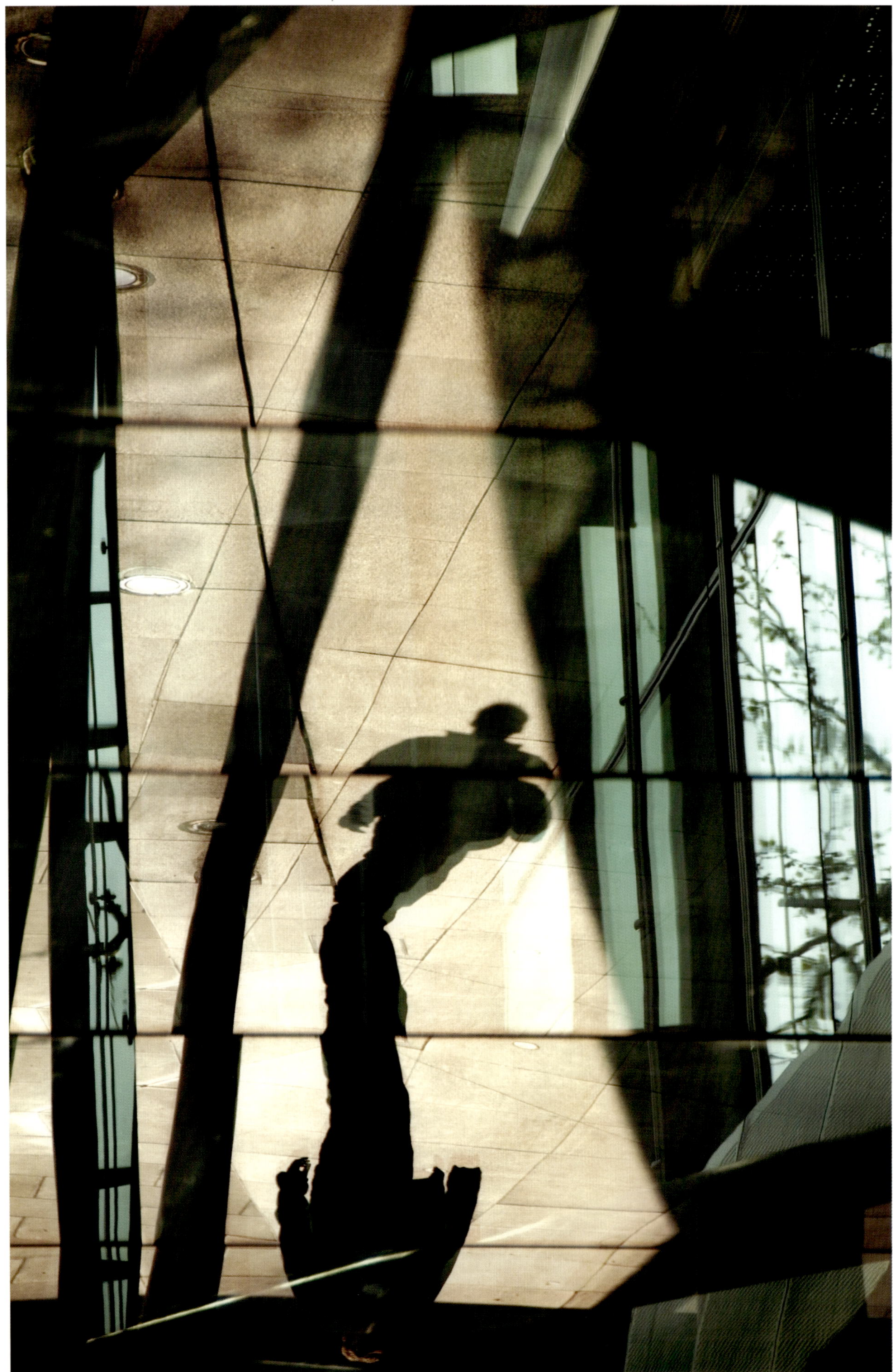

Reflections in a glass canopy over the pavement, in the Euston Road

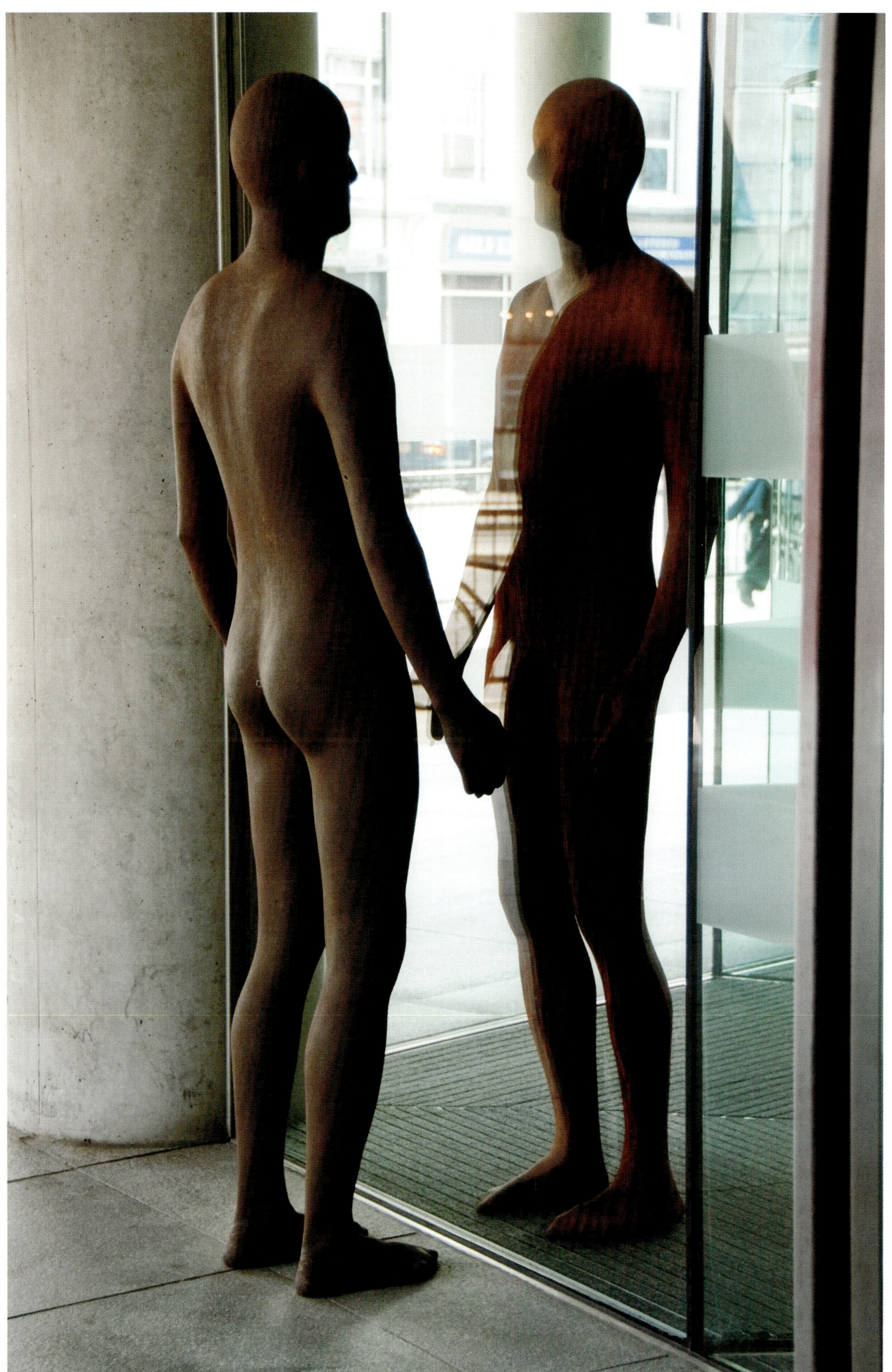

Reflection, a sculpture by Antony Gormley, in the Euston Road:
two figures, one inside, one out, gaze at each other through a glass window

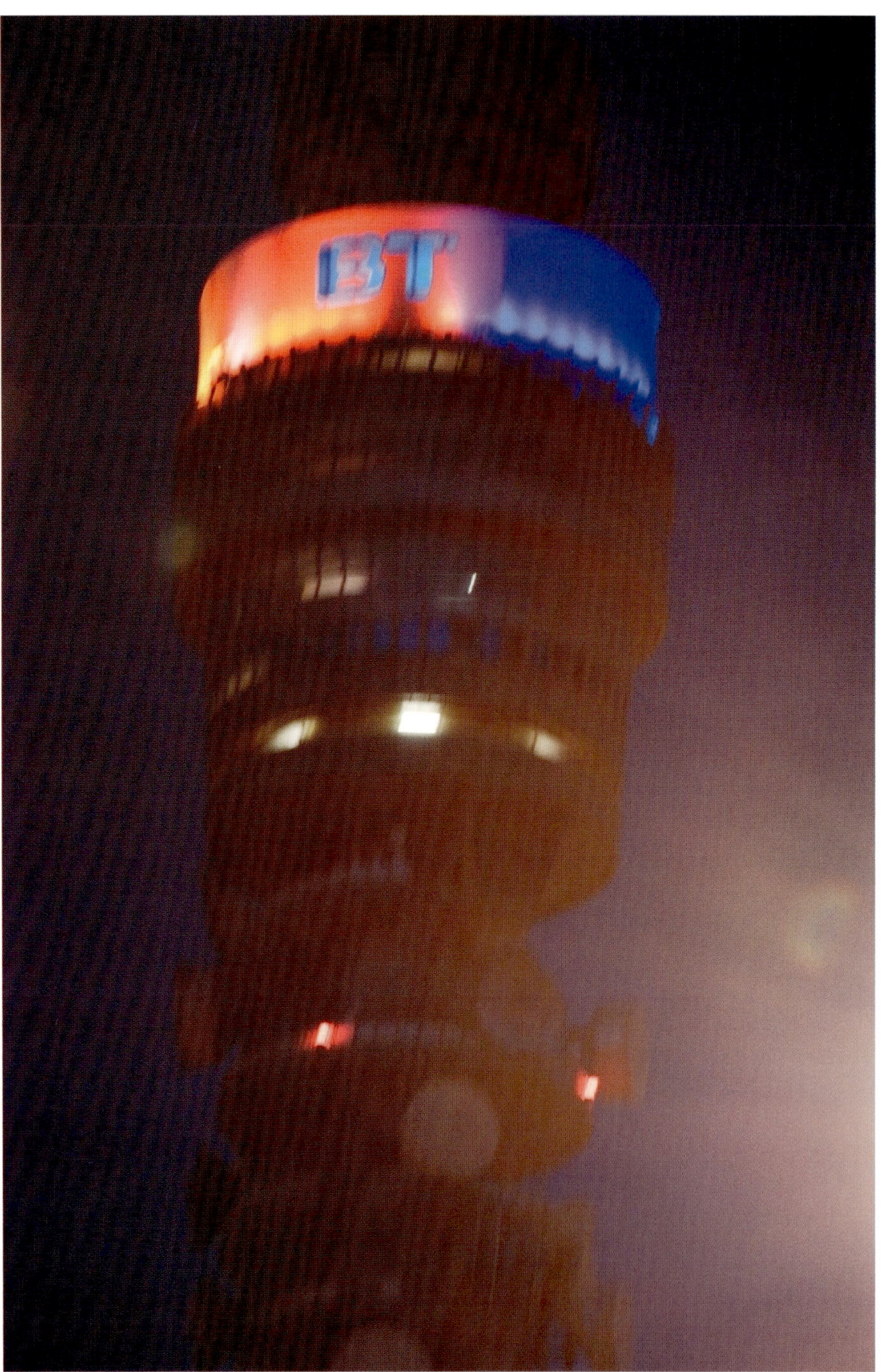

The Telecom Tower

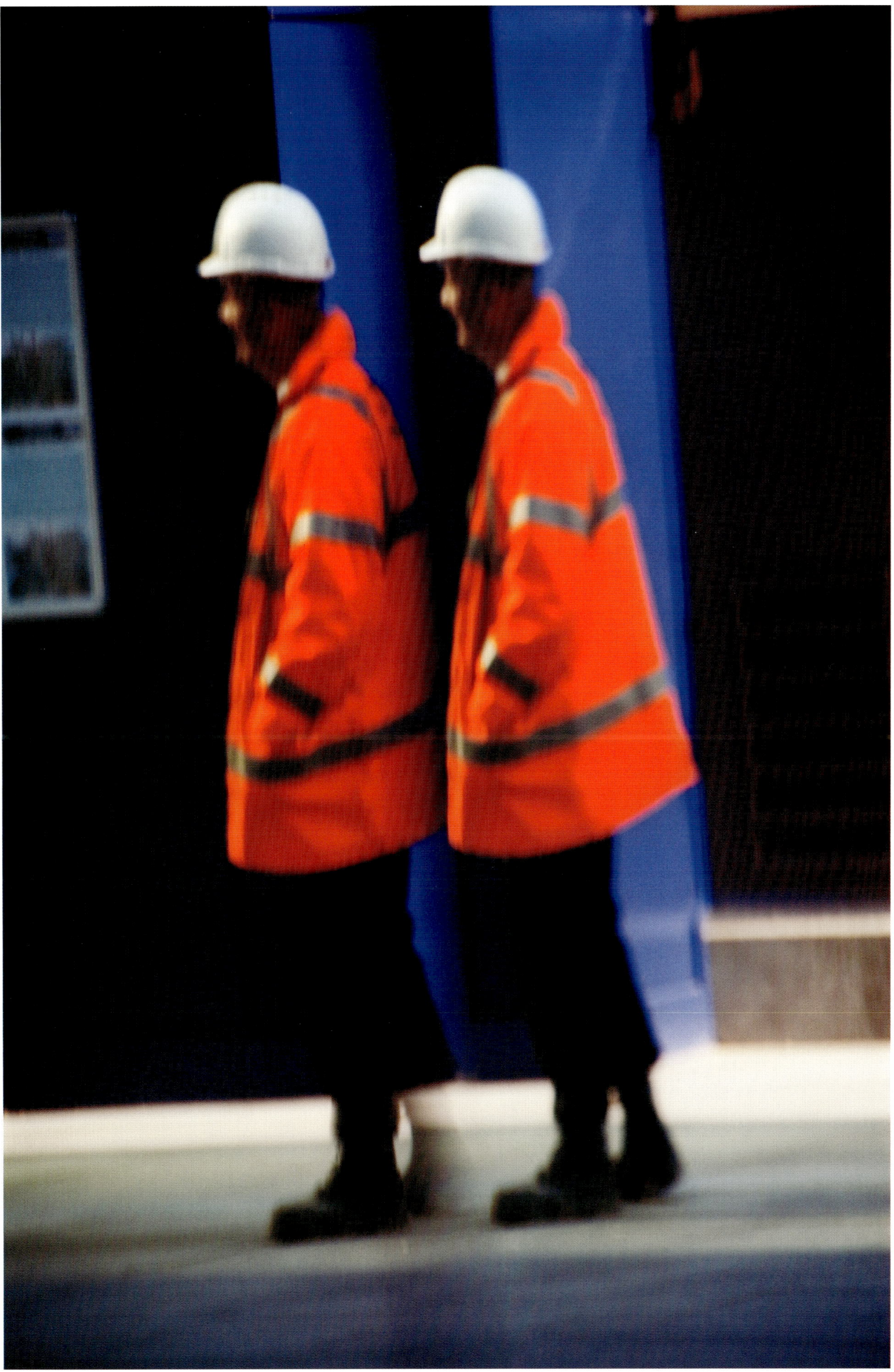

A site worker reflected in a window on a Euston Road site

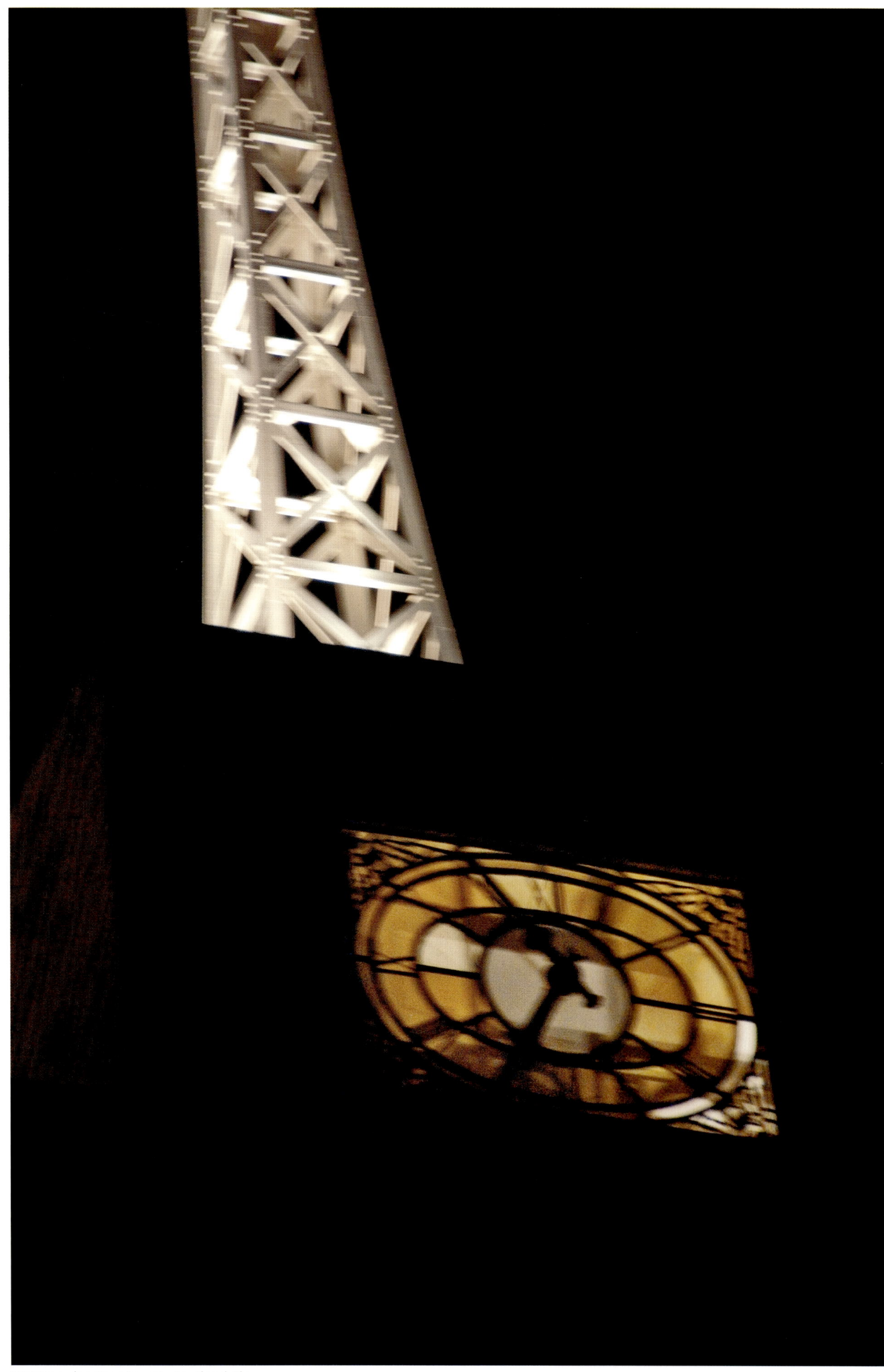

BBC Broadcasting House, Portland Place

All Souls Church,
Langham Place

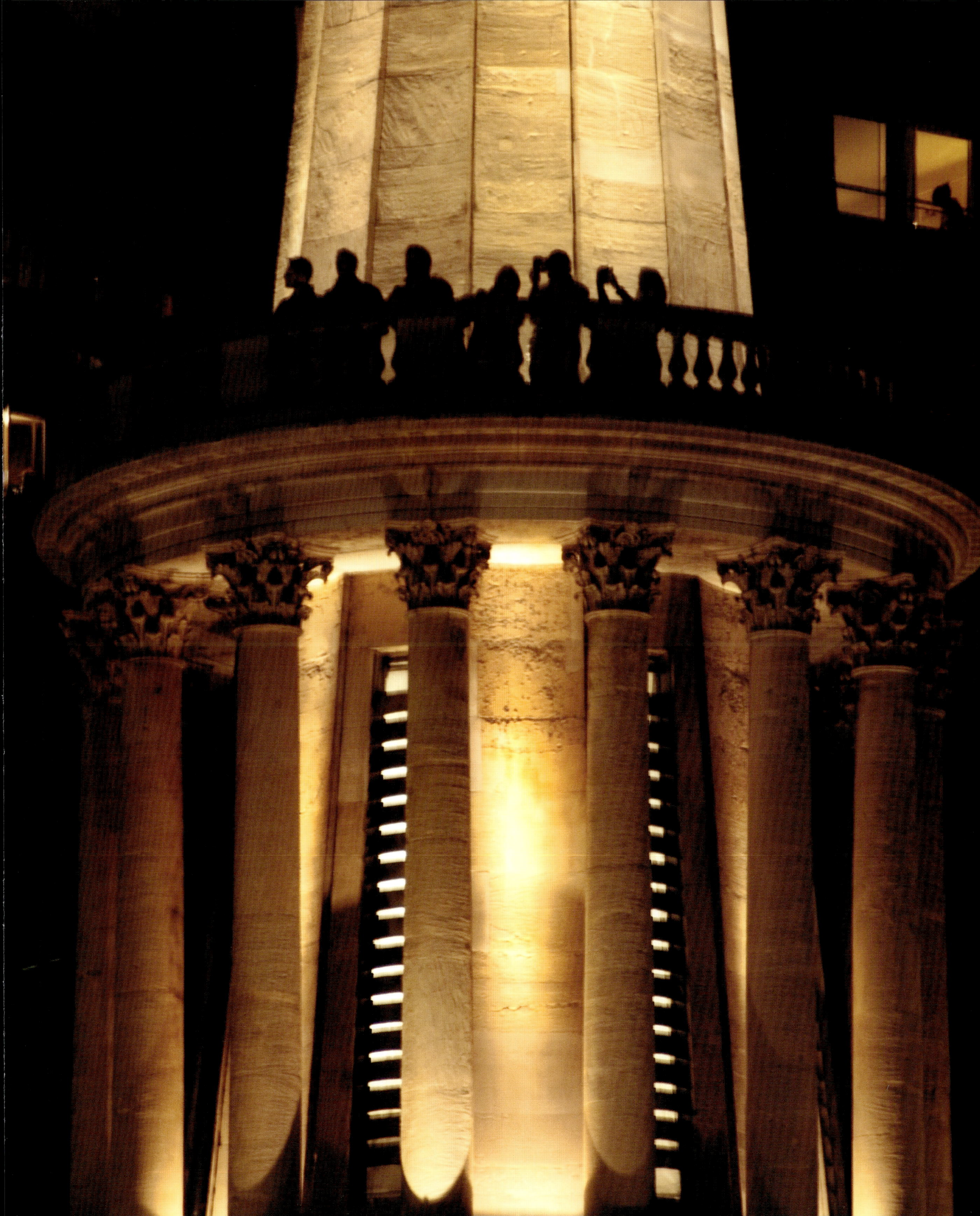

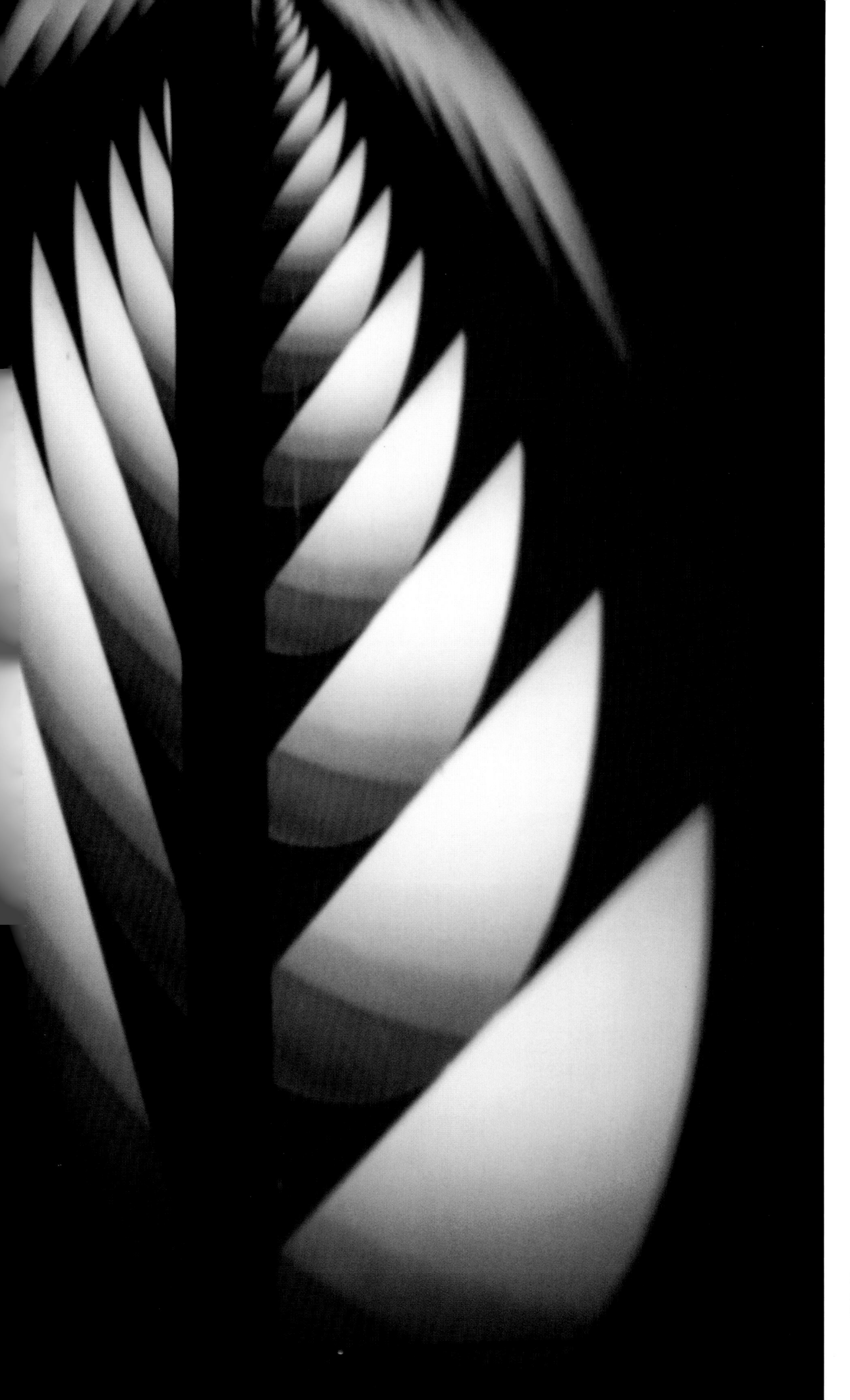

Erco Lighting, Dover Street:
a light pattern projected
inside the shop

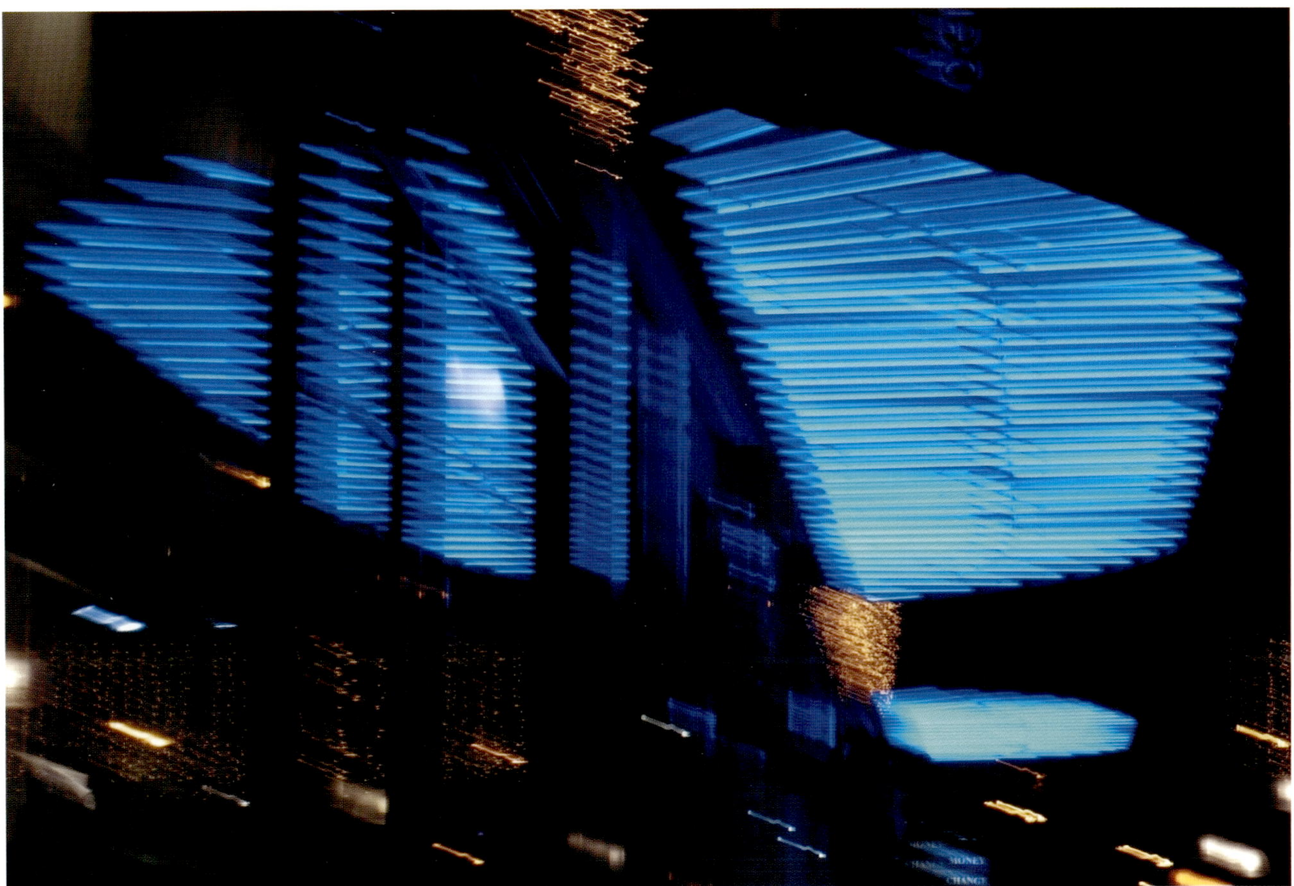

The blue-lit canopy of an Oxford Street shop

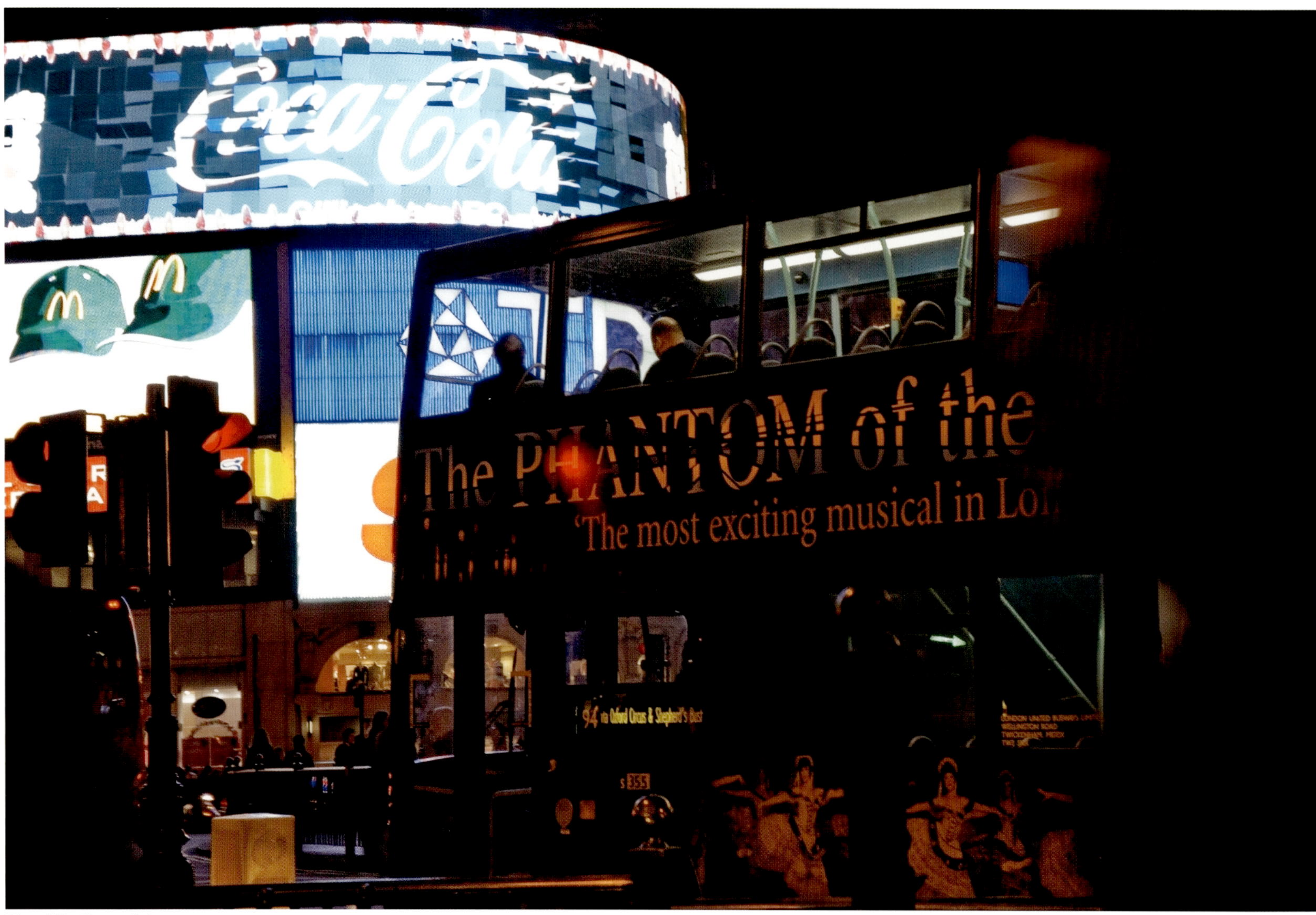

Piccadilly Circus lights

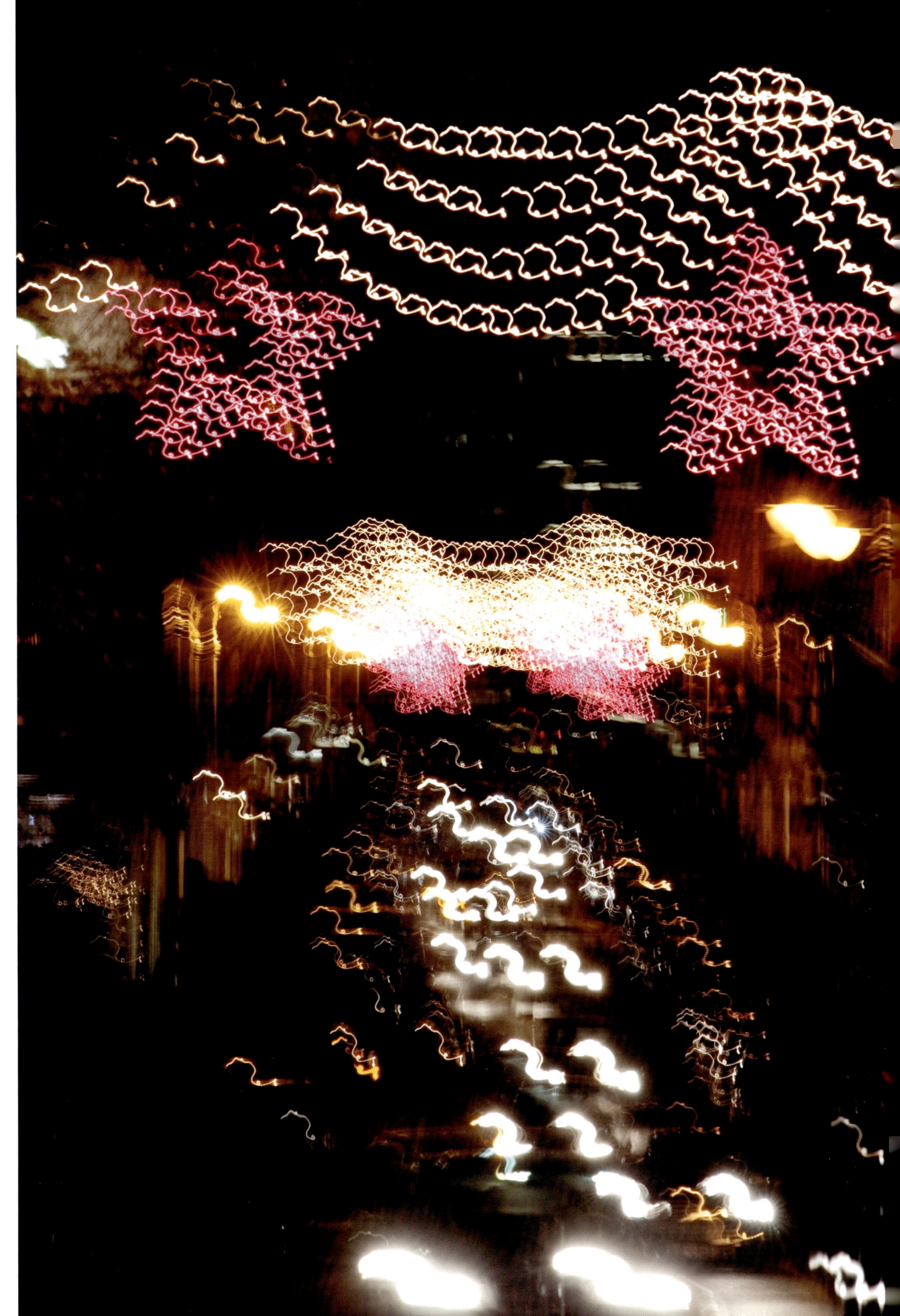

Christmas lights in
Bond Street

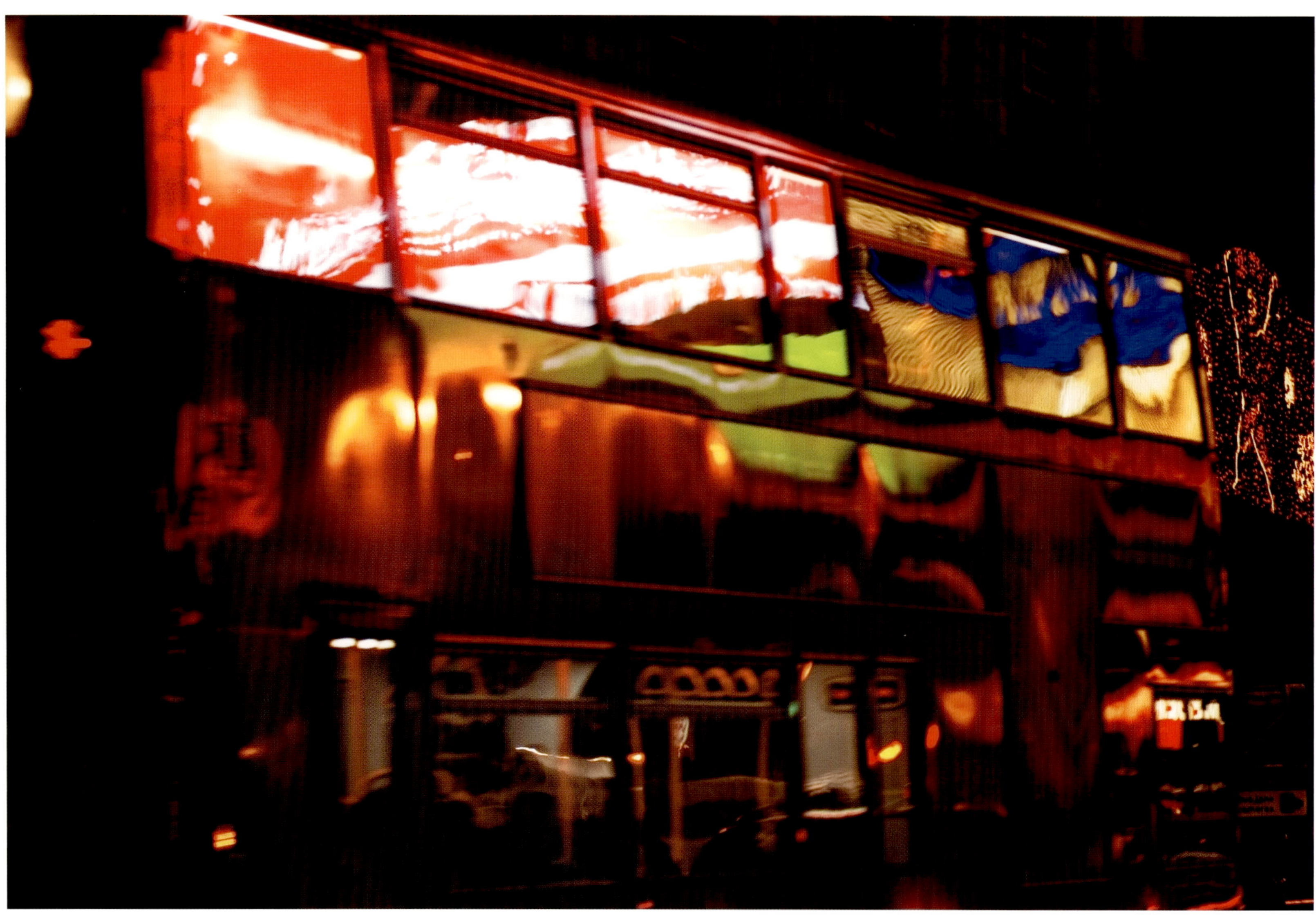

Lights reflected in a double-decker bus

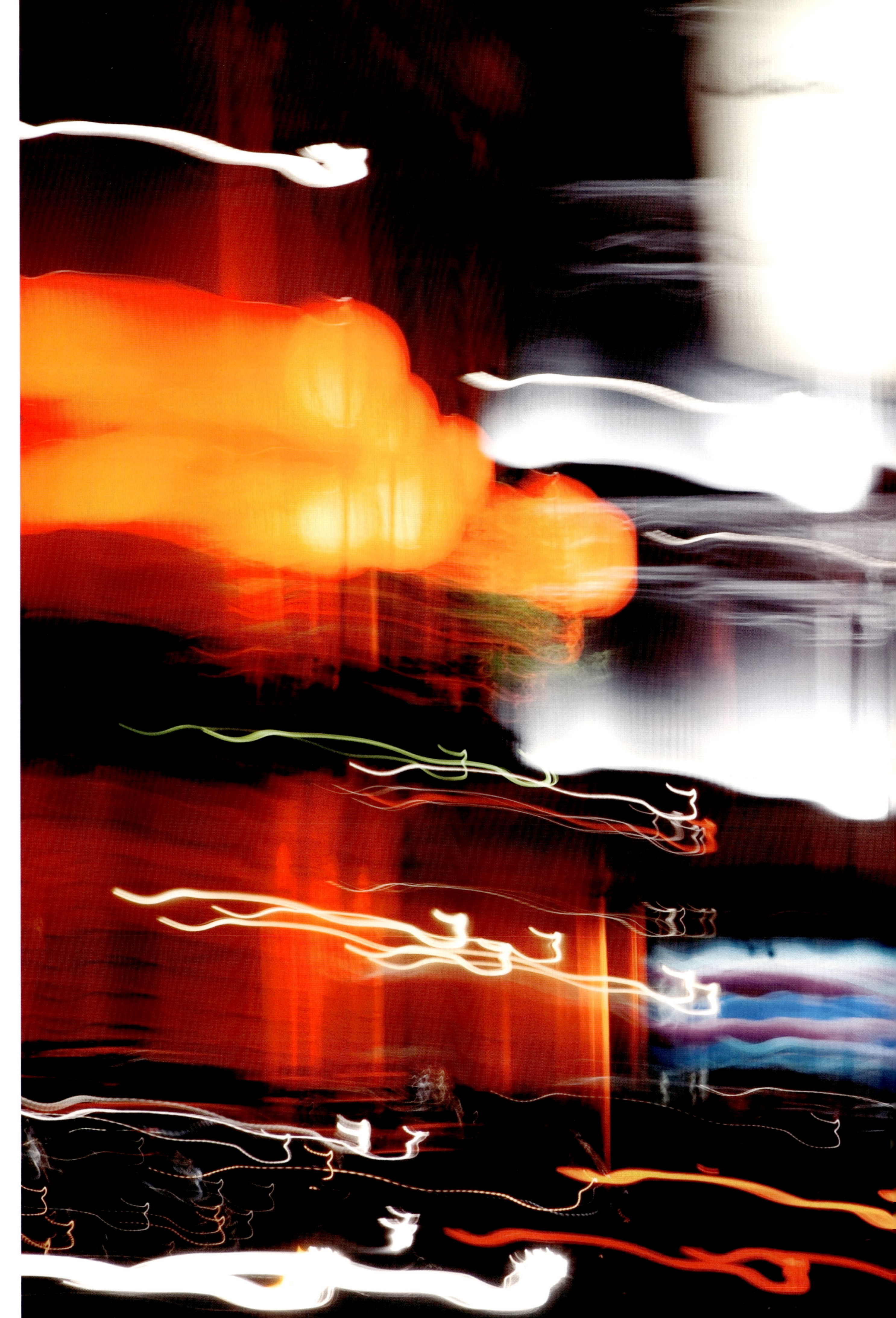

Burlington Gardens
Christmas lighting

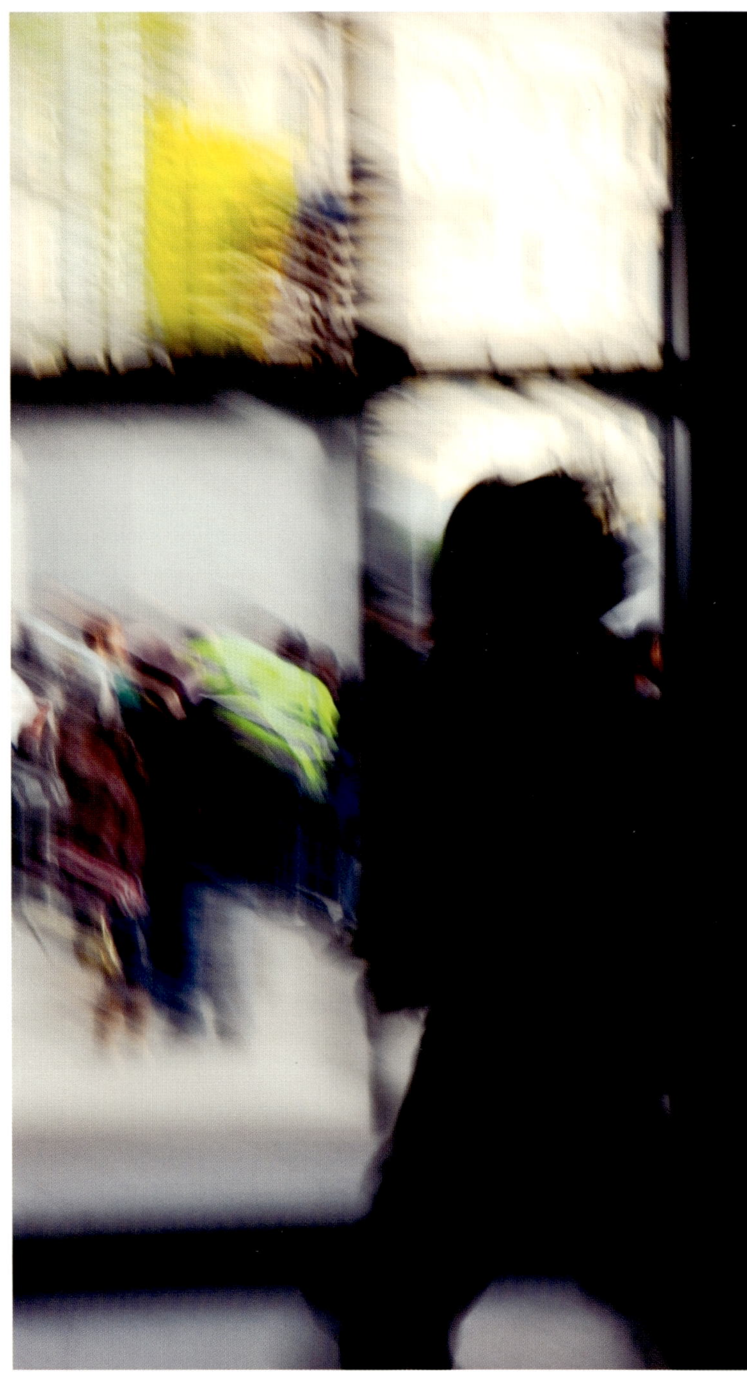

Opposite Trafalgar Square's fourth plinth, displaying Thomas Schütte's *Model for a Hotel*
Above The fourth plinth photographed from the National Gallery

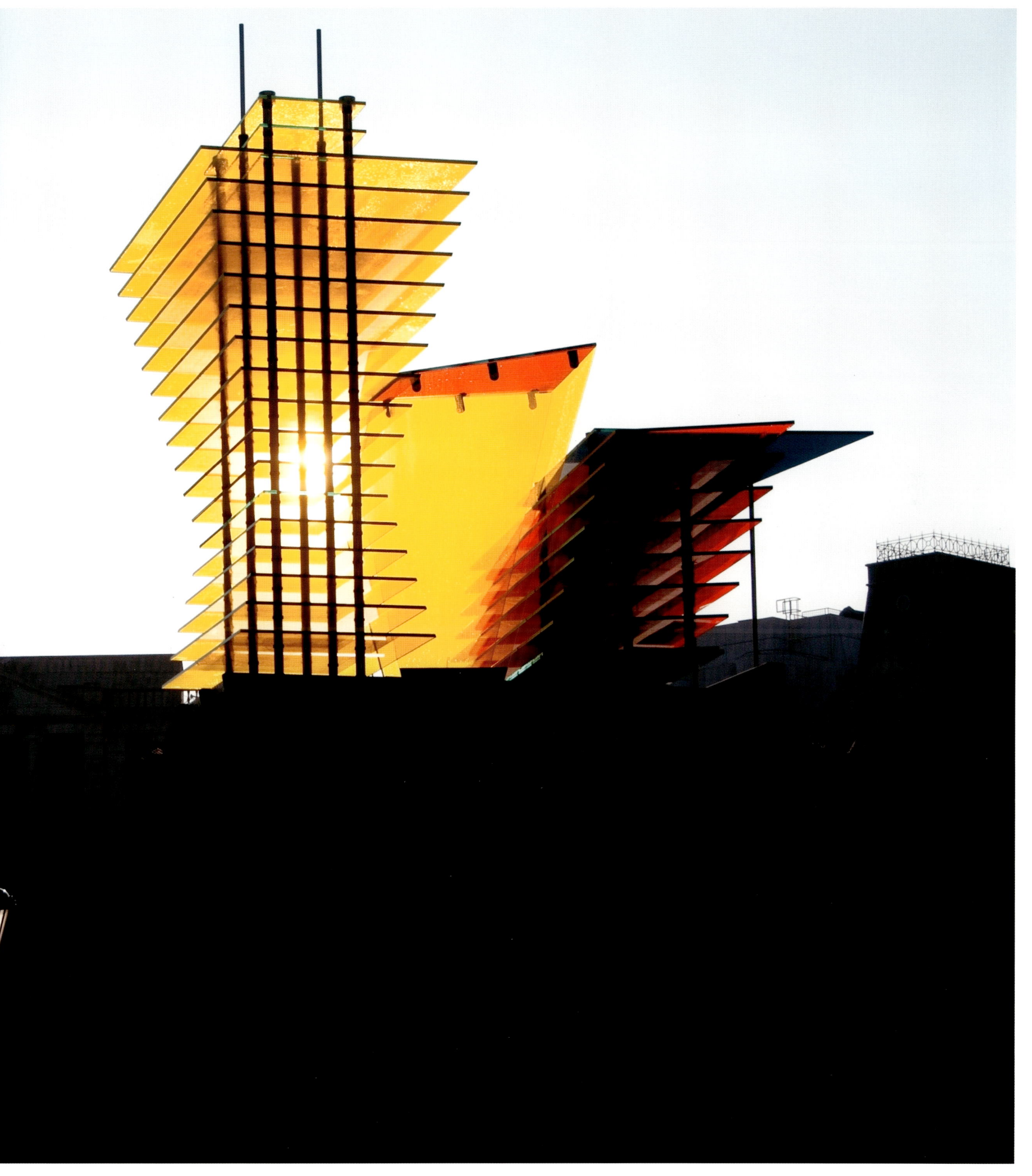

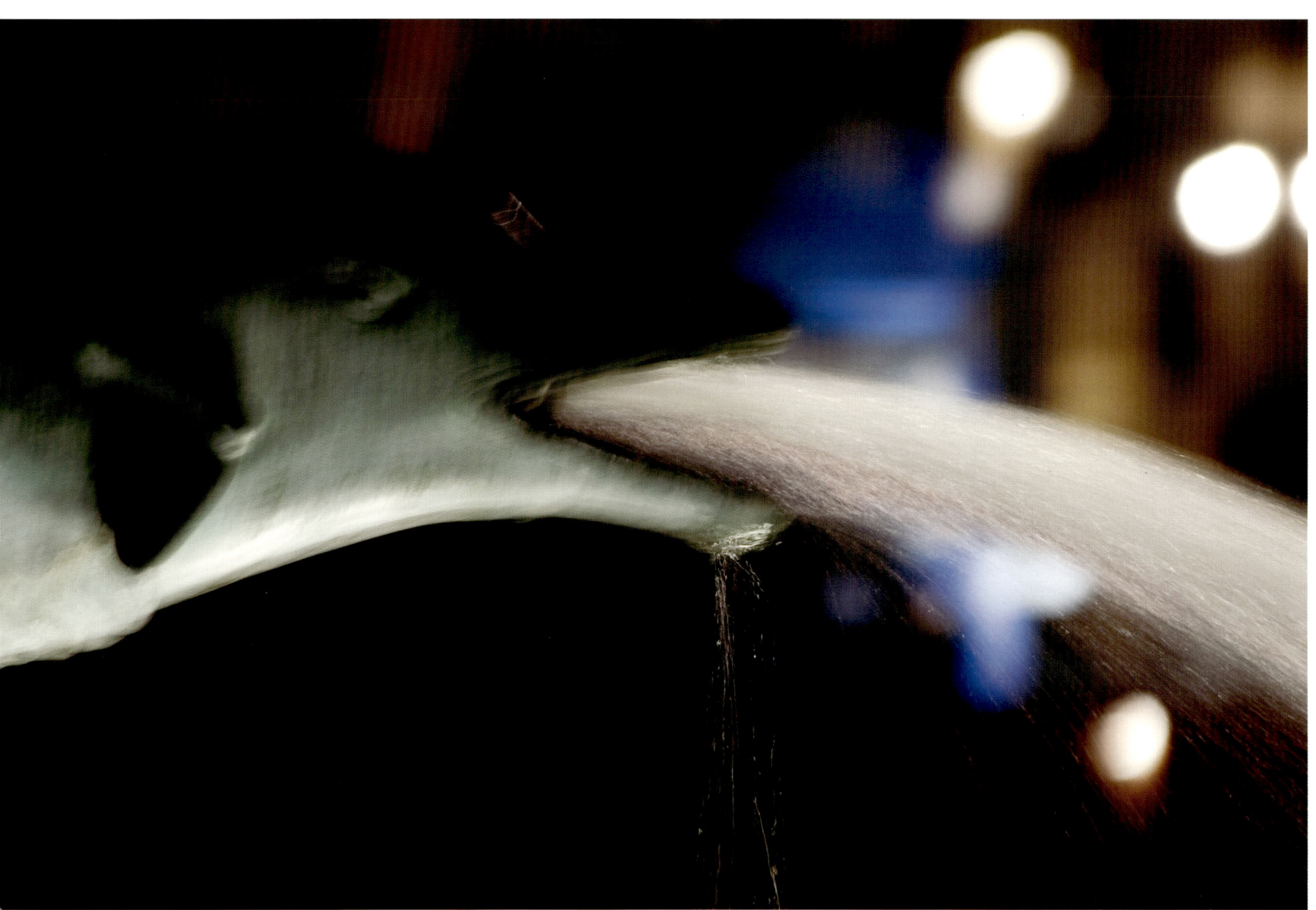

Above, opposite and on pages 50-51
Fountains in Trafalgar Square

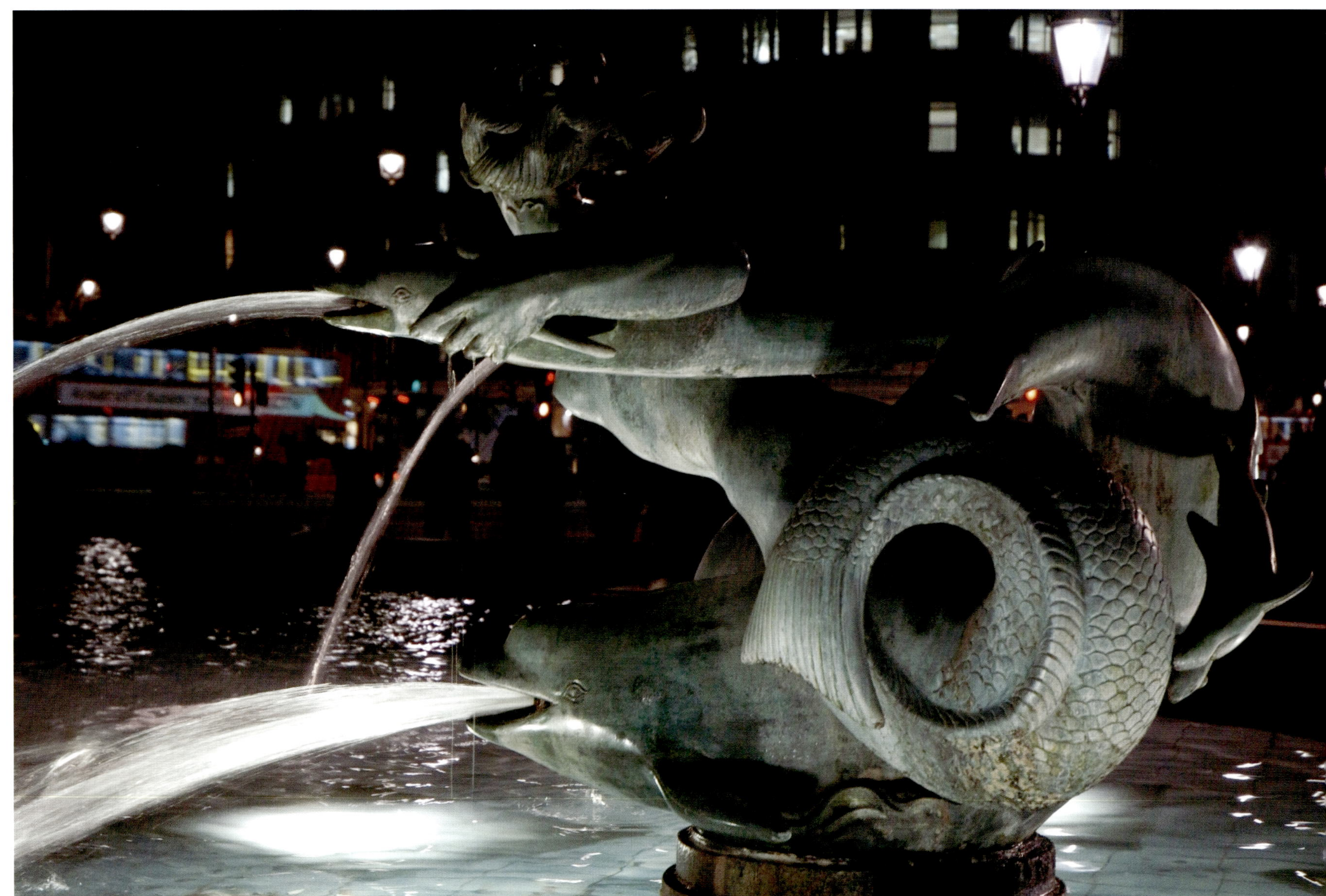

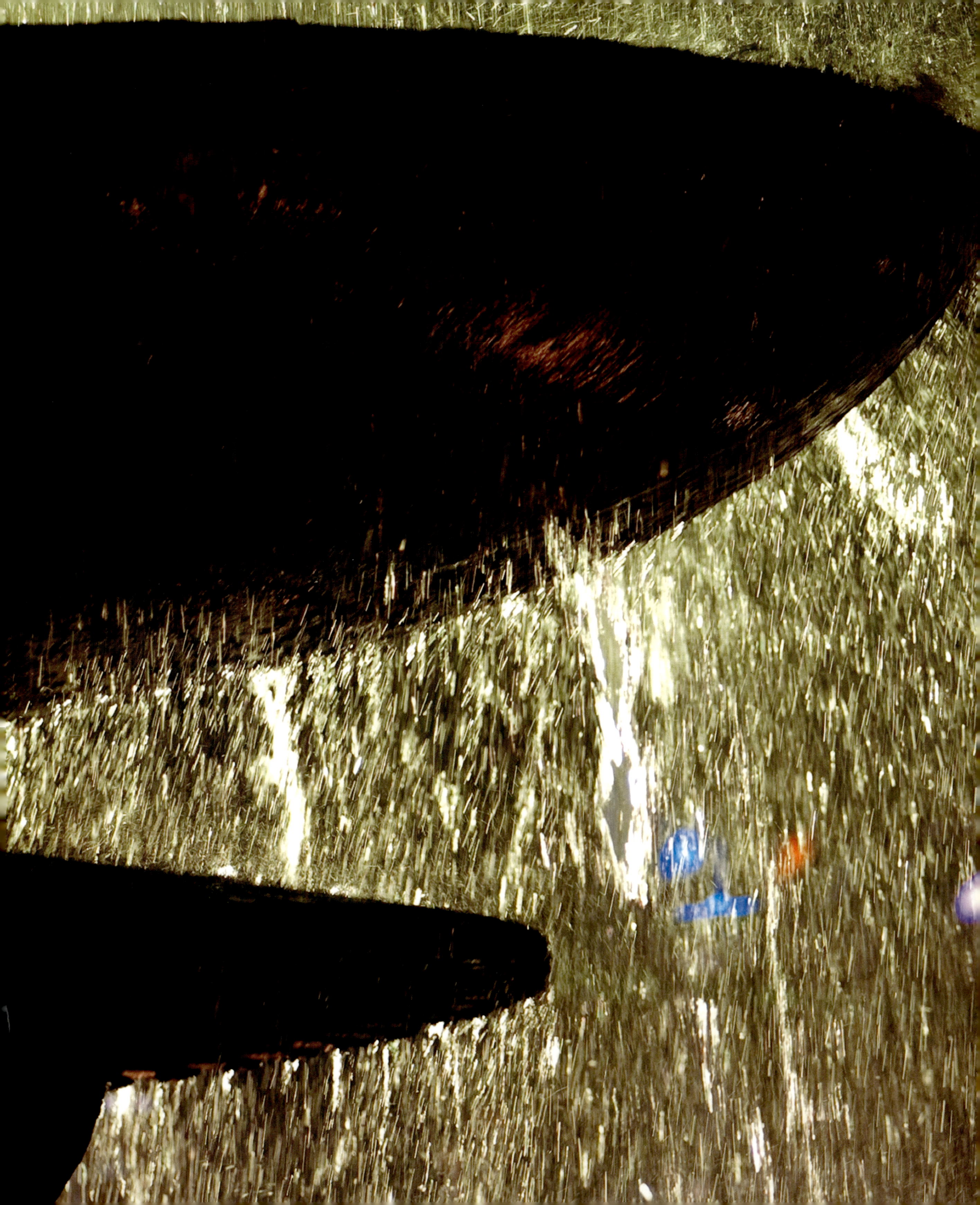

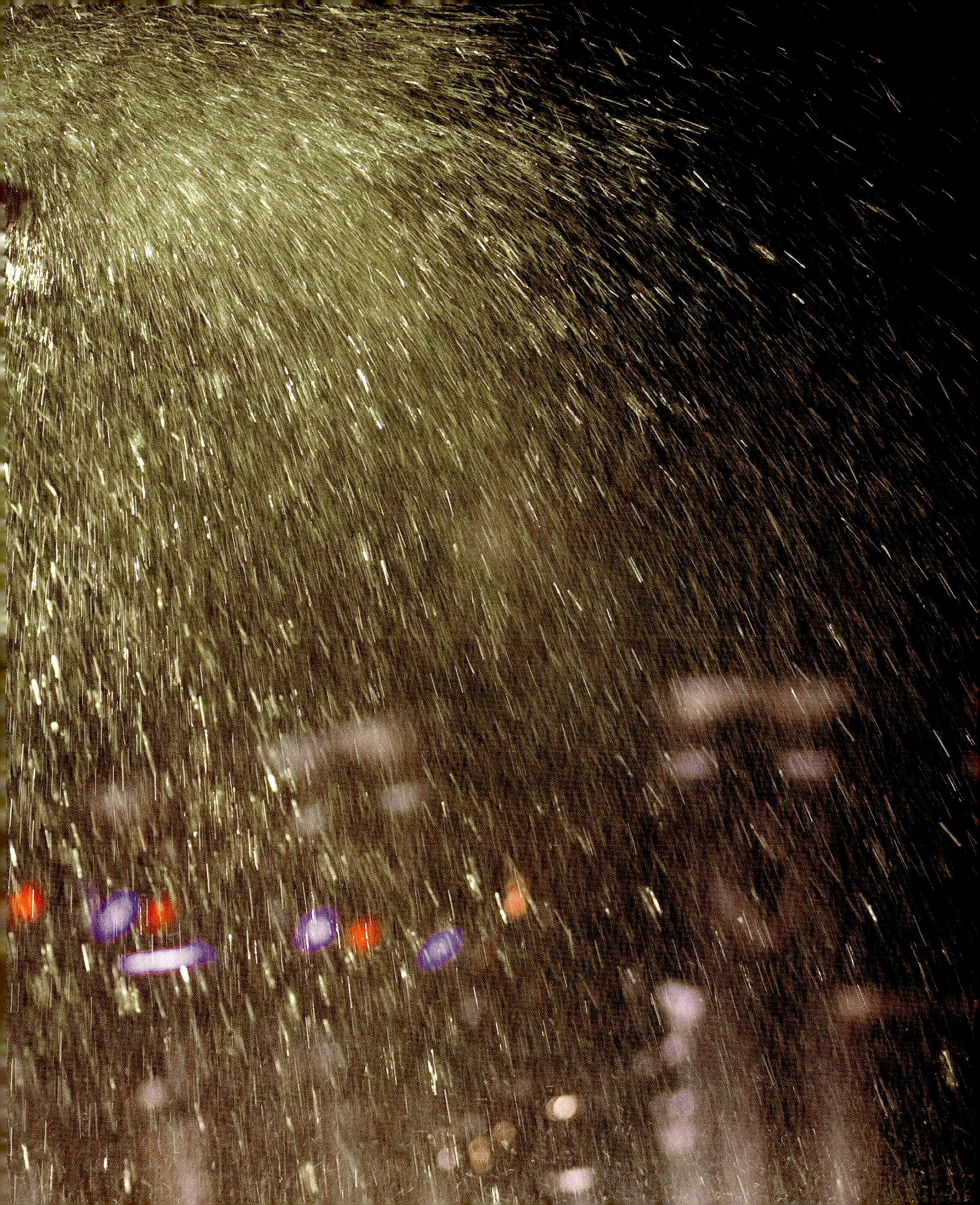

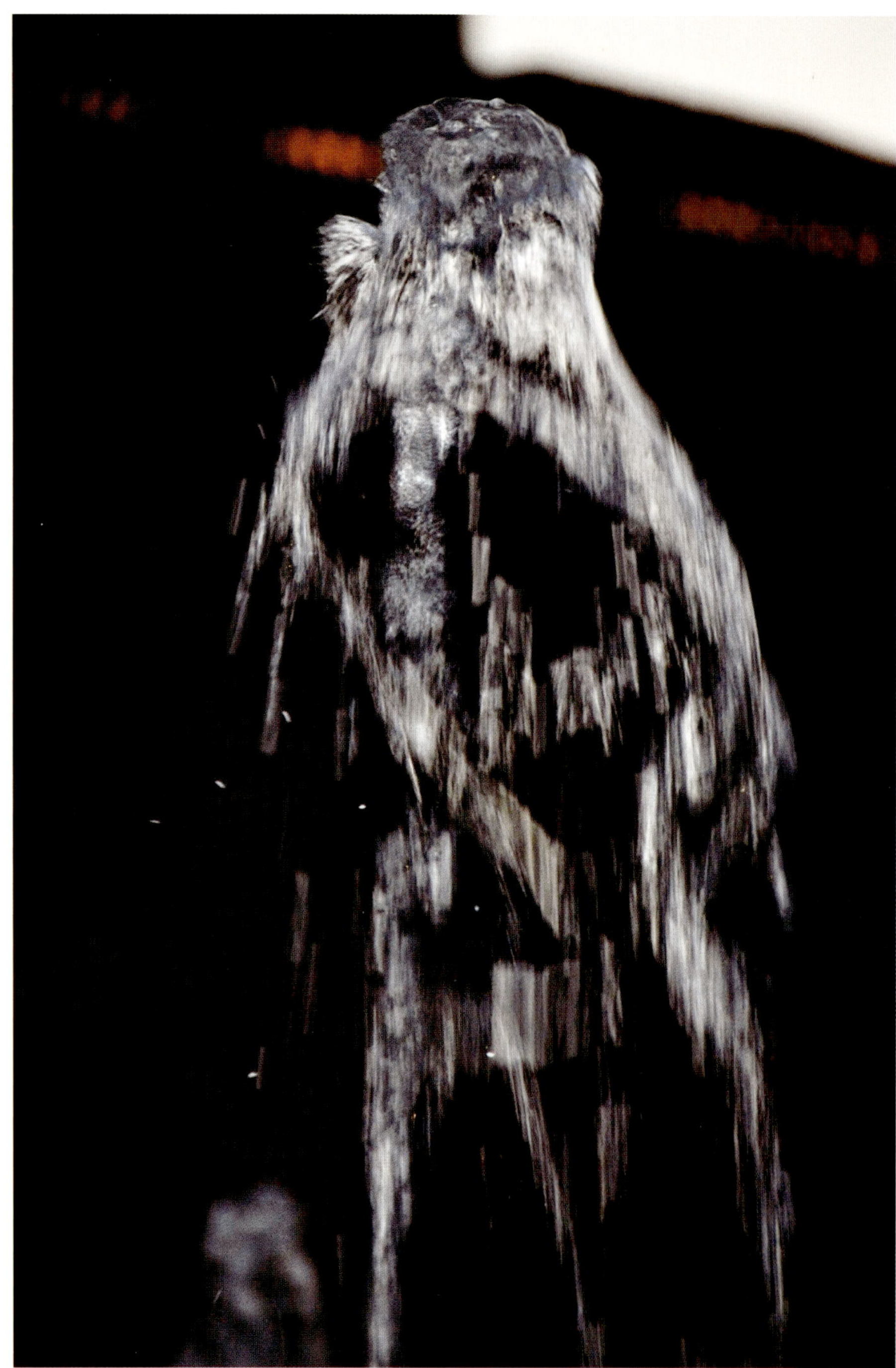

Above, opposite and on pages 54 and 55
Fountains in the courtyard at Somerset House

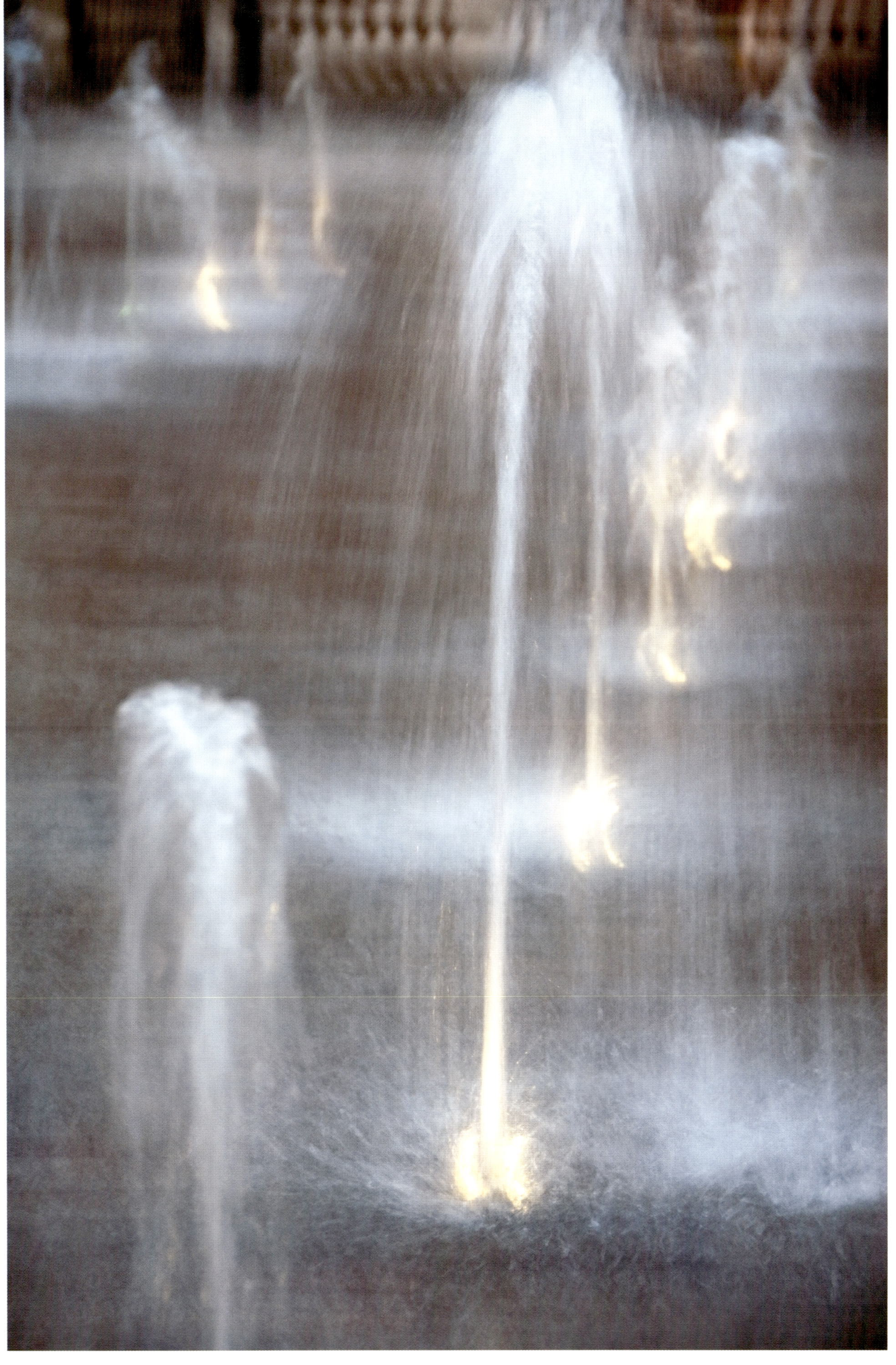

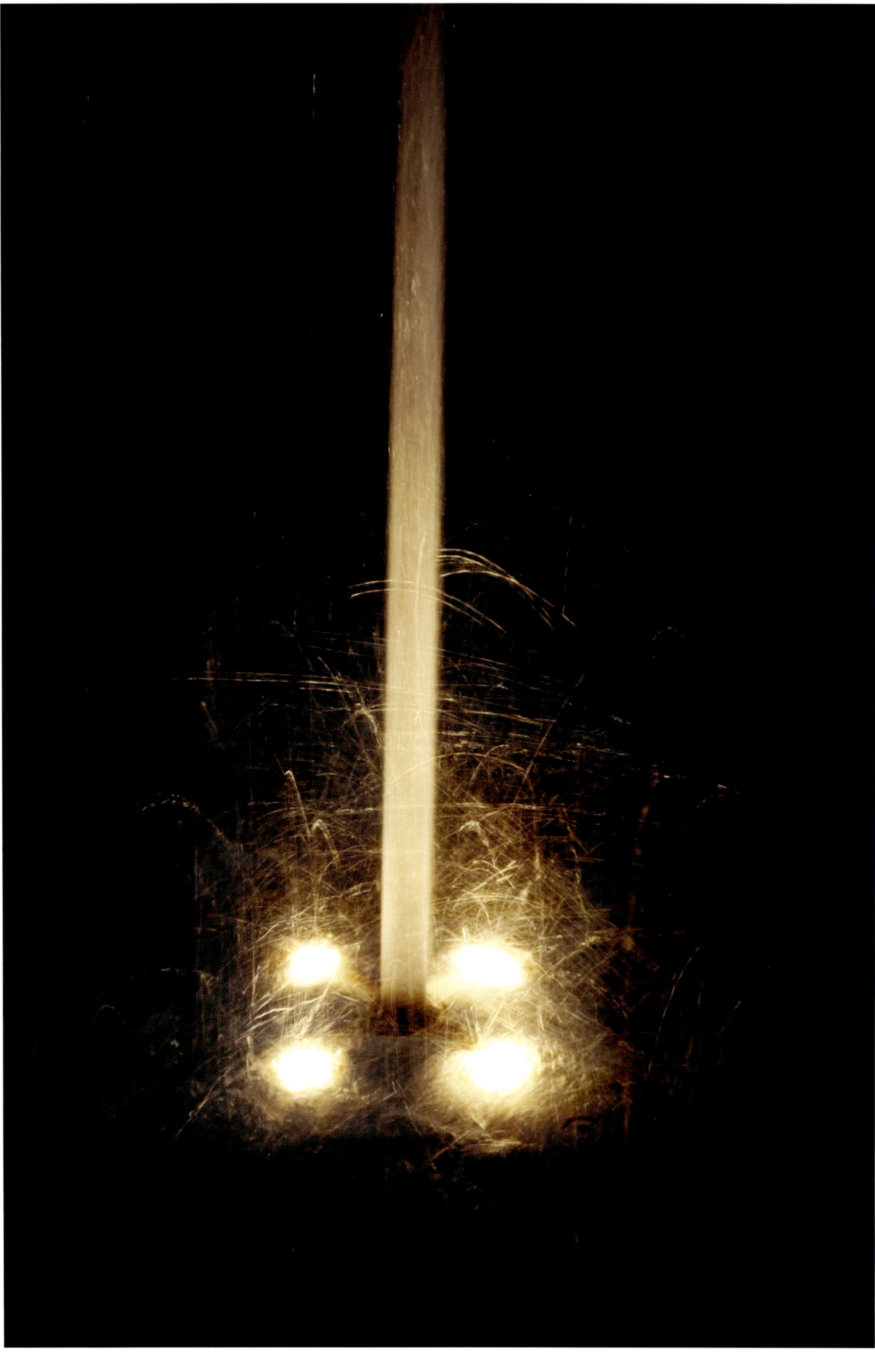

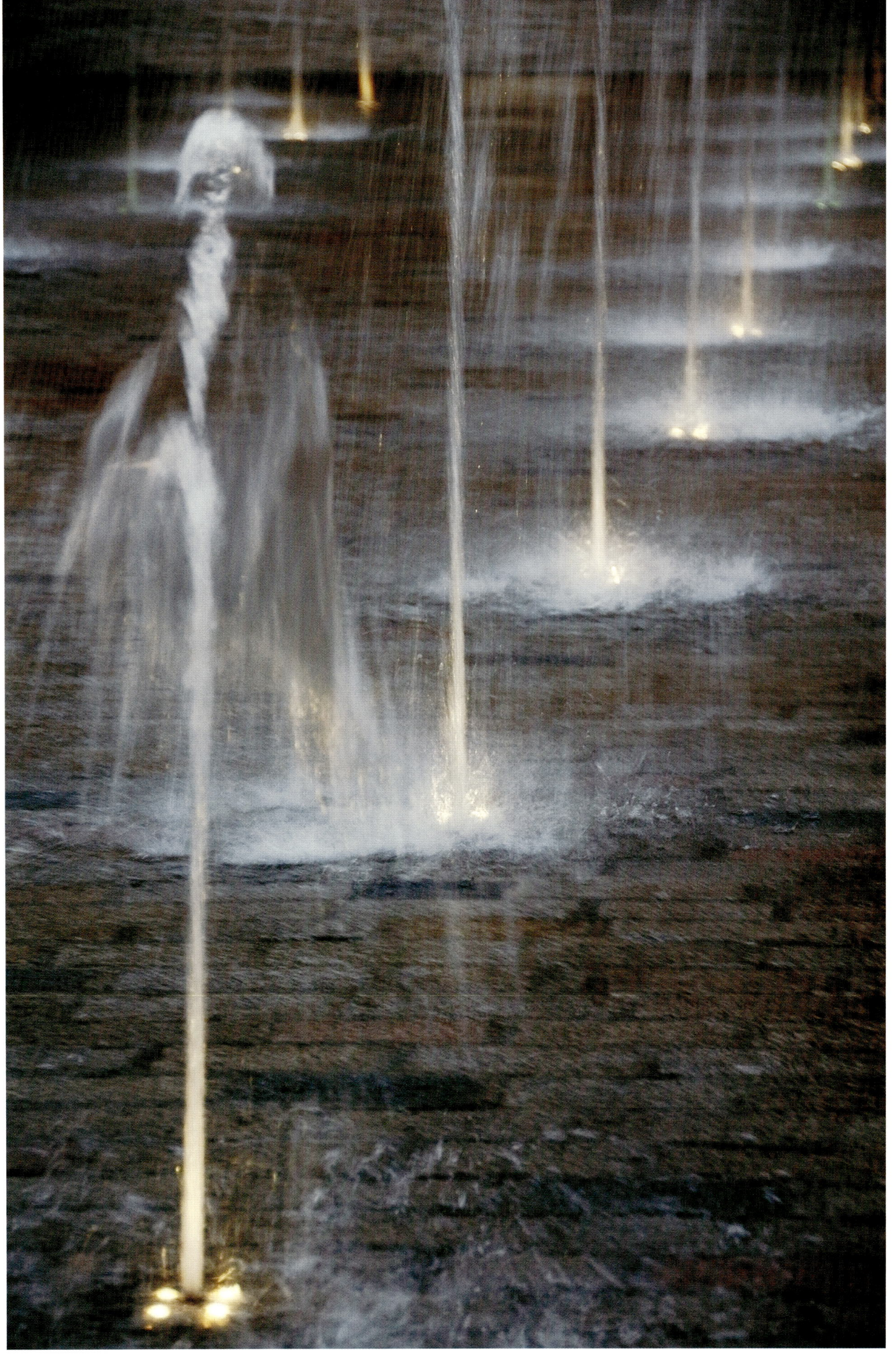

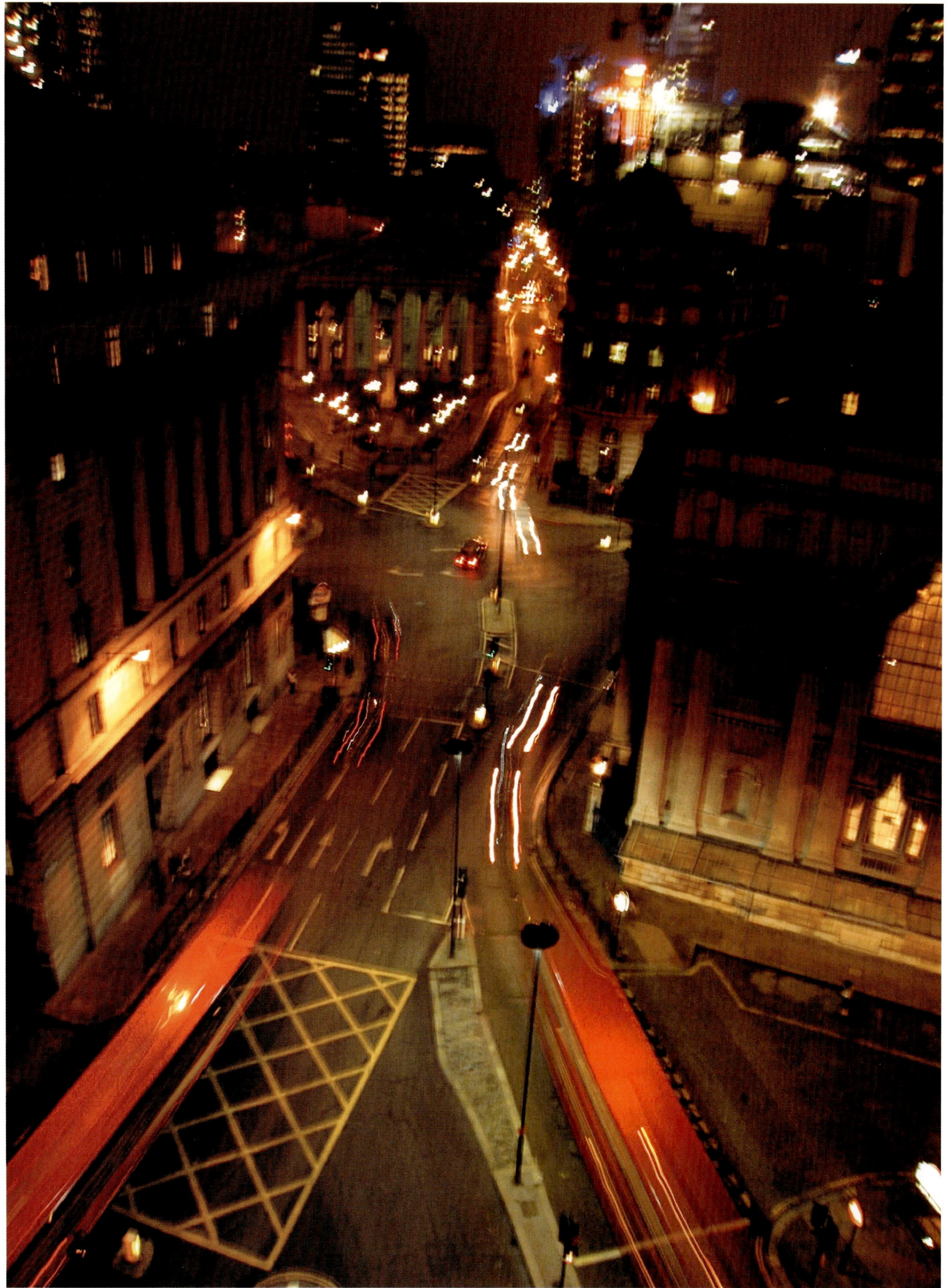

The Mansion House and the Royal Exchange, in the City of London

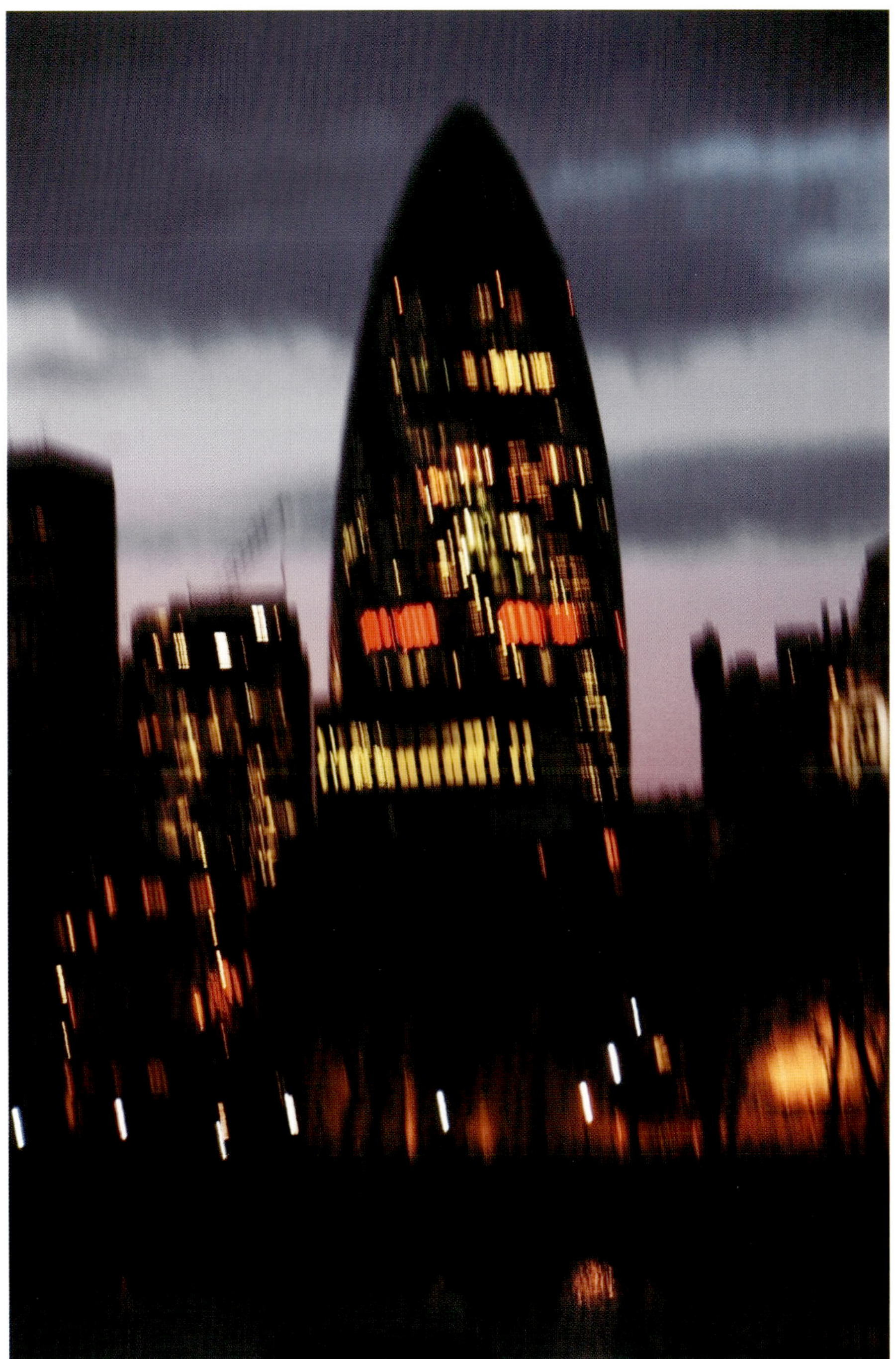

The Gherkin: the Swiss Re building at 30 St Mary Axe, designed by Norman Foster

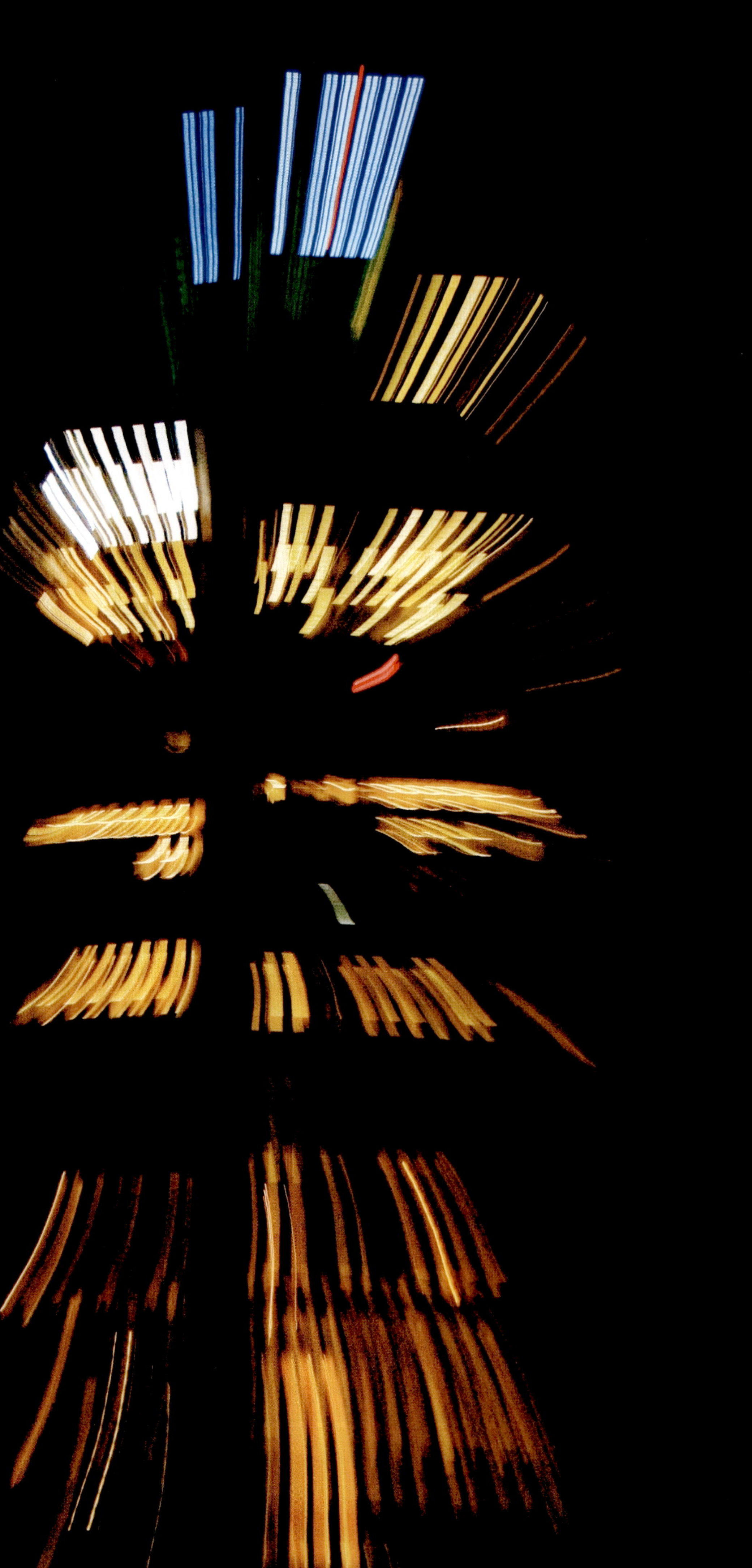

Tower 42, also known as the NatWest Tower, designed by Norman Foster

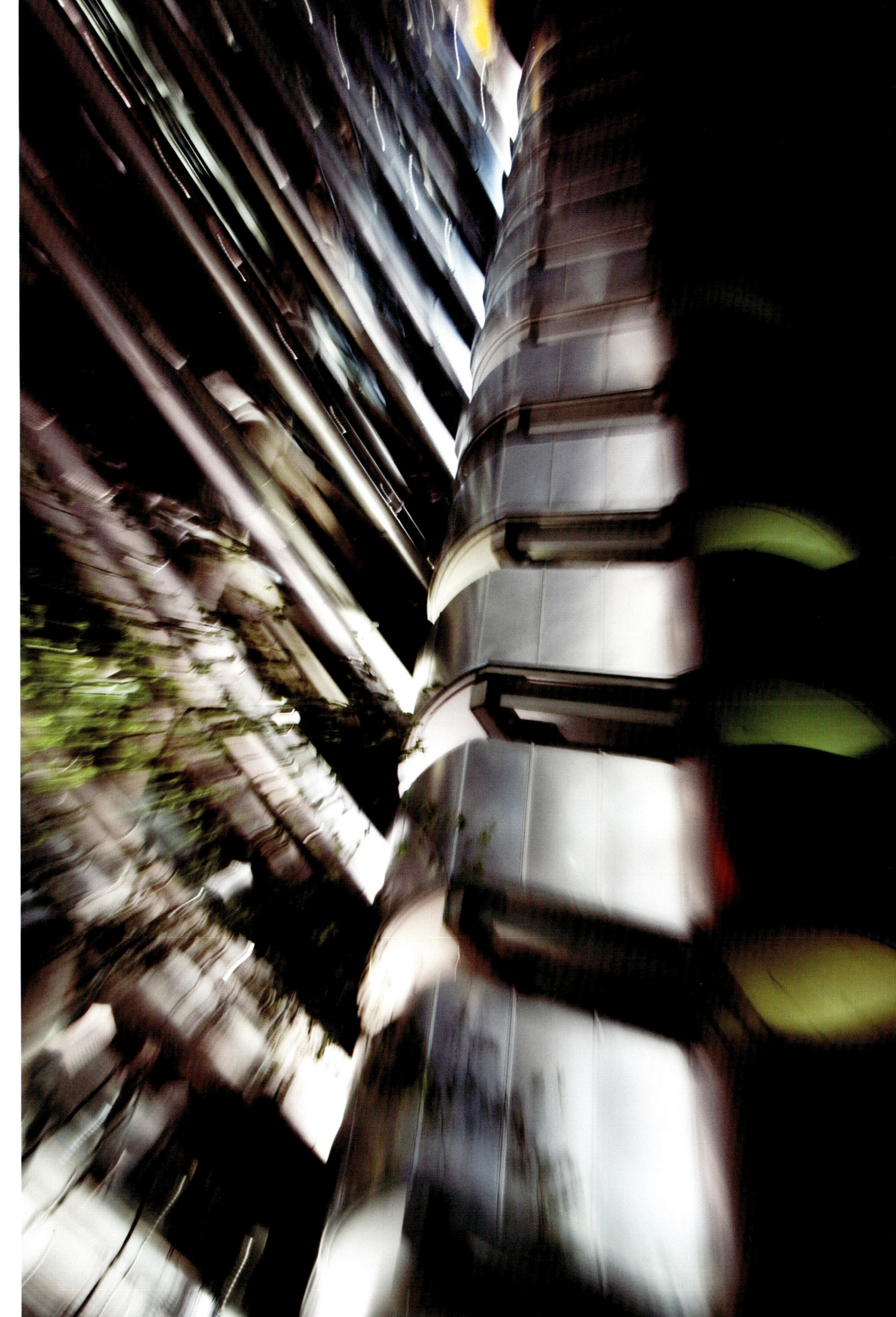

The Lloyds Building, designed by Richard Rogers

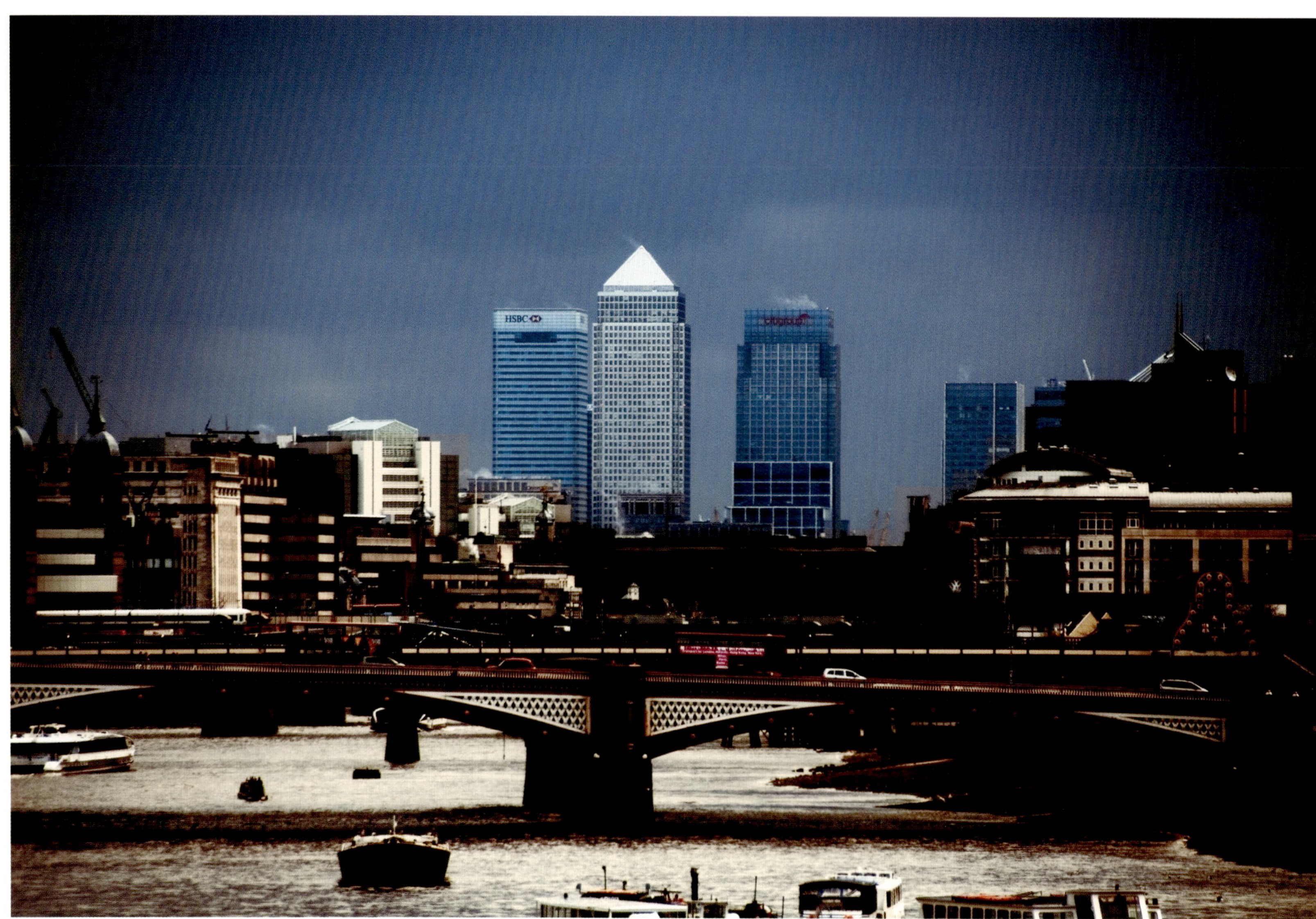

Canary Wharf from Waterloo Bridge

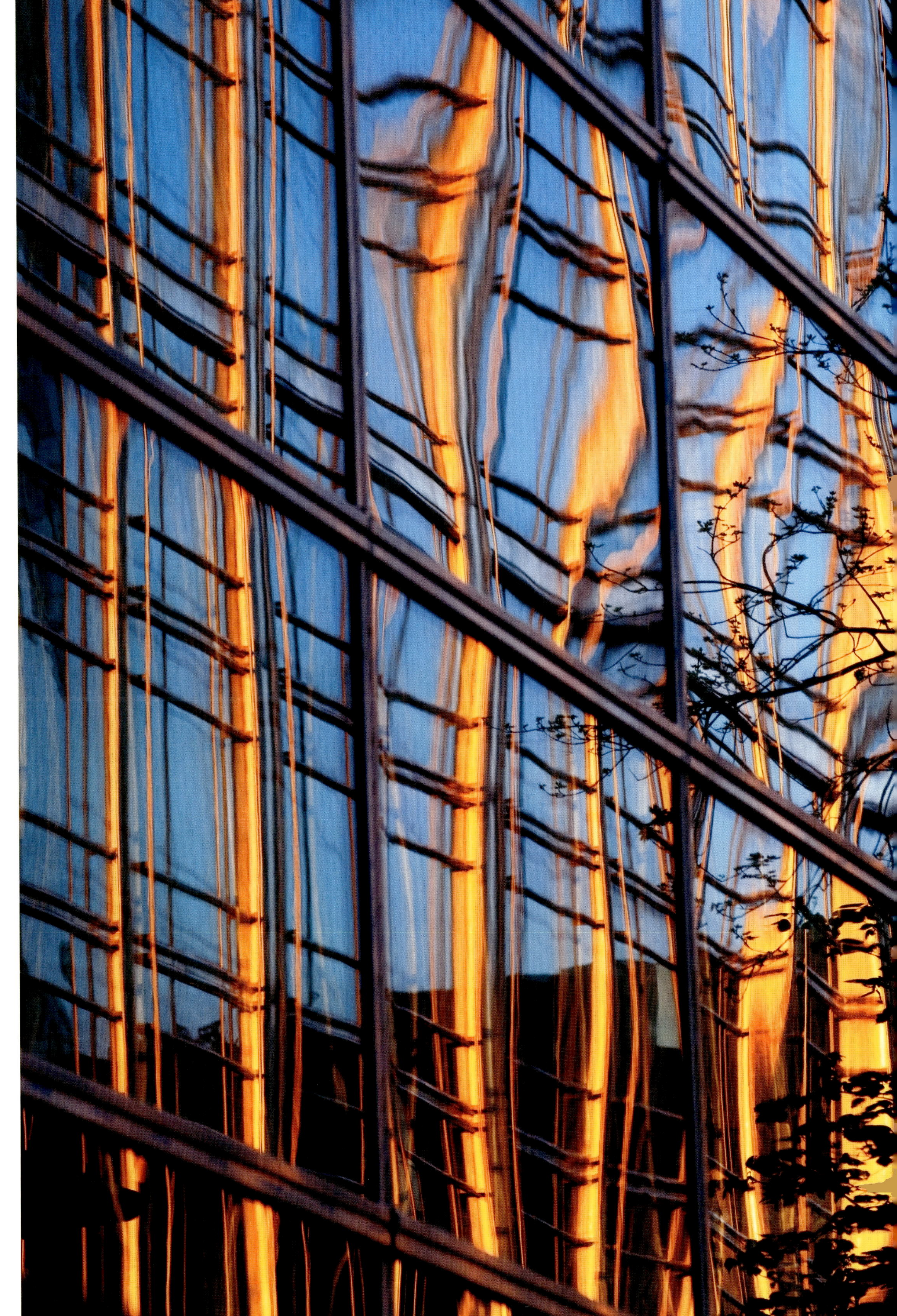

Sunset reflections in the windows of an office block in Canary Wharf's South Colonnade

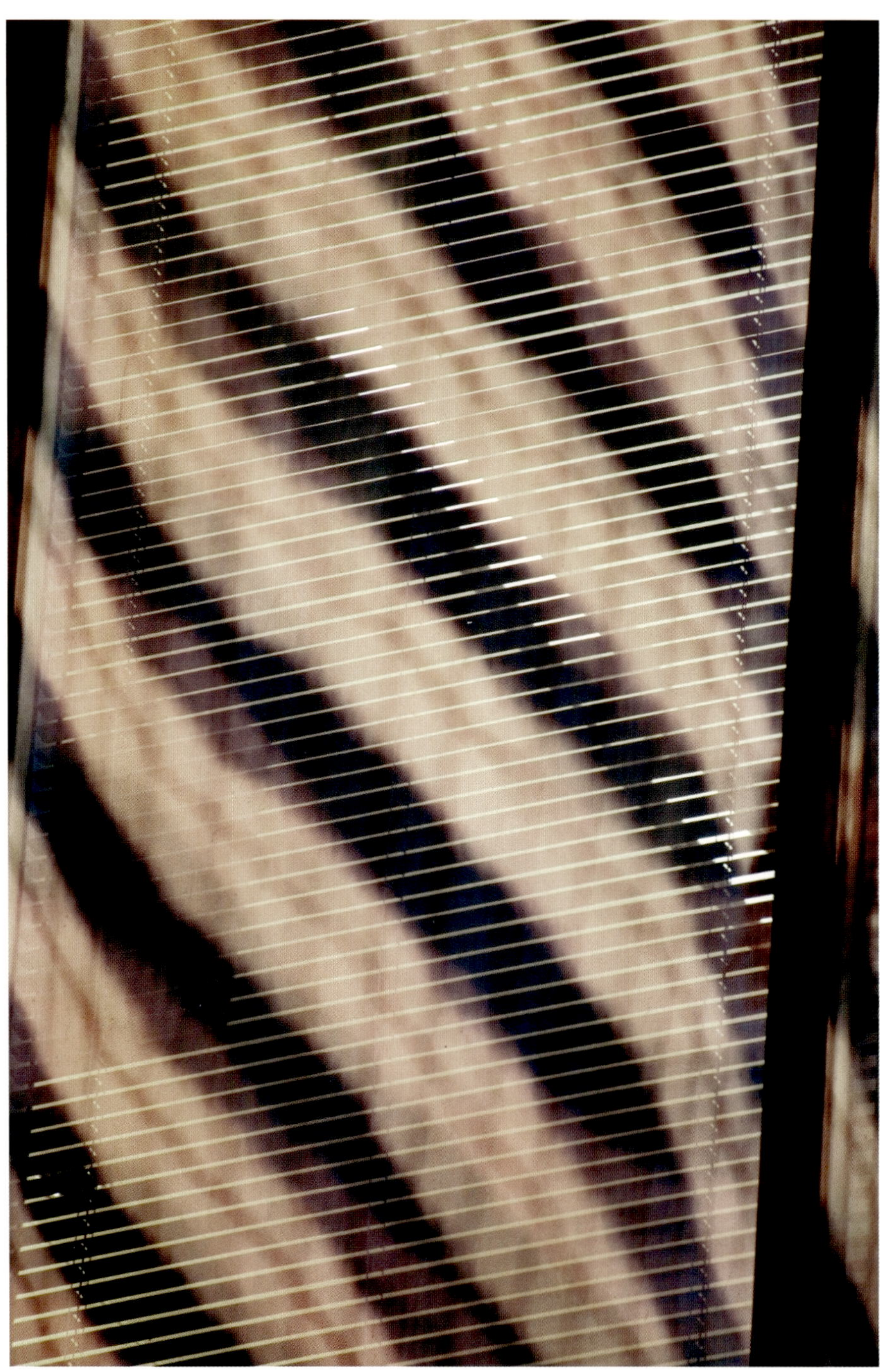

Above and opposite
Reflections in the windows of South Colonnade office blocks

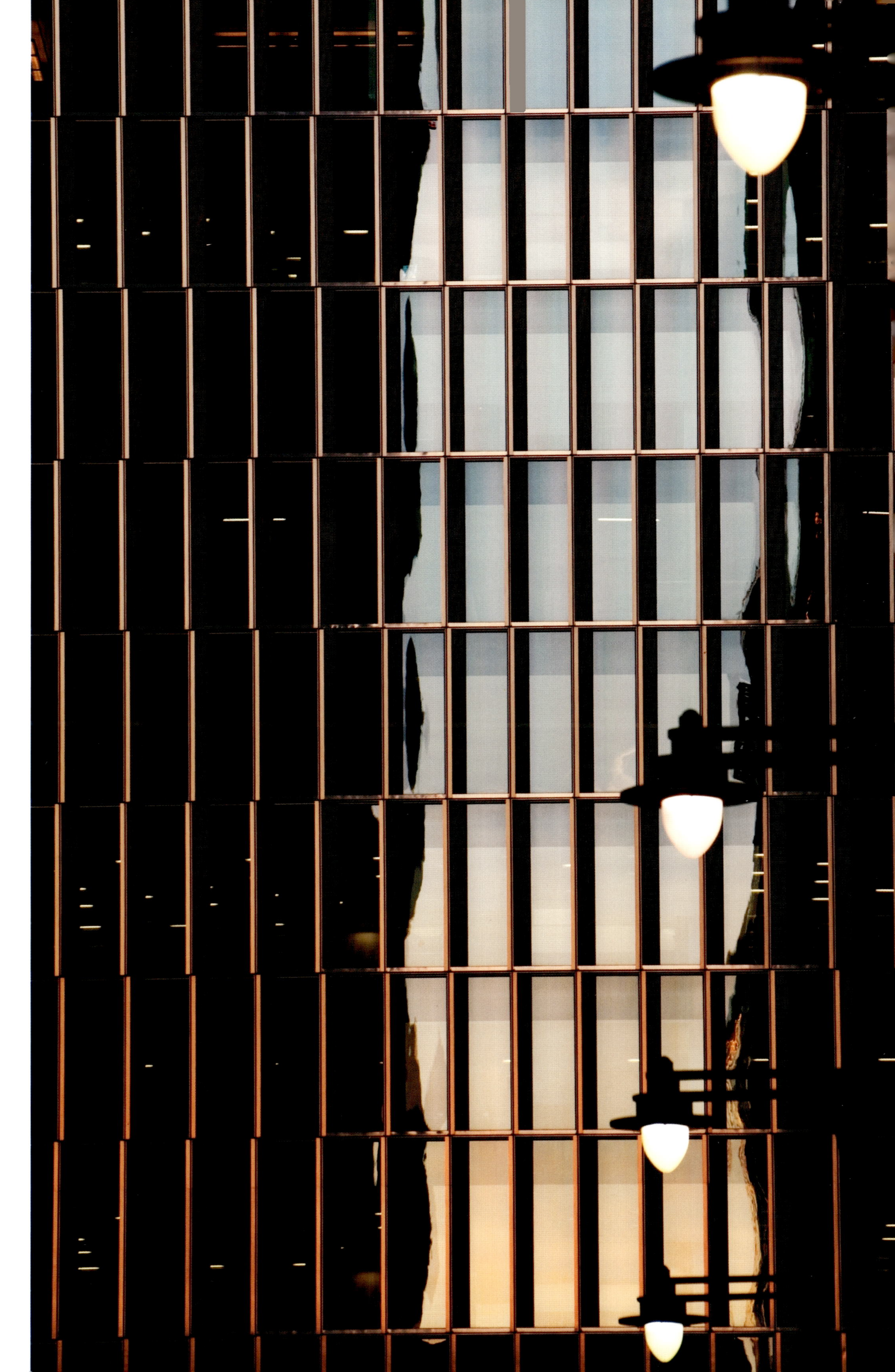

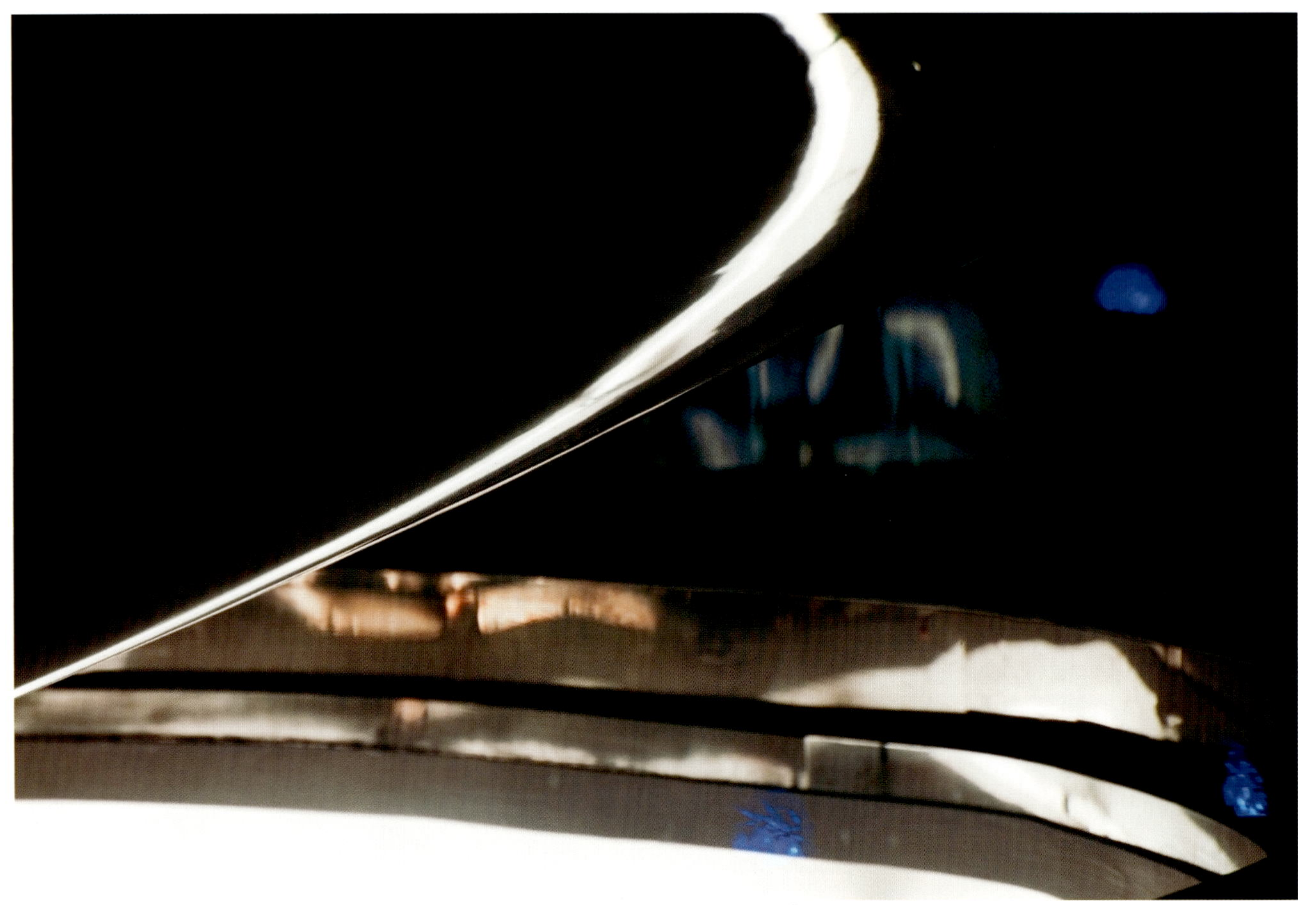

Big Blue, sculpture by Ron Arad, outside Canary Wharf Tower

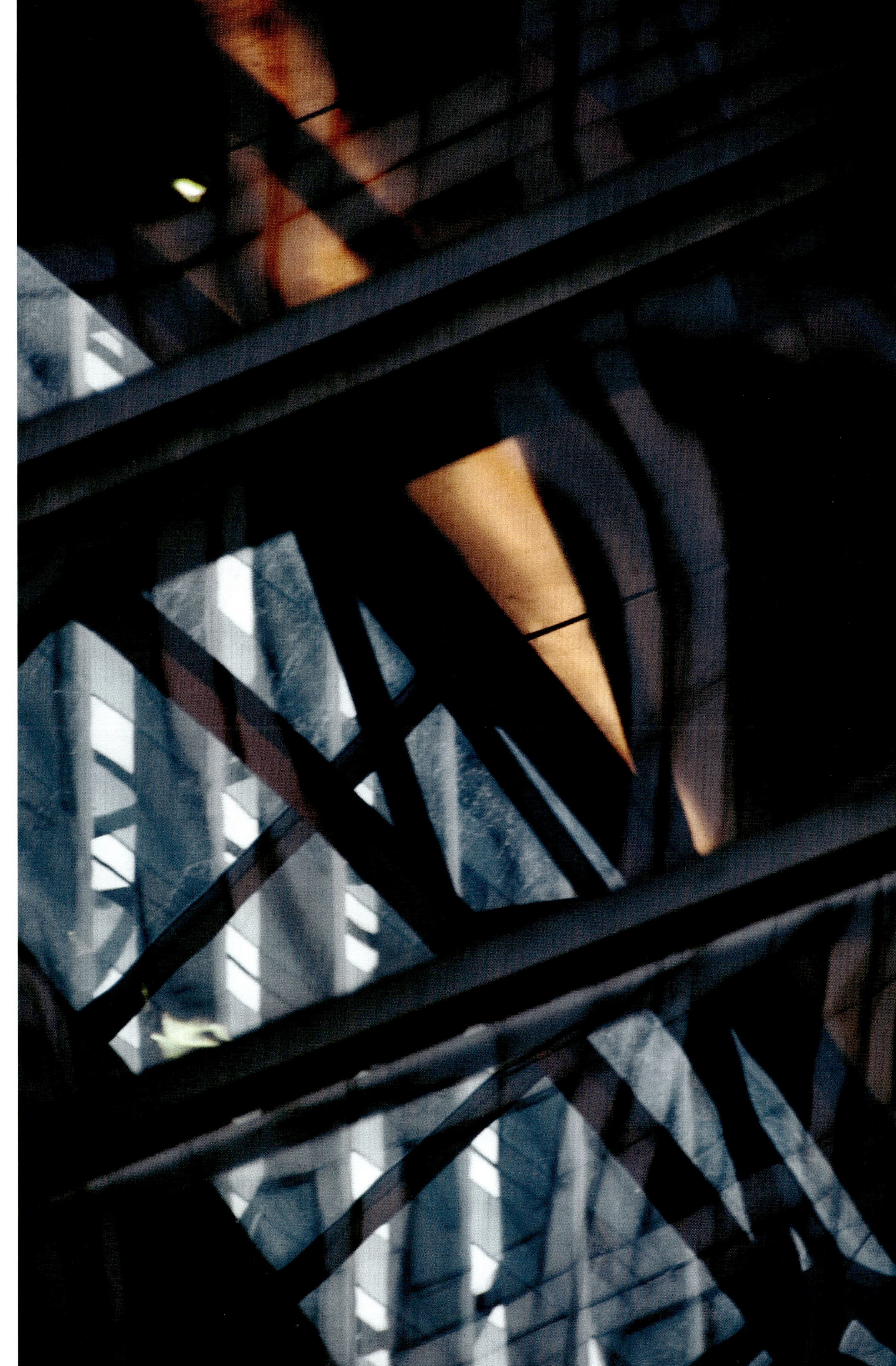

Window reflections in
the North Colonnade

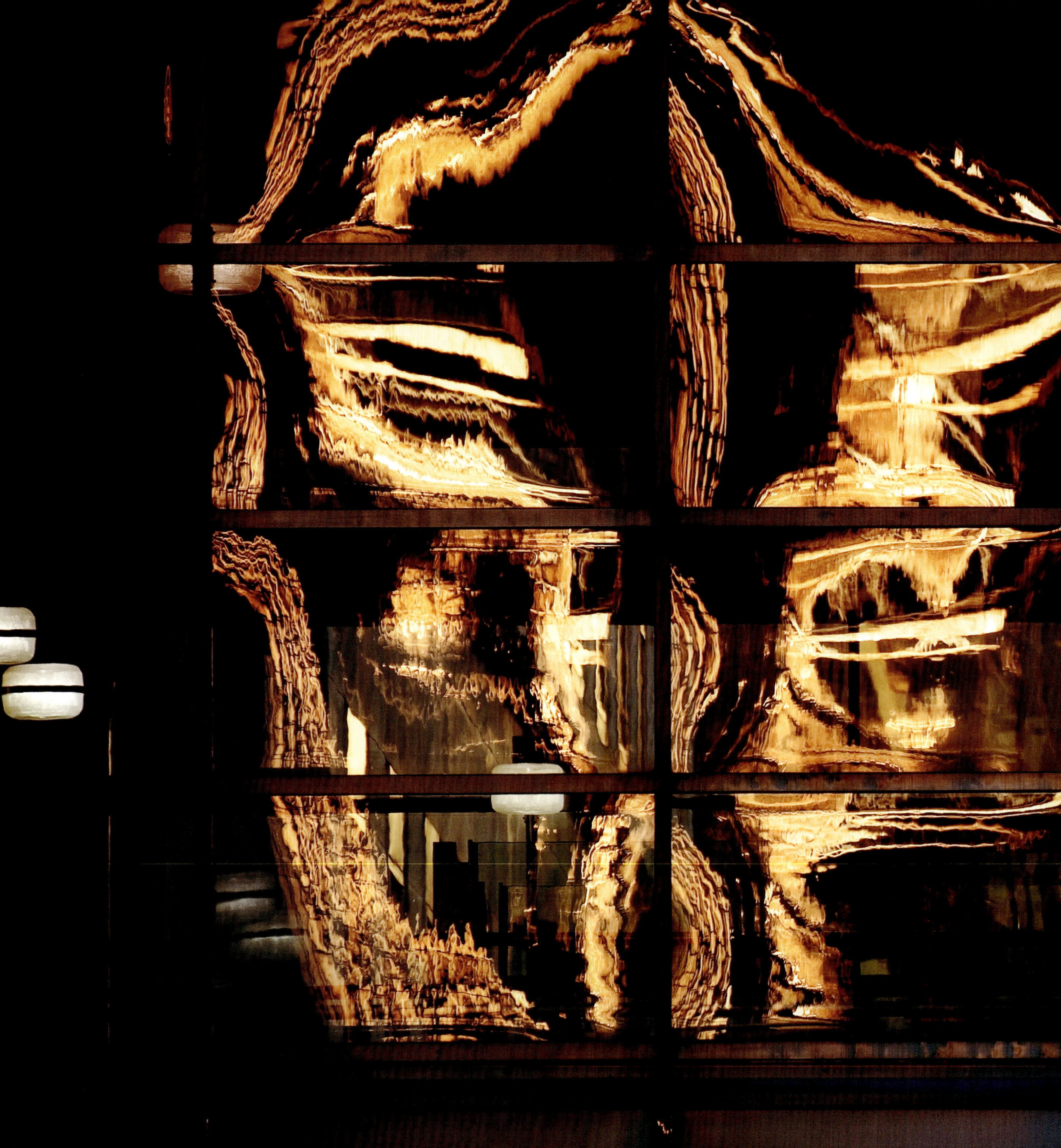

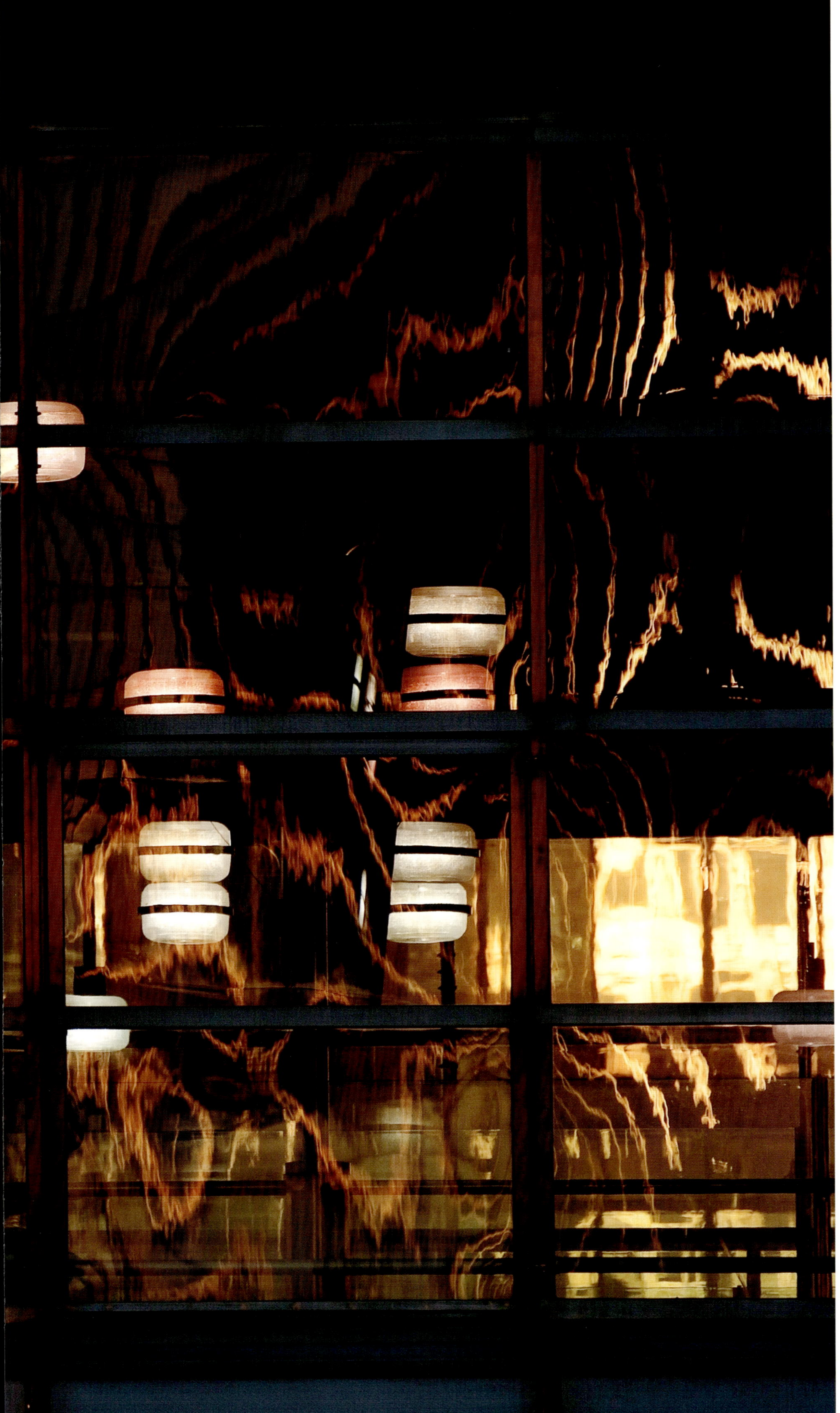

Sunset reflected through windows on the South Colonnade

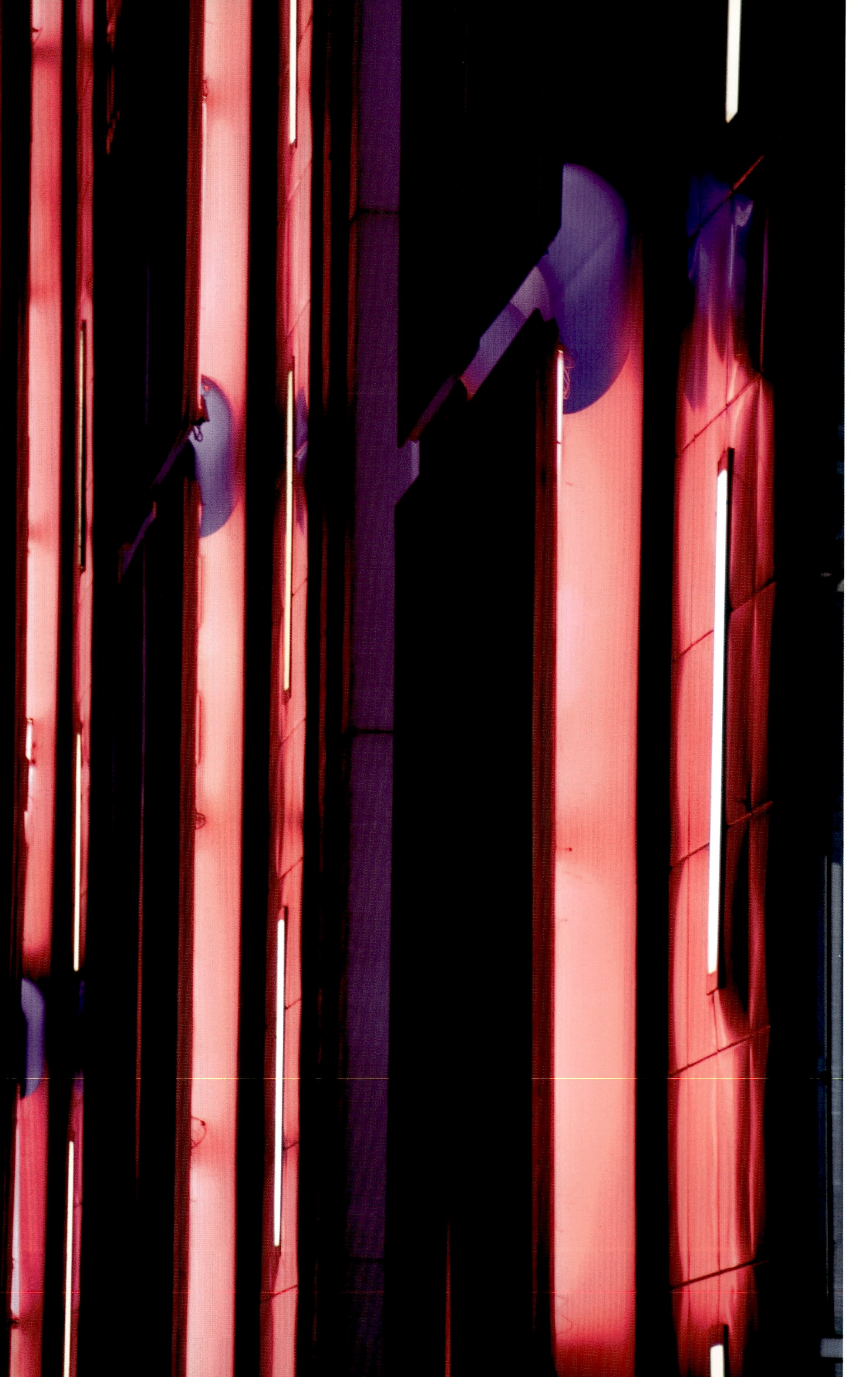

Ceiling lighting for a
North Colonnade
pedestrian crossing

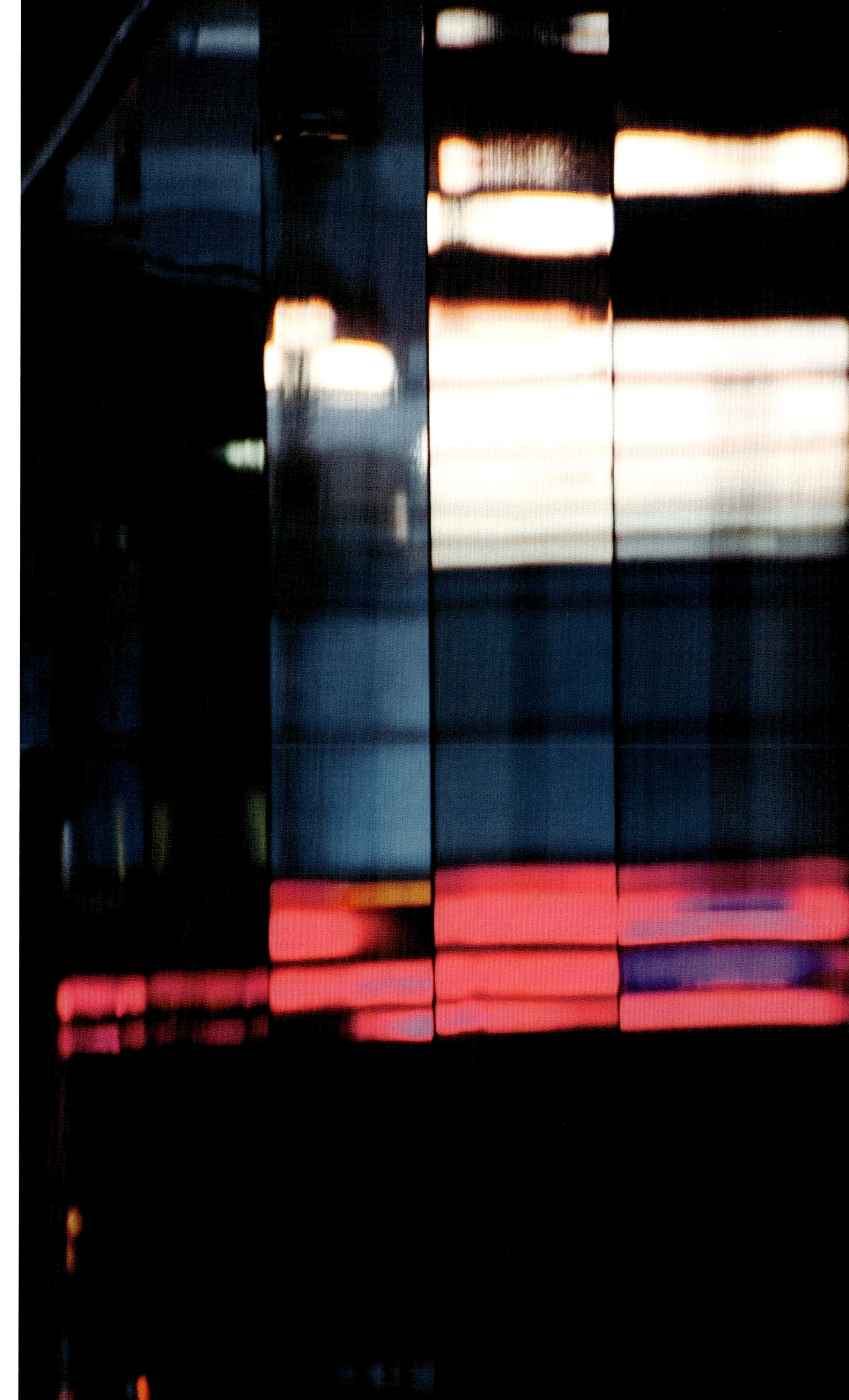

Lighting reflected in
an office block on the
North Colonnade

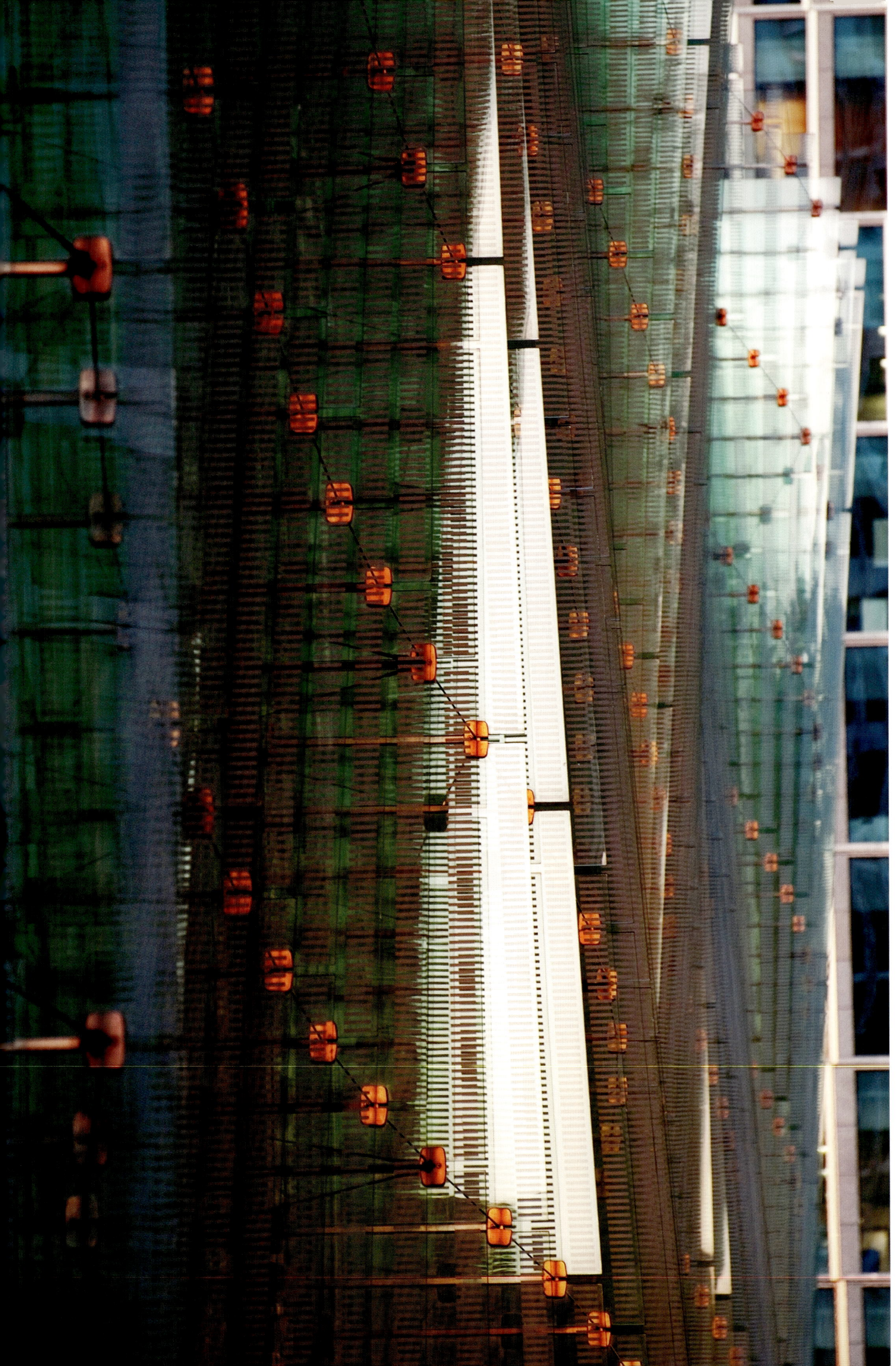

South Colonnade,
Canary Wharf

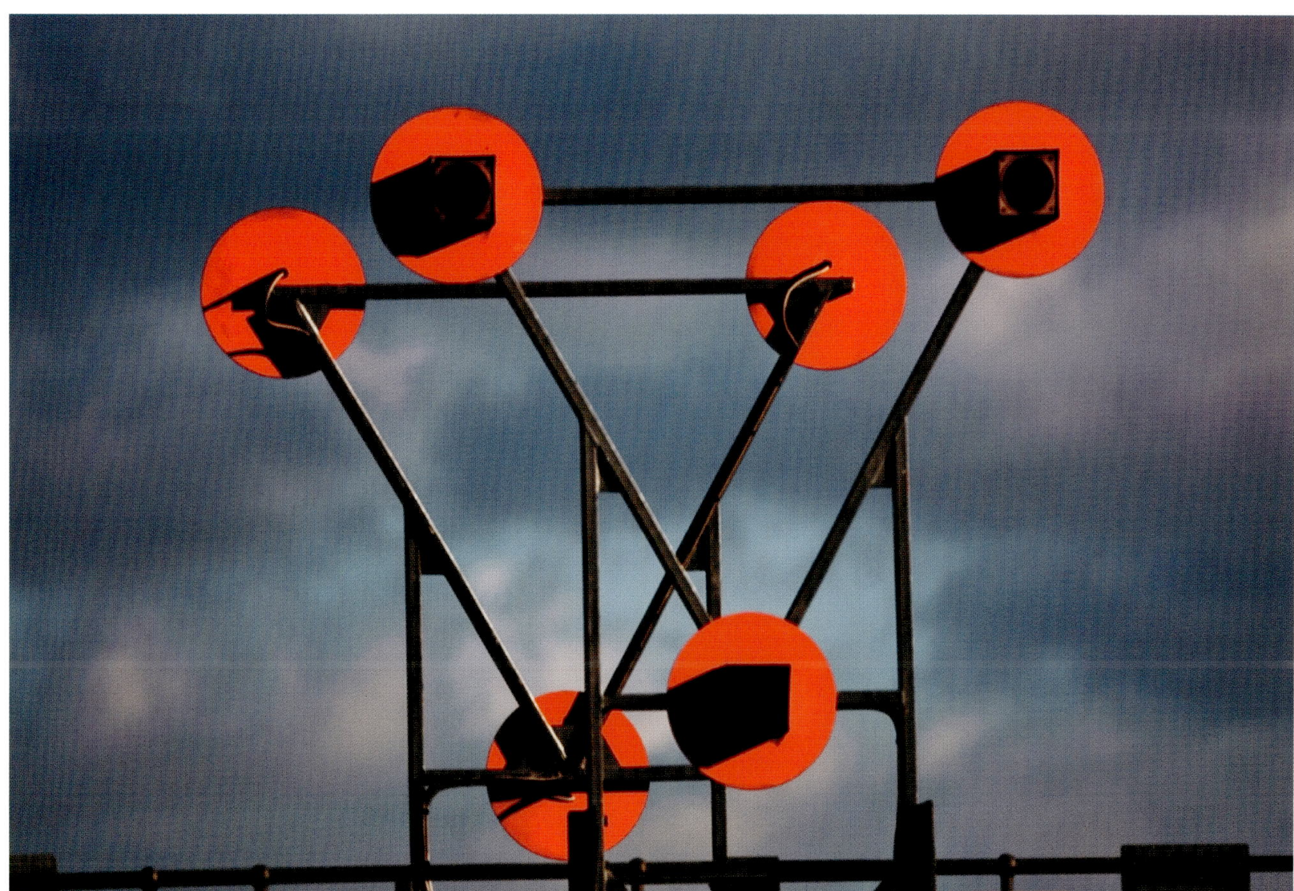

Thames Barrier signs: ‘Closed to Navigation’

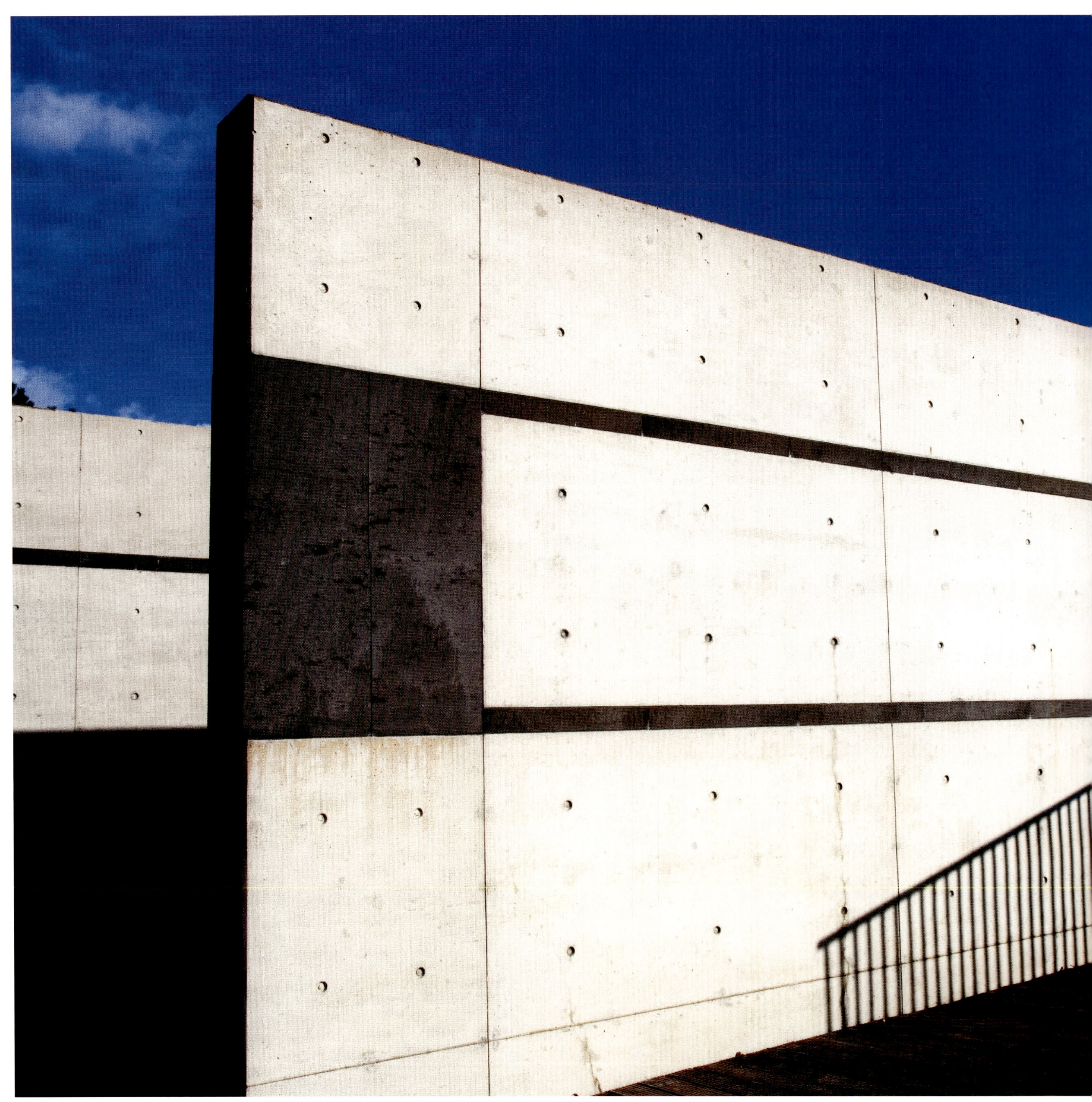

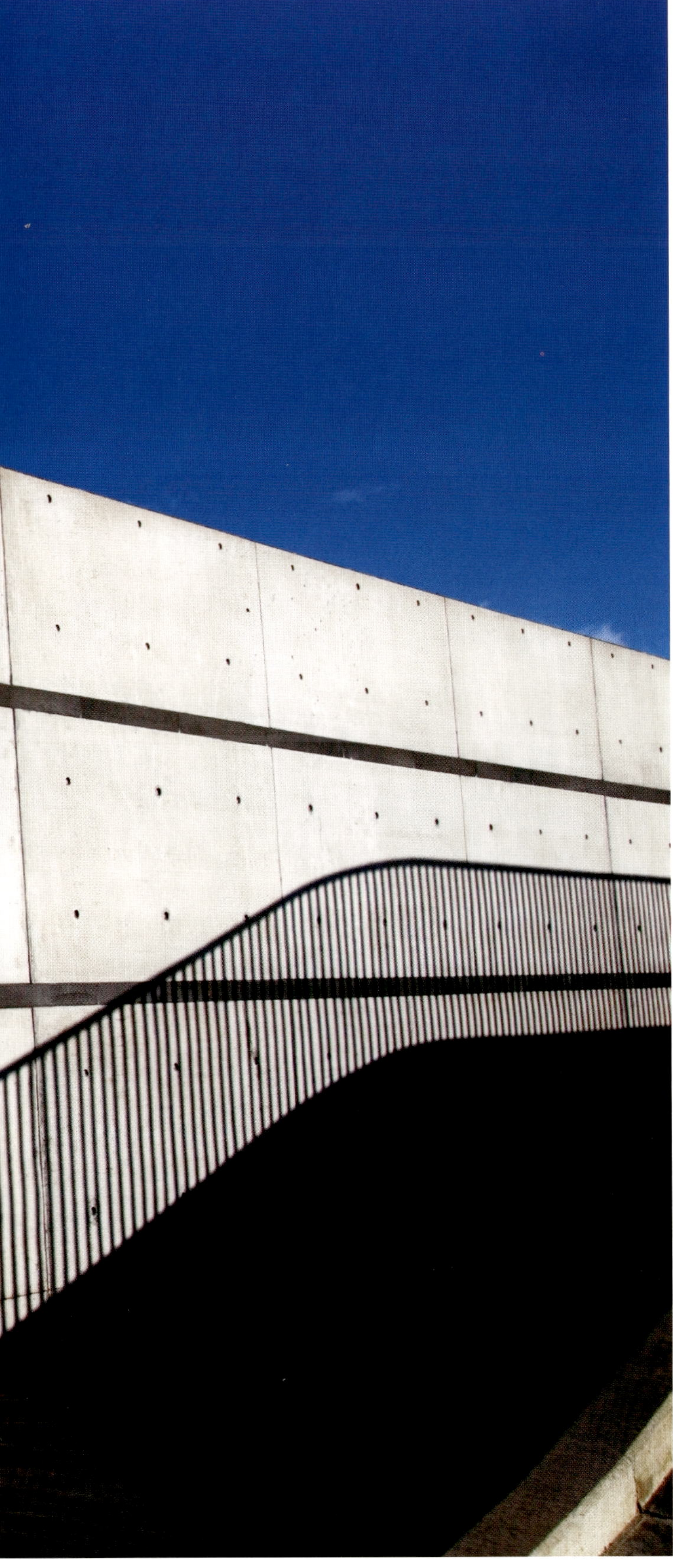

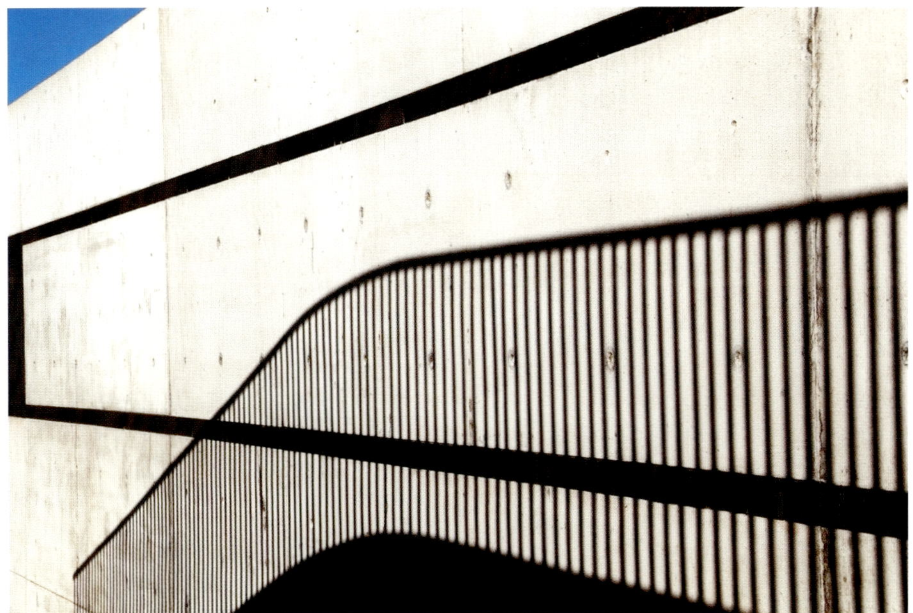

Above and left
White walls and railing shadows,
Thames Barrier Park

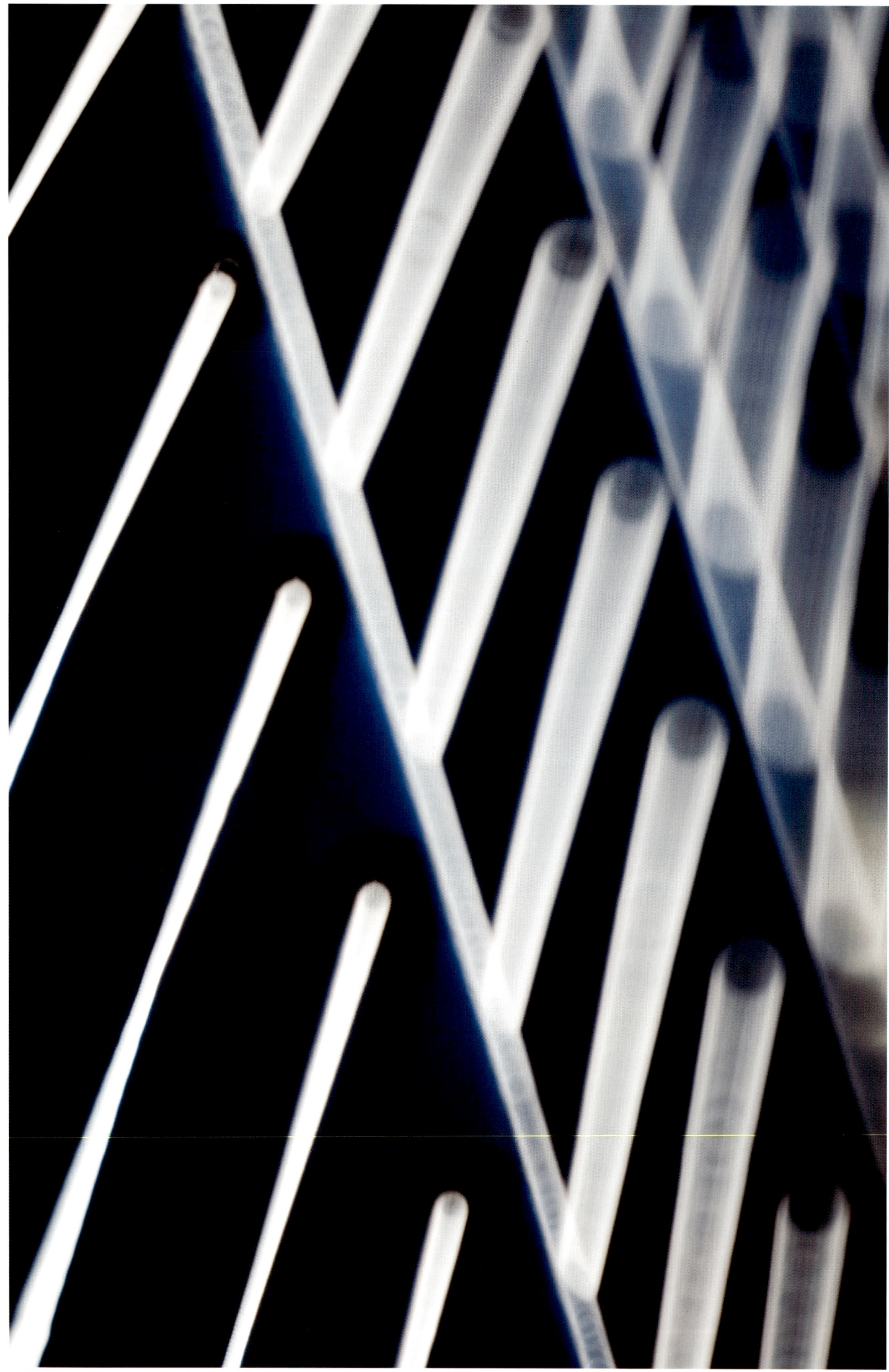

Railings, Thames Barrier Park

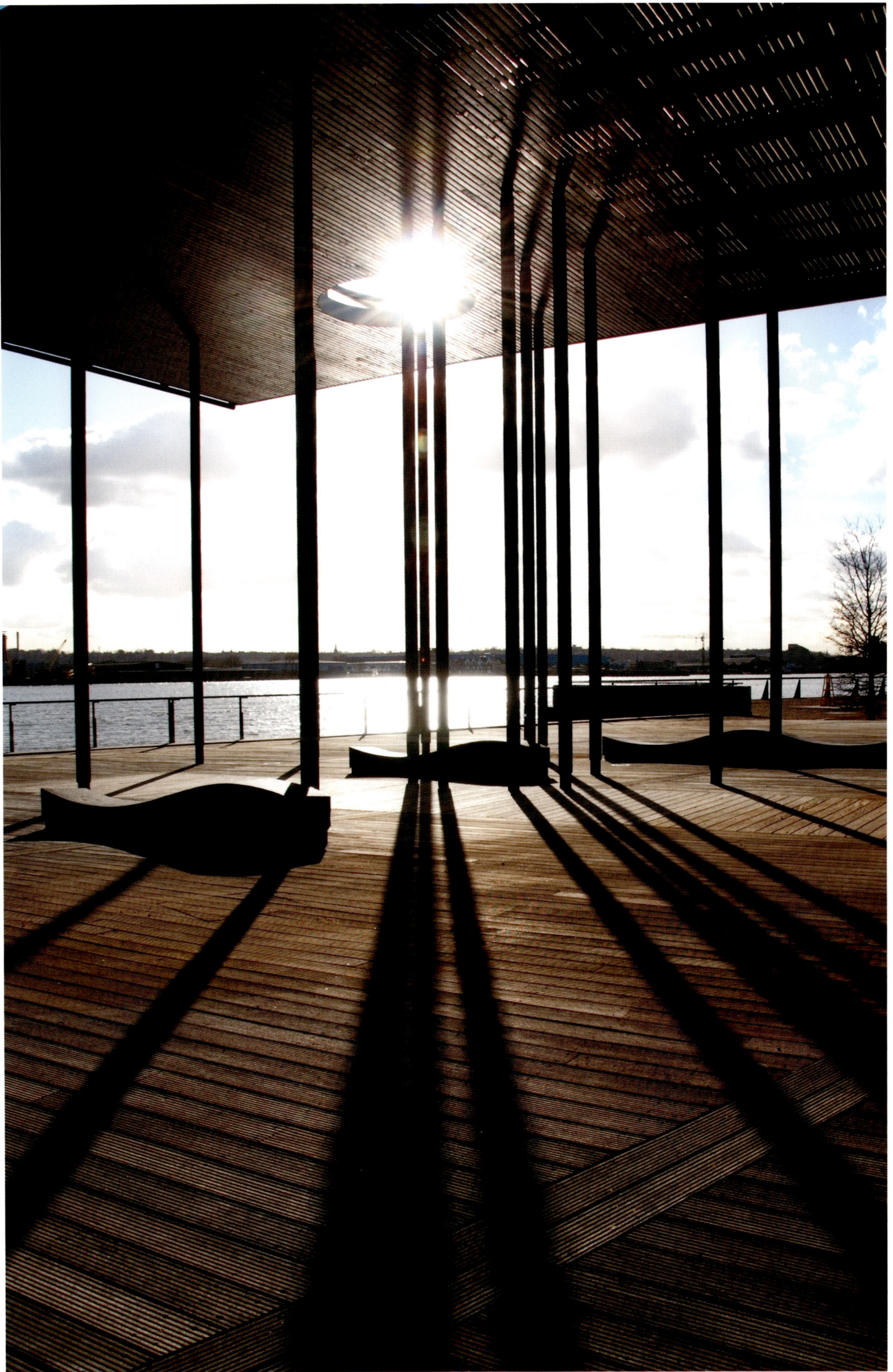

Above Pavilion, Thames Barrier Park

Pages 76–77 Antony Gormley's *Quantum Cloud*, on the end of the O2 pier

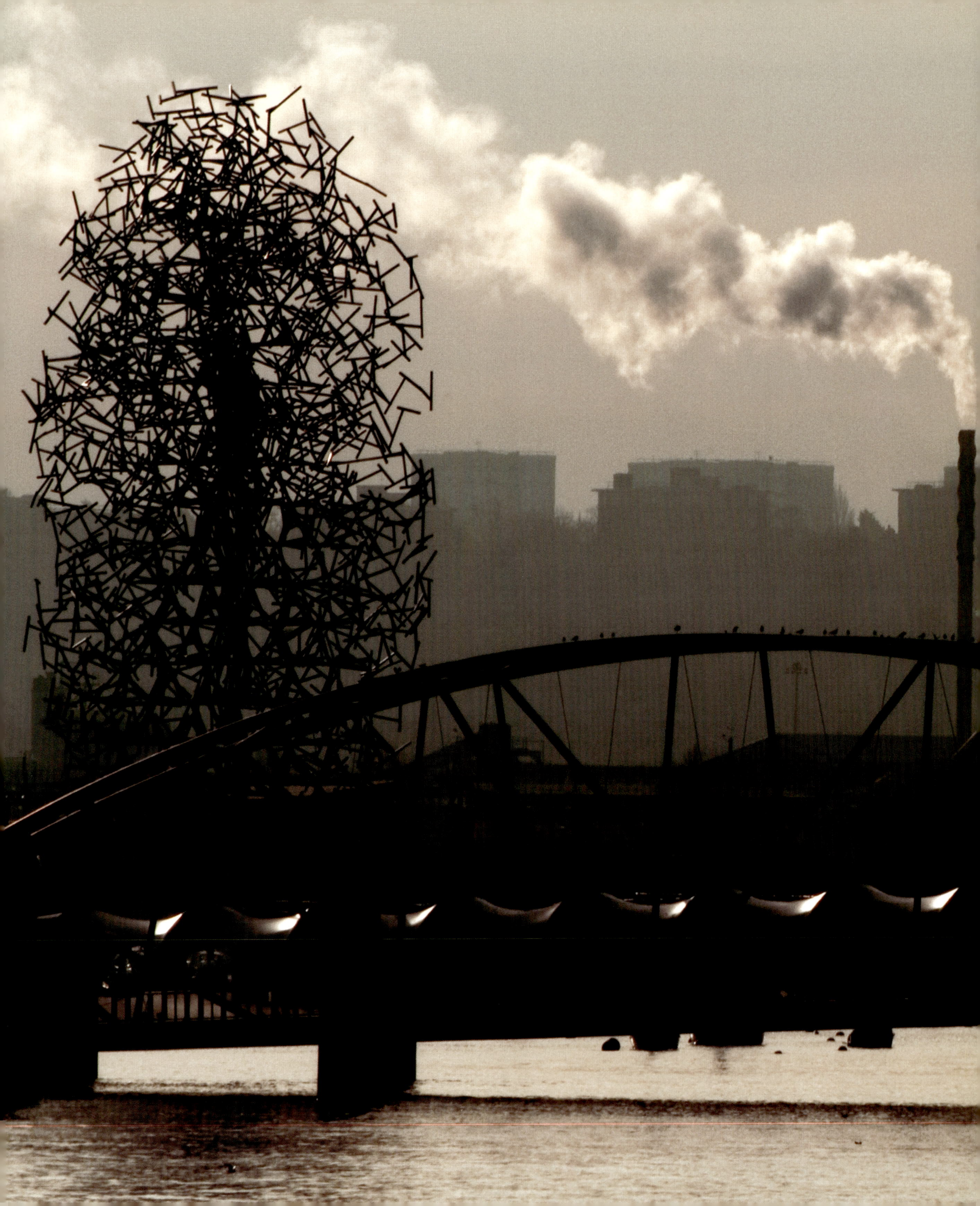

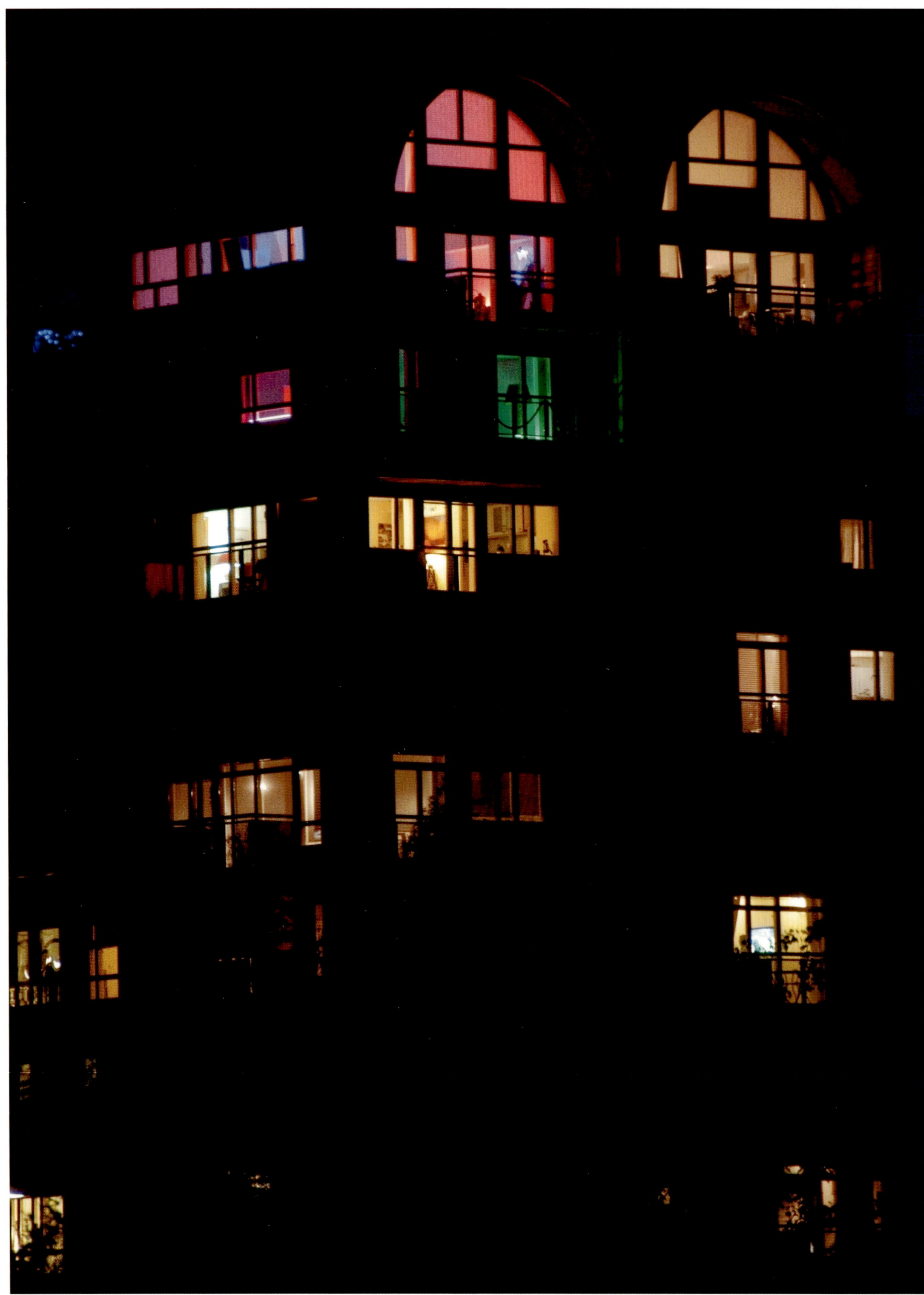

Greenwich Millennium Village housing, designed by Ralph Erskine

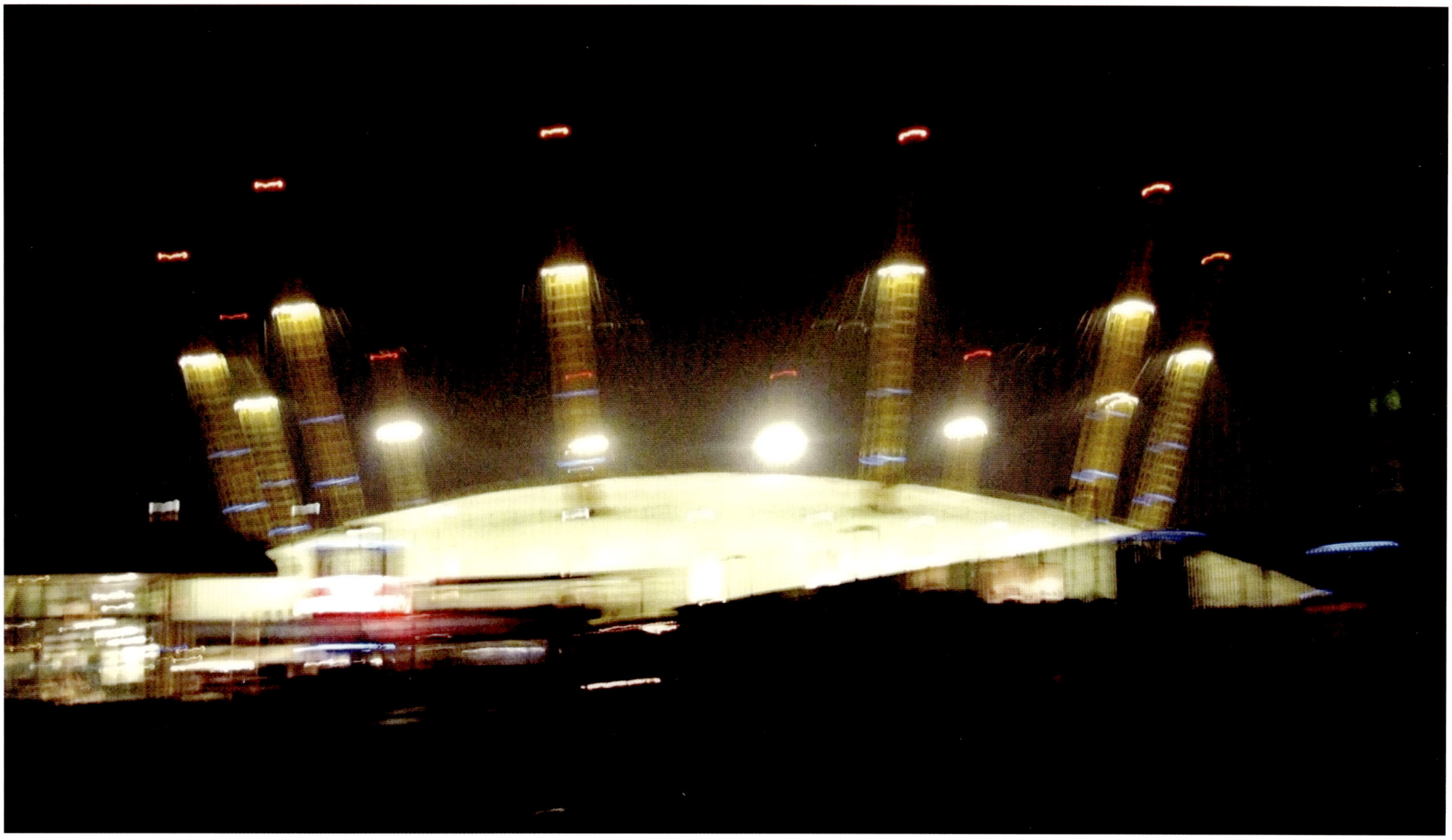

The O2 (the Dome) at night

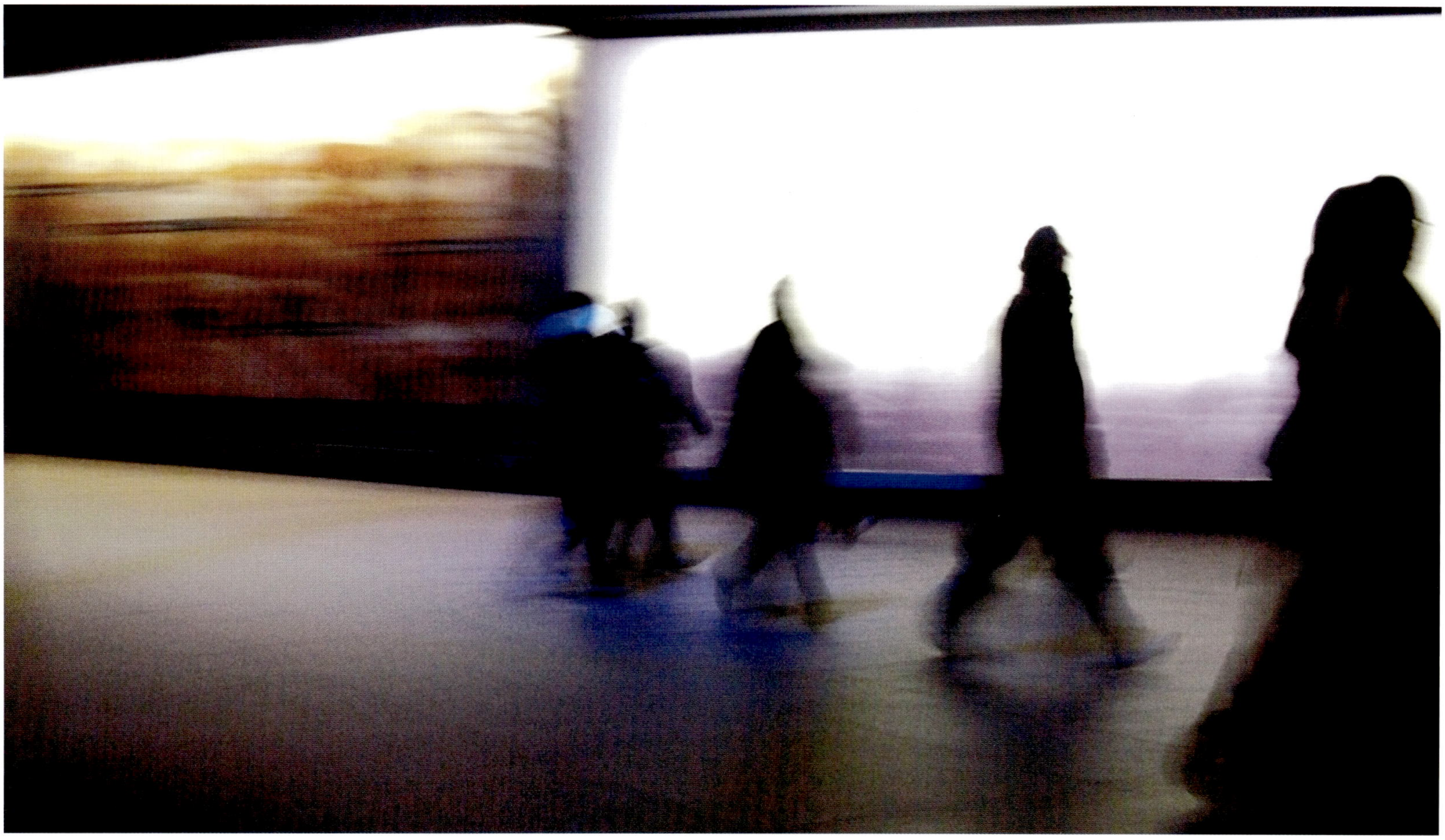

Walkway to the O2

Pages 80–81 The O2 at night

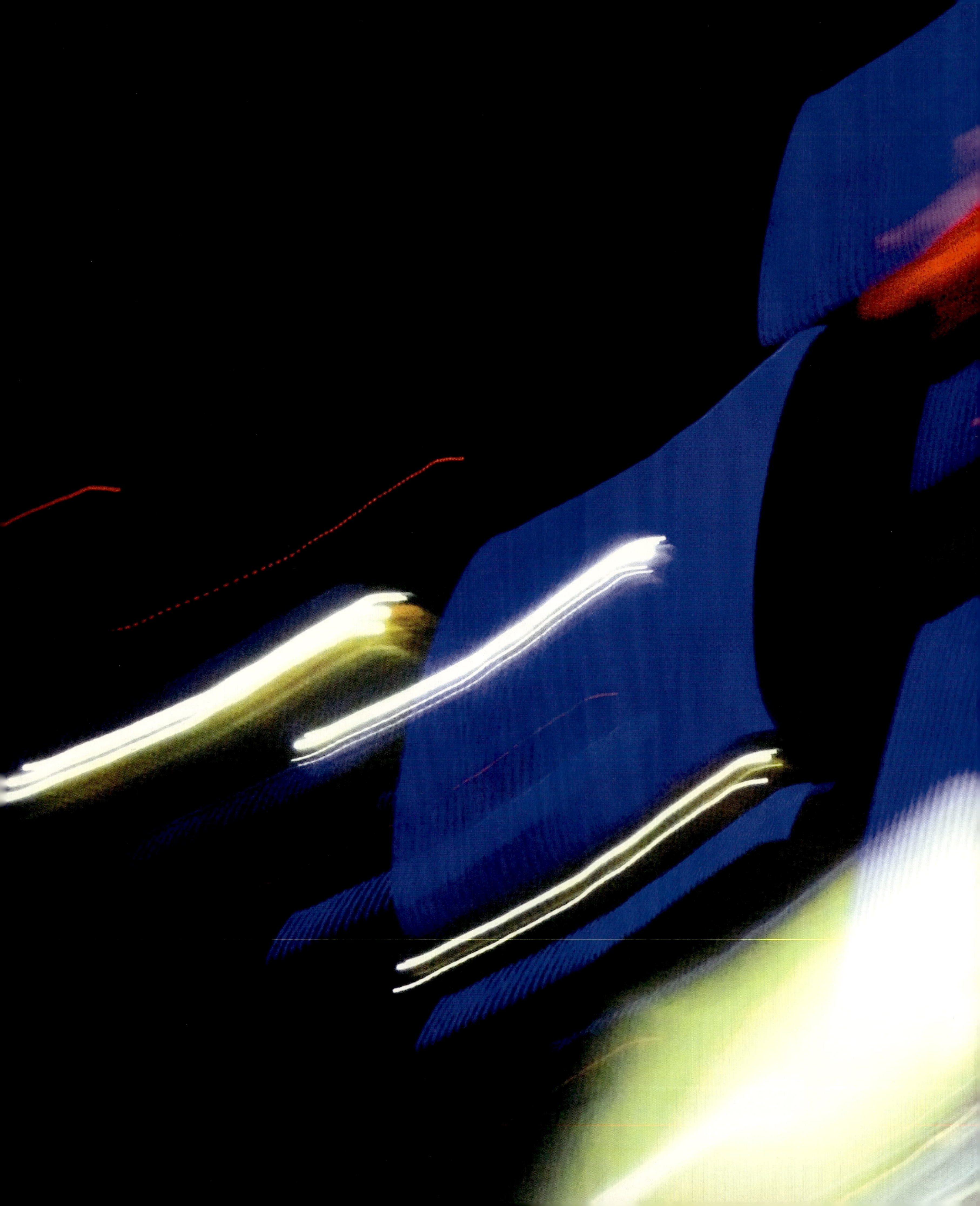

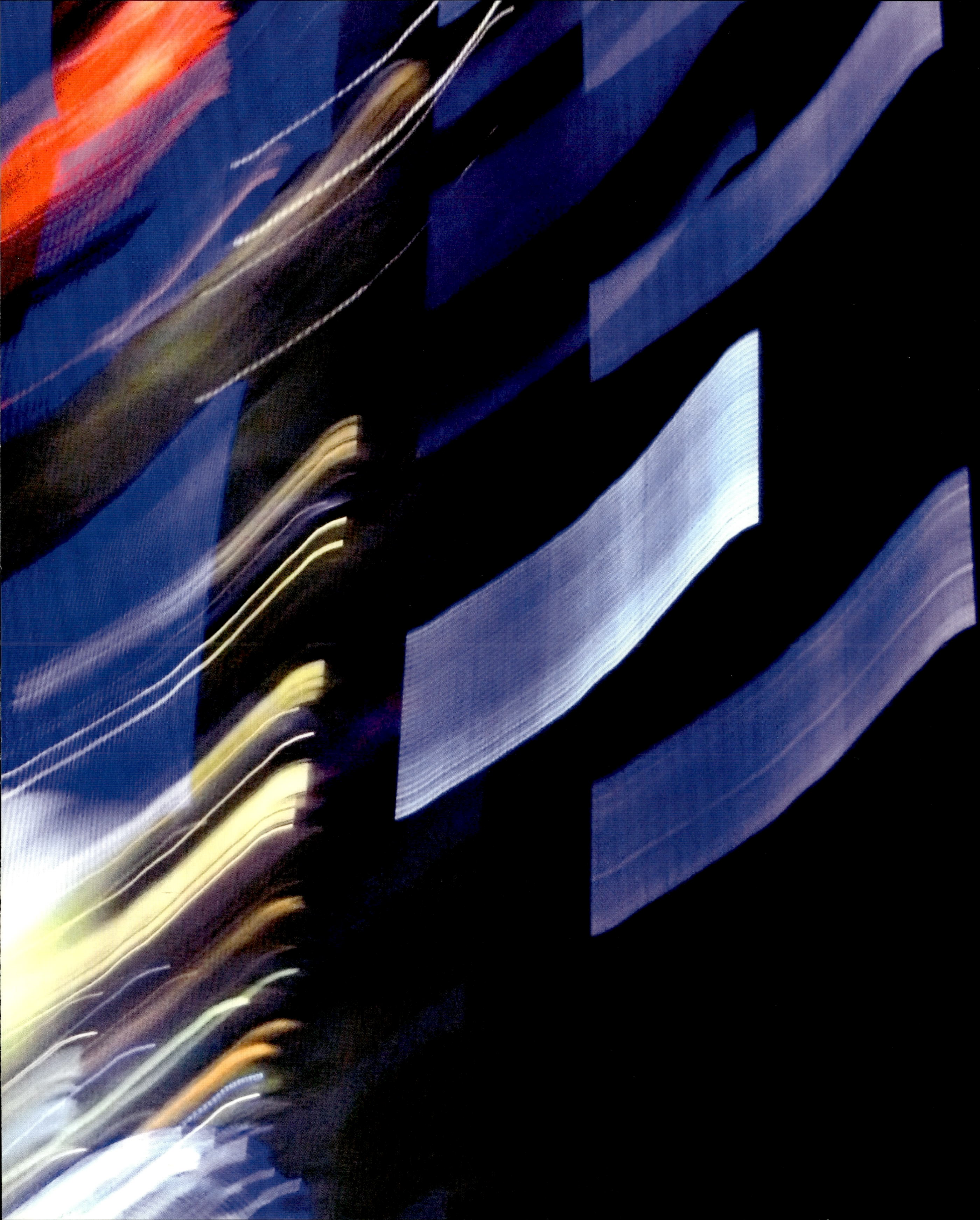

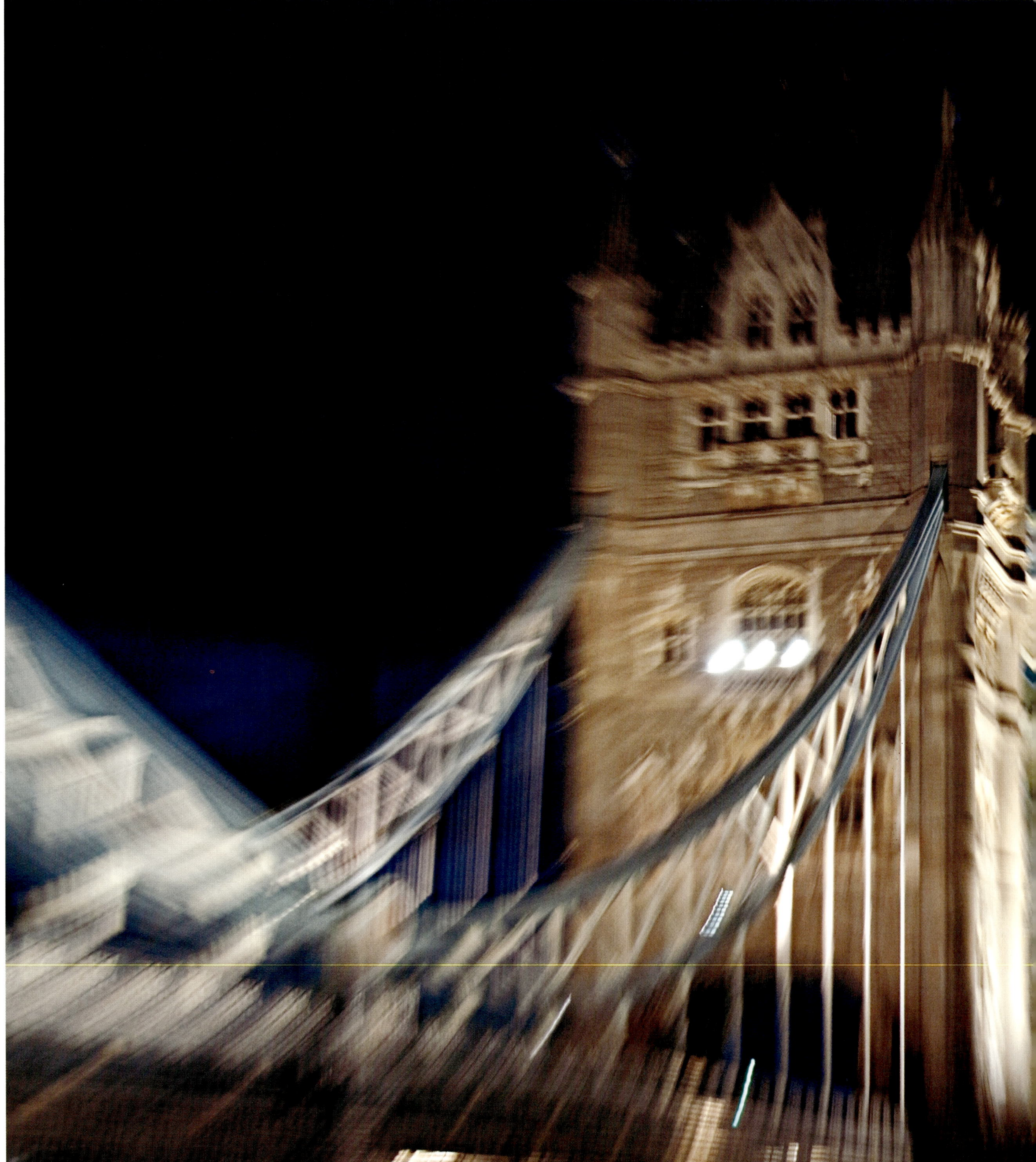

Tower Bridge

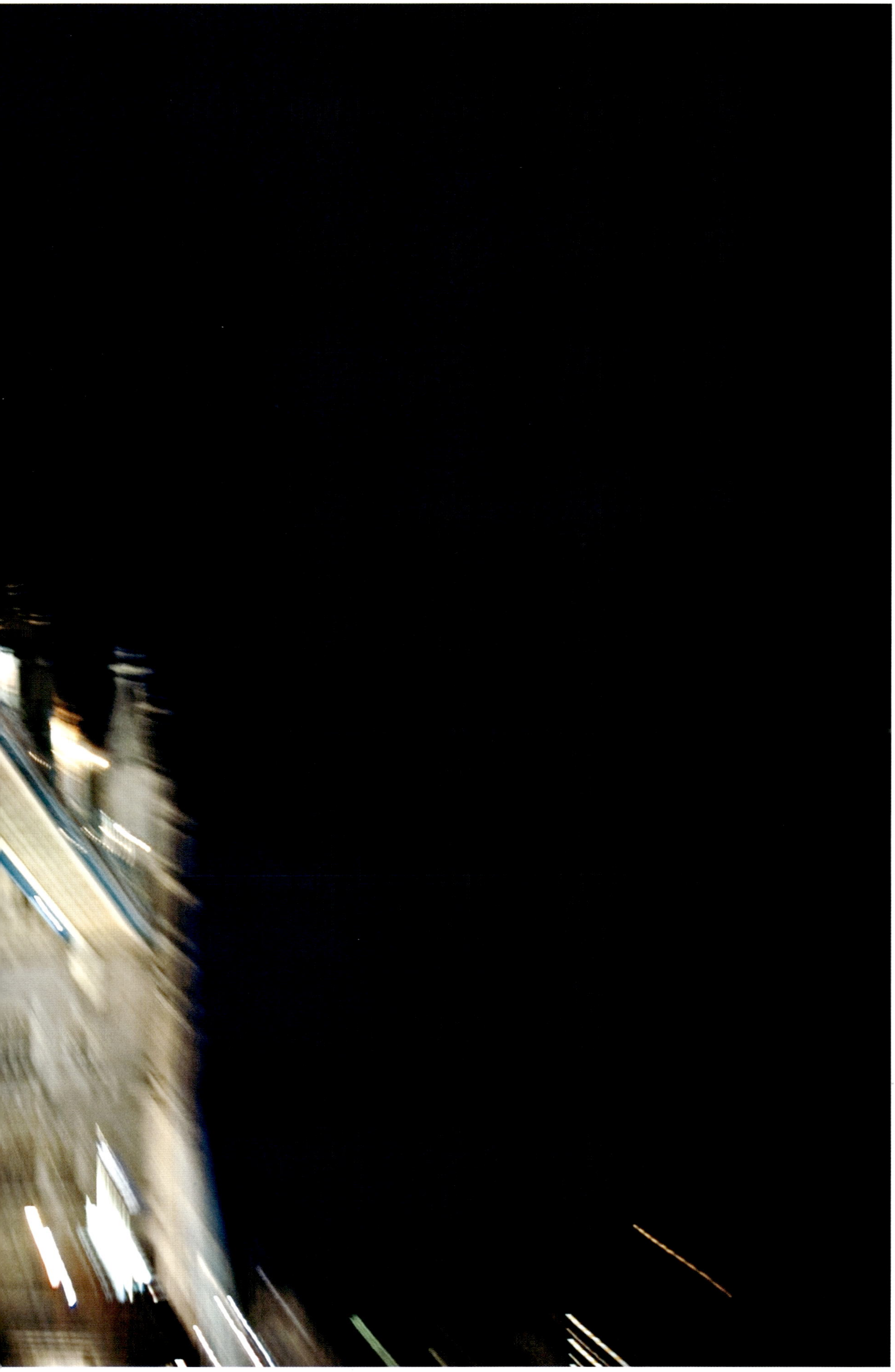

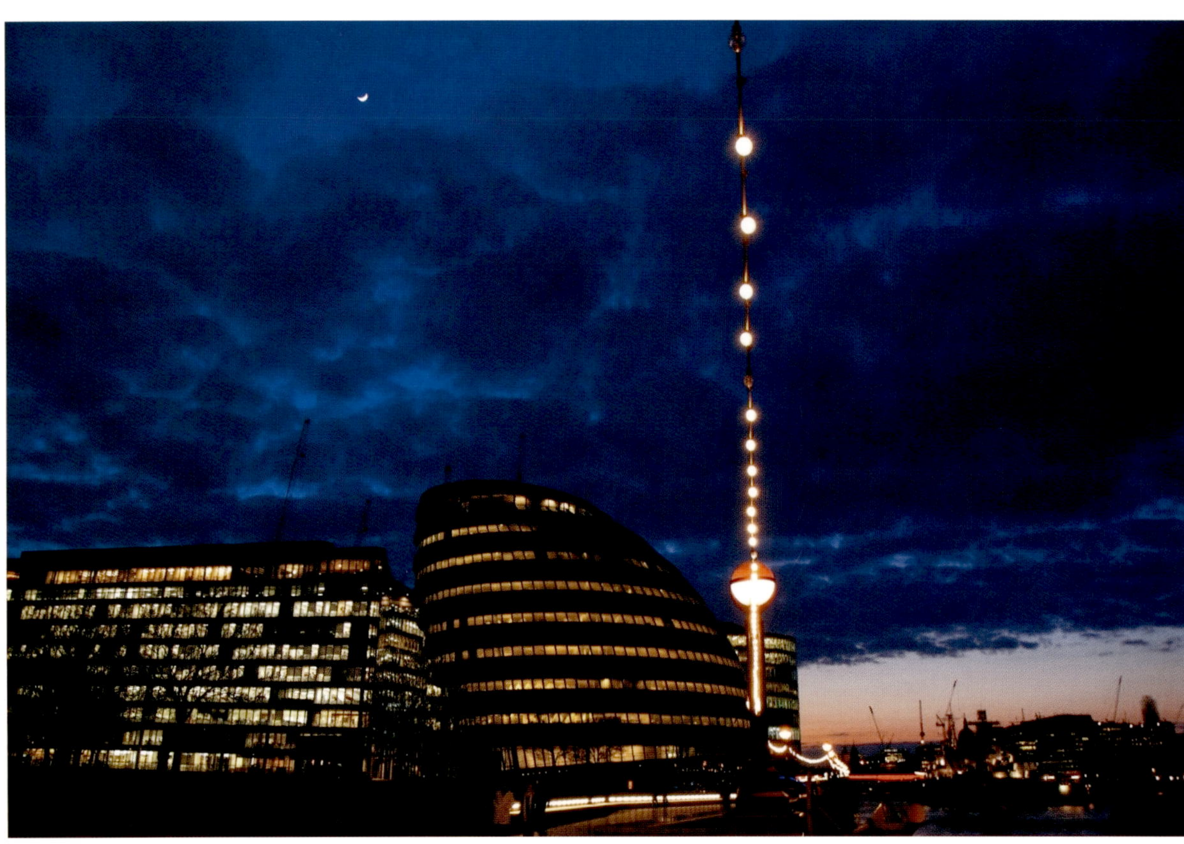

Above and opposite
City Hall

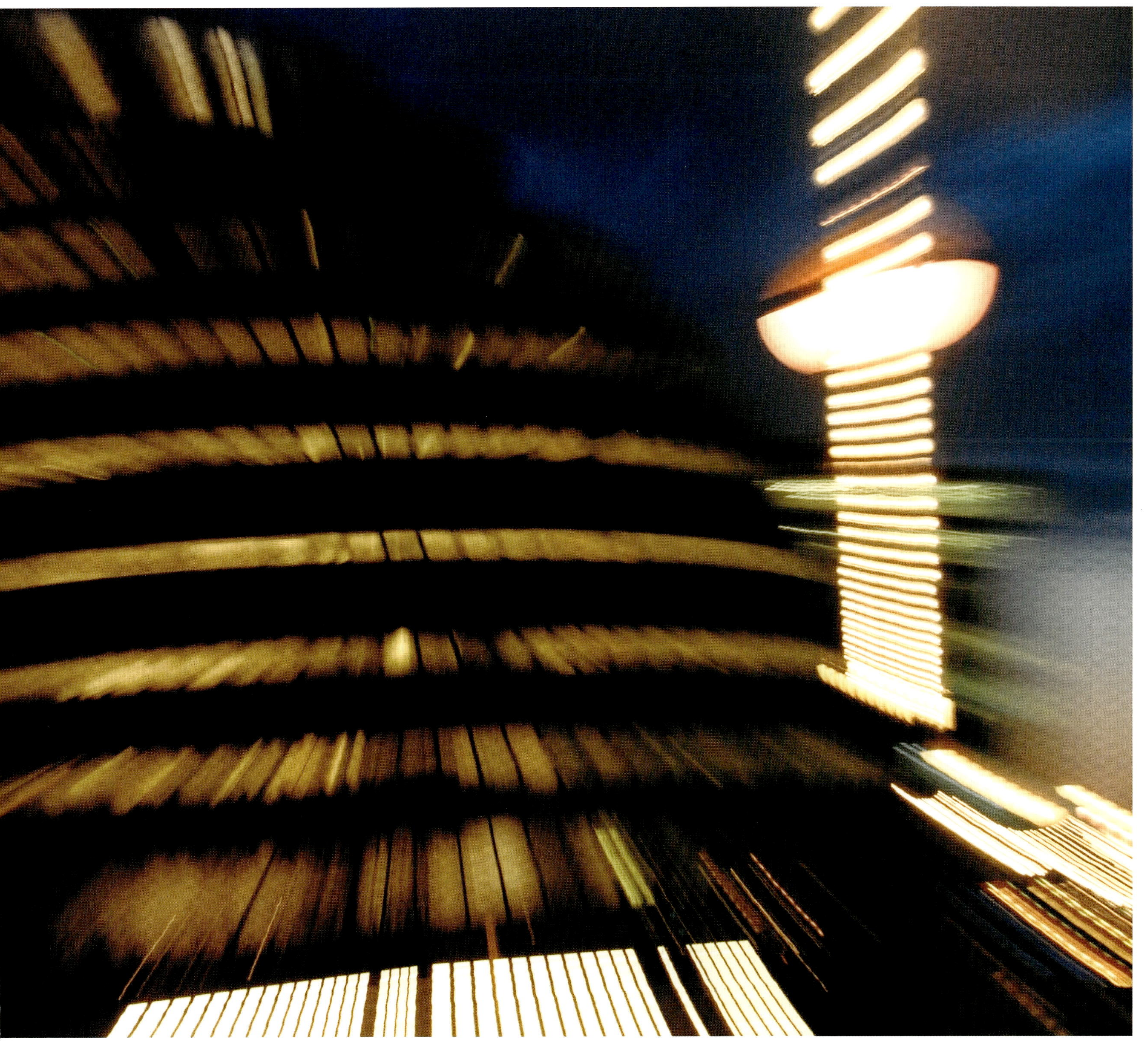

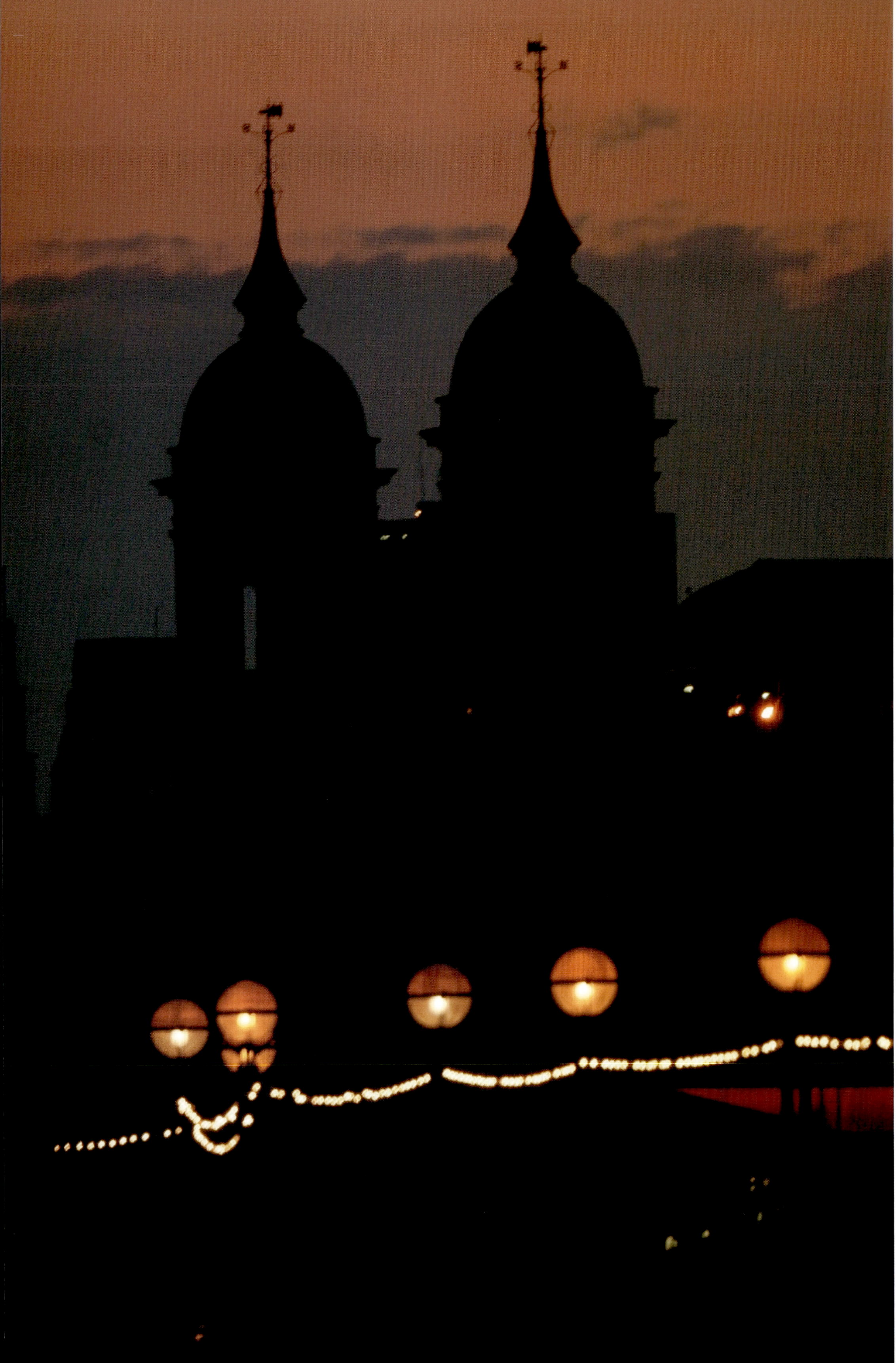

Cannon Street Station

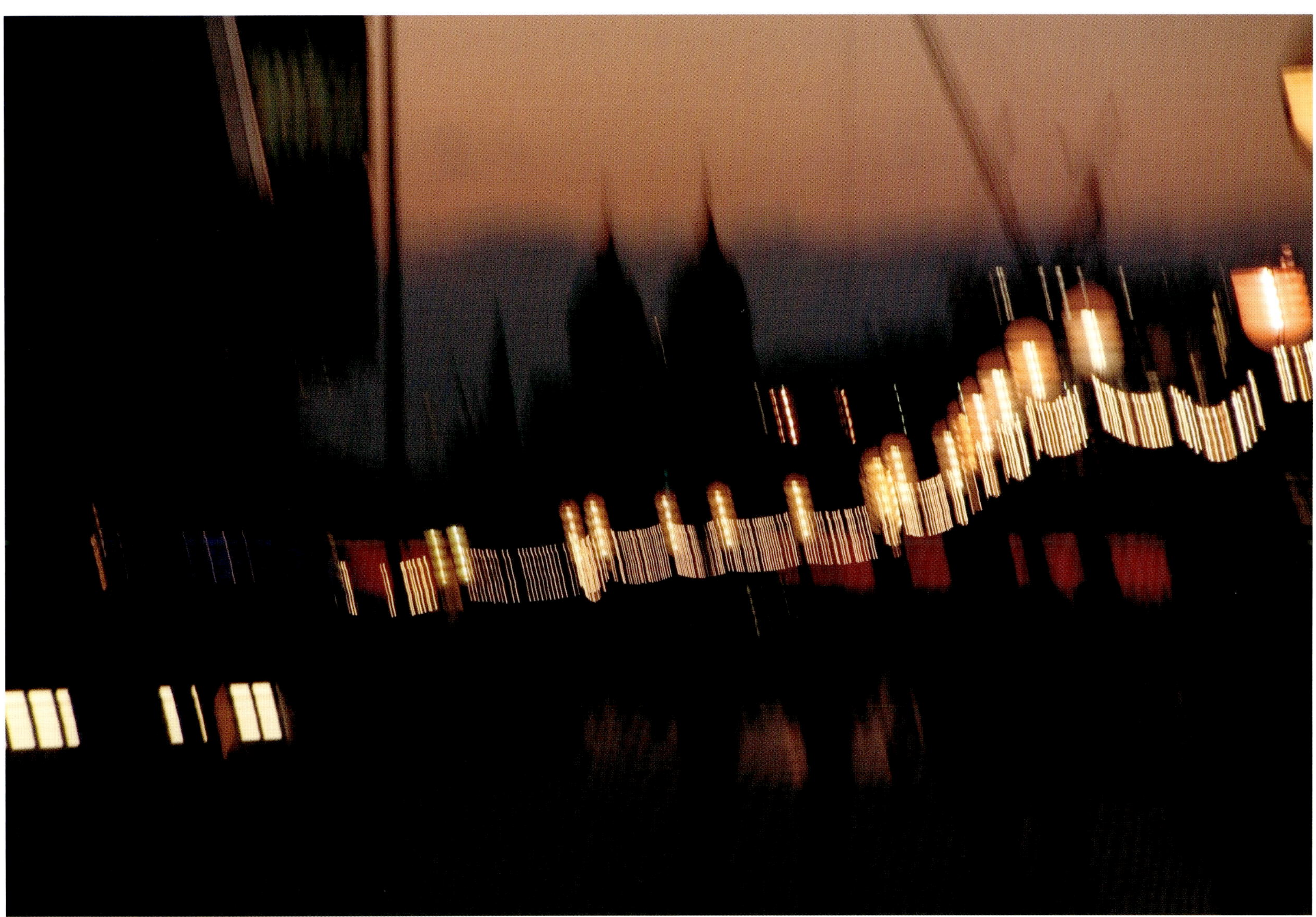

The Thames Path walkway by City Hall

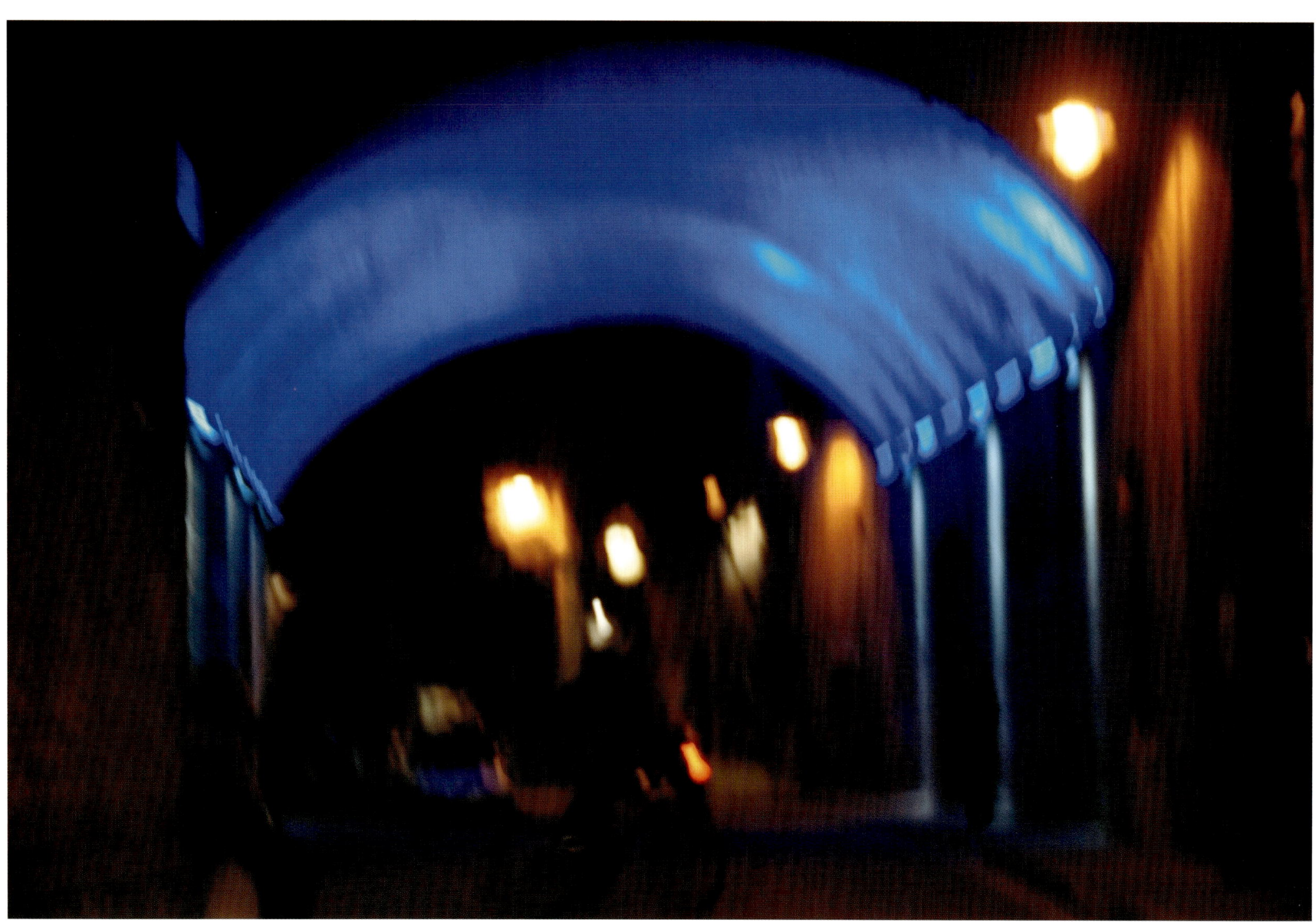

The blue-lit Stoney Street Rail Bridge, Borough Market

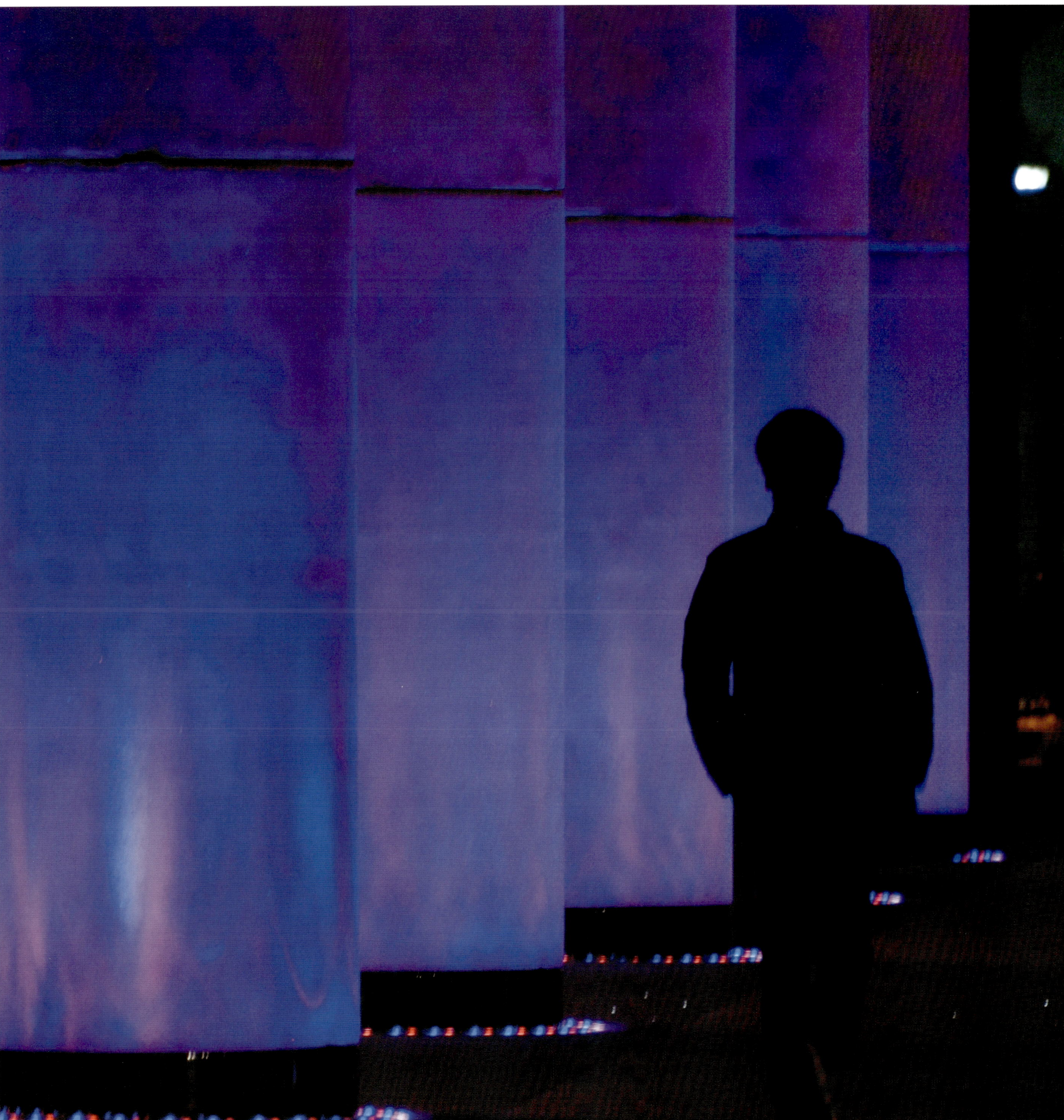

Park Plaza Hotel, County Hall

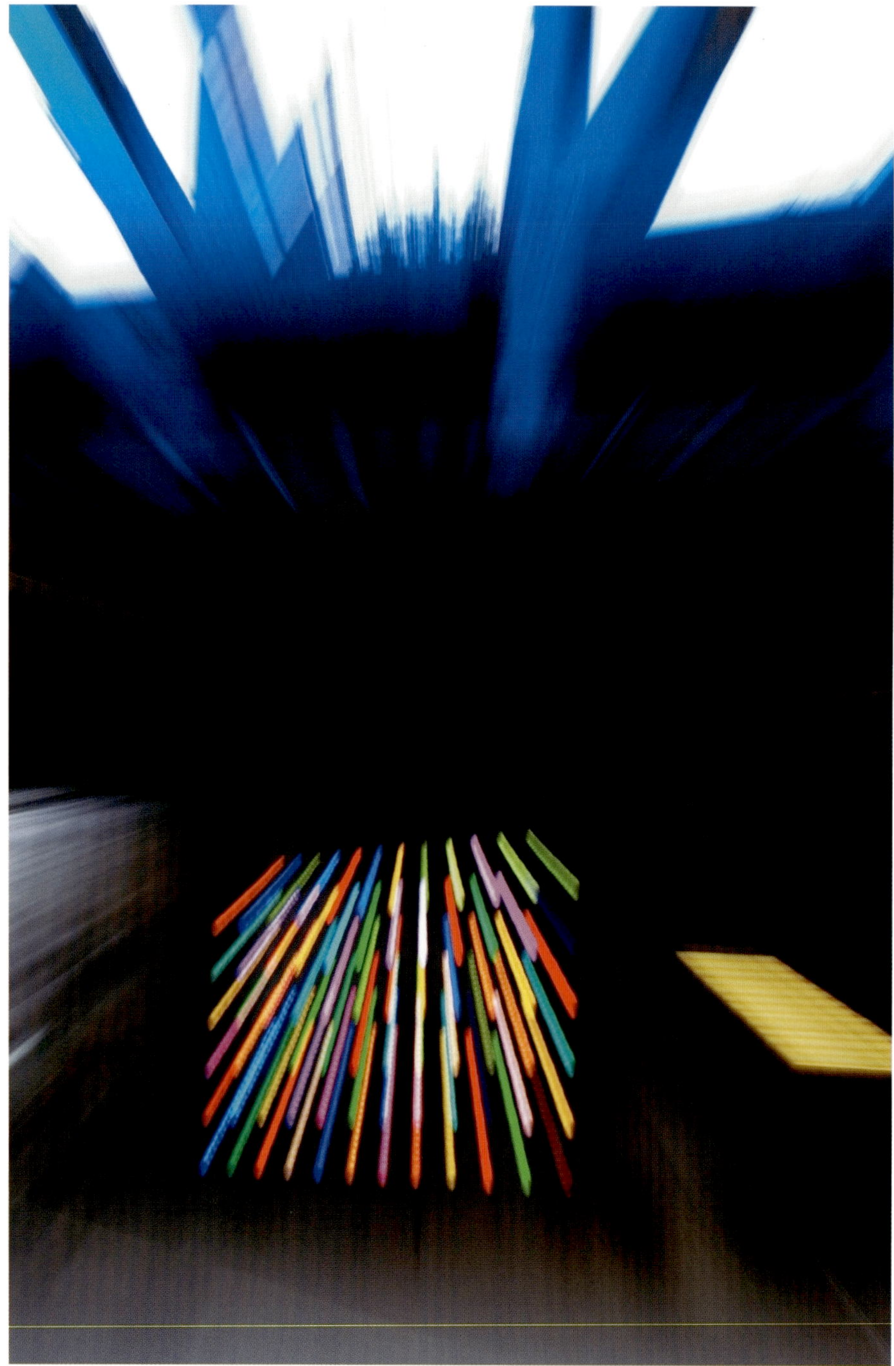

Above and opposite
Southwark Street: 'Smarties' lighting installation by Southwark Council and Antonia Simpson

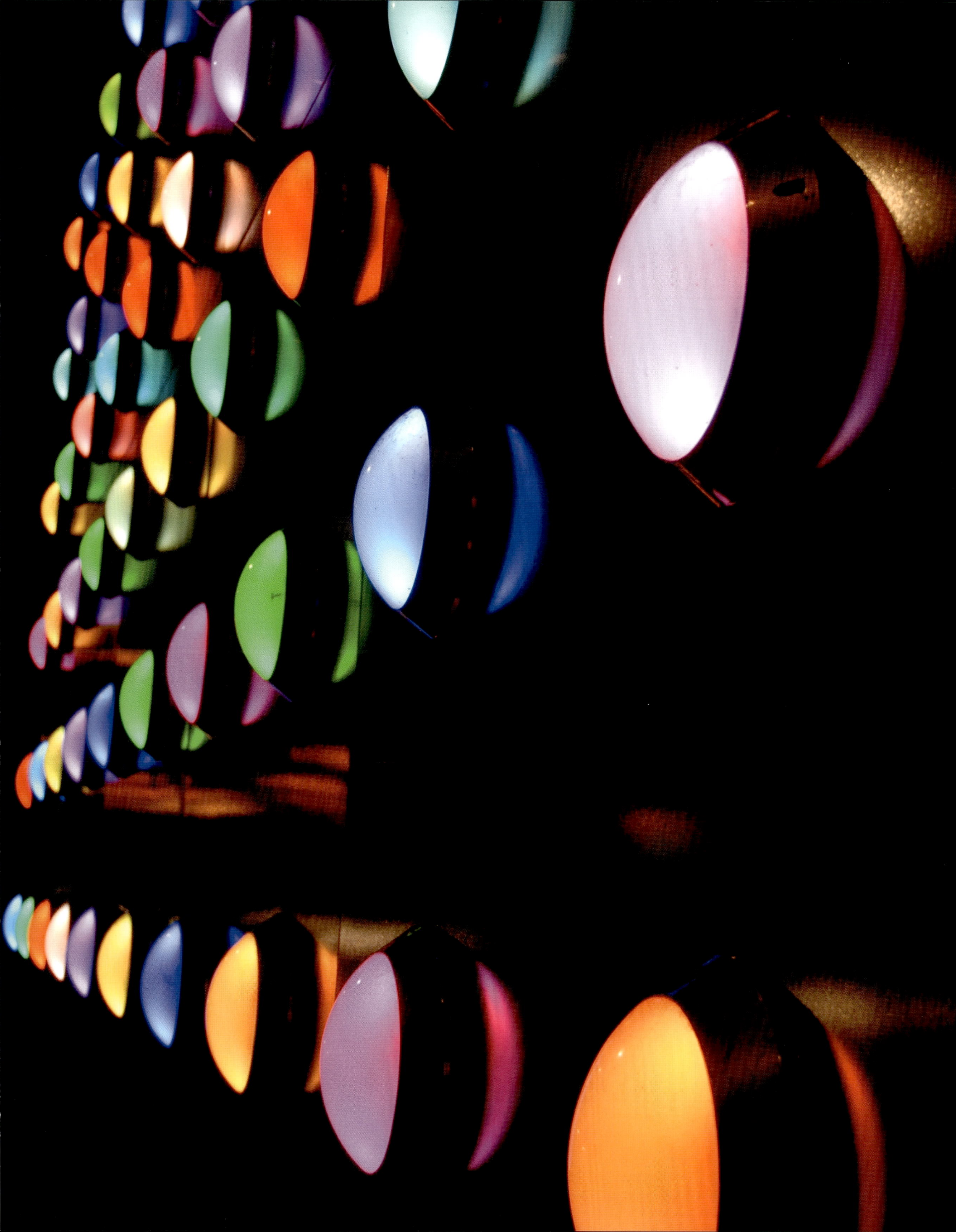

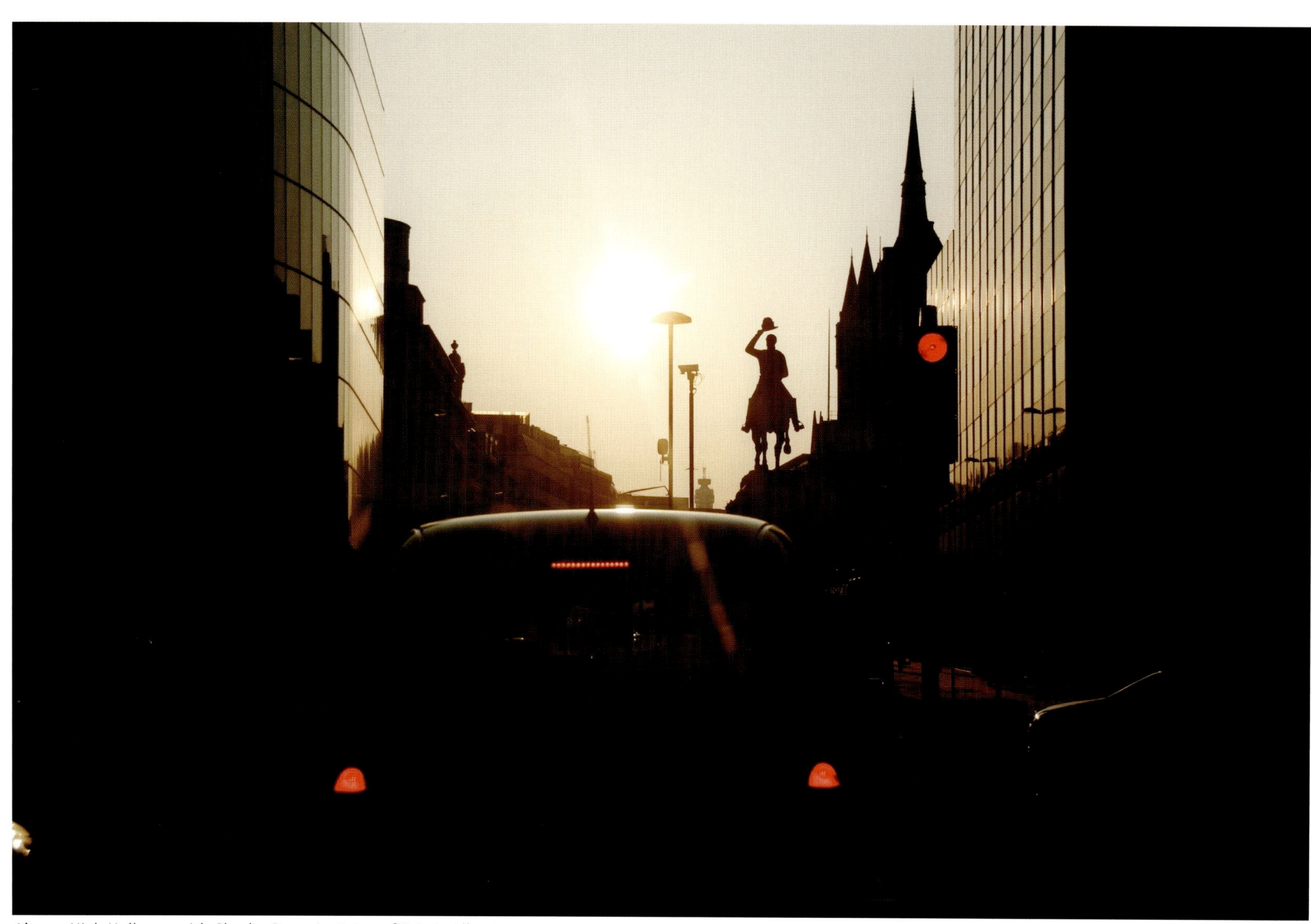

Above High Holborn, with Charles Bacon's statue of Prince Albert
Opposite St Paul's Cathedral and the Millennium Bridge
Pages 94–95 The Millennium Bridge and the City of London

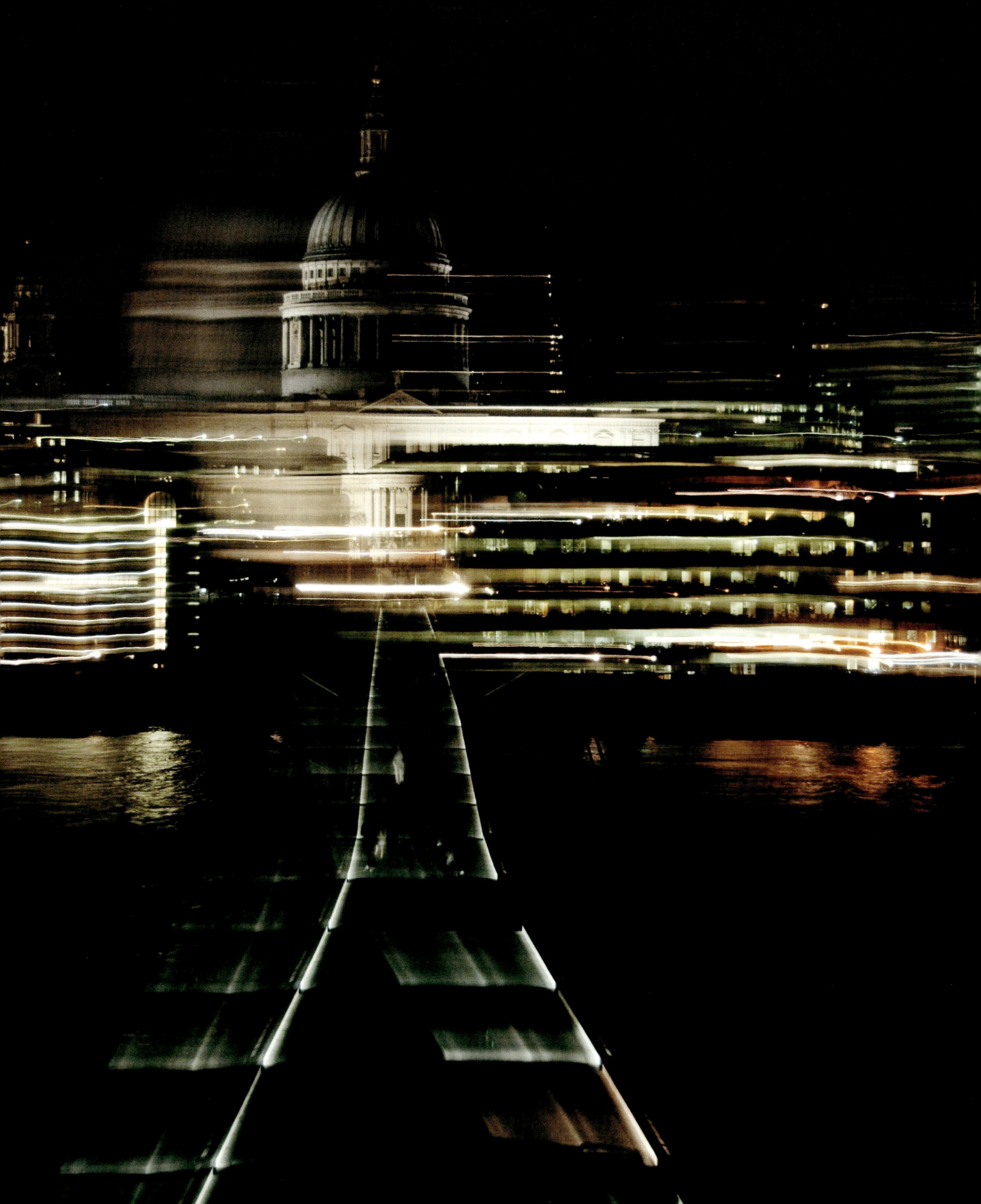

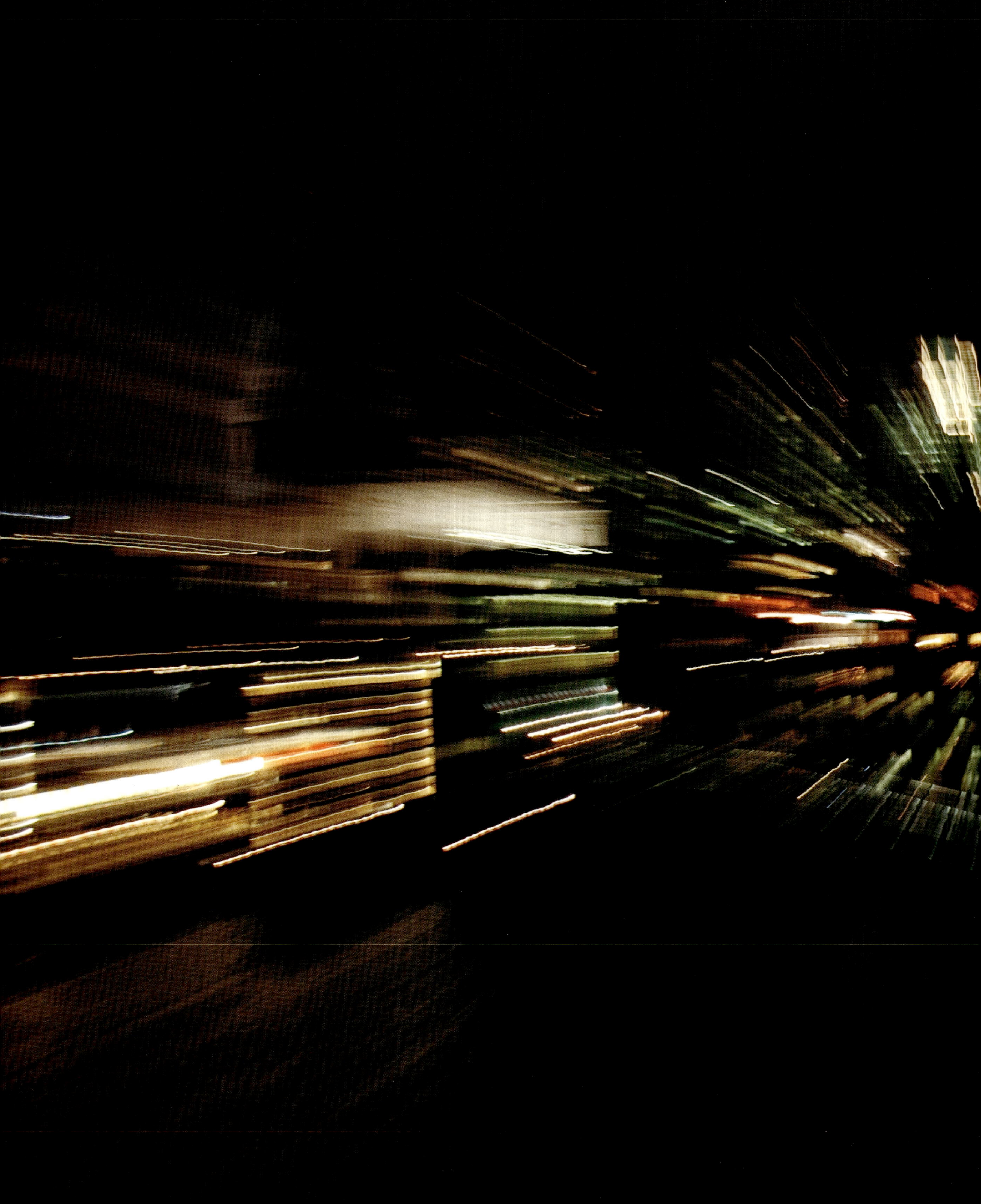

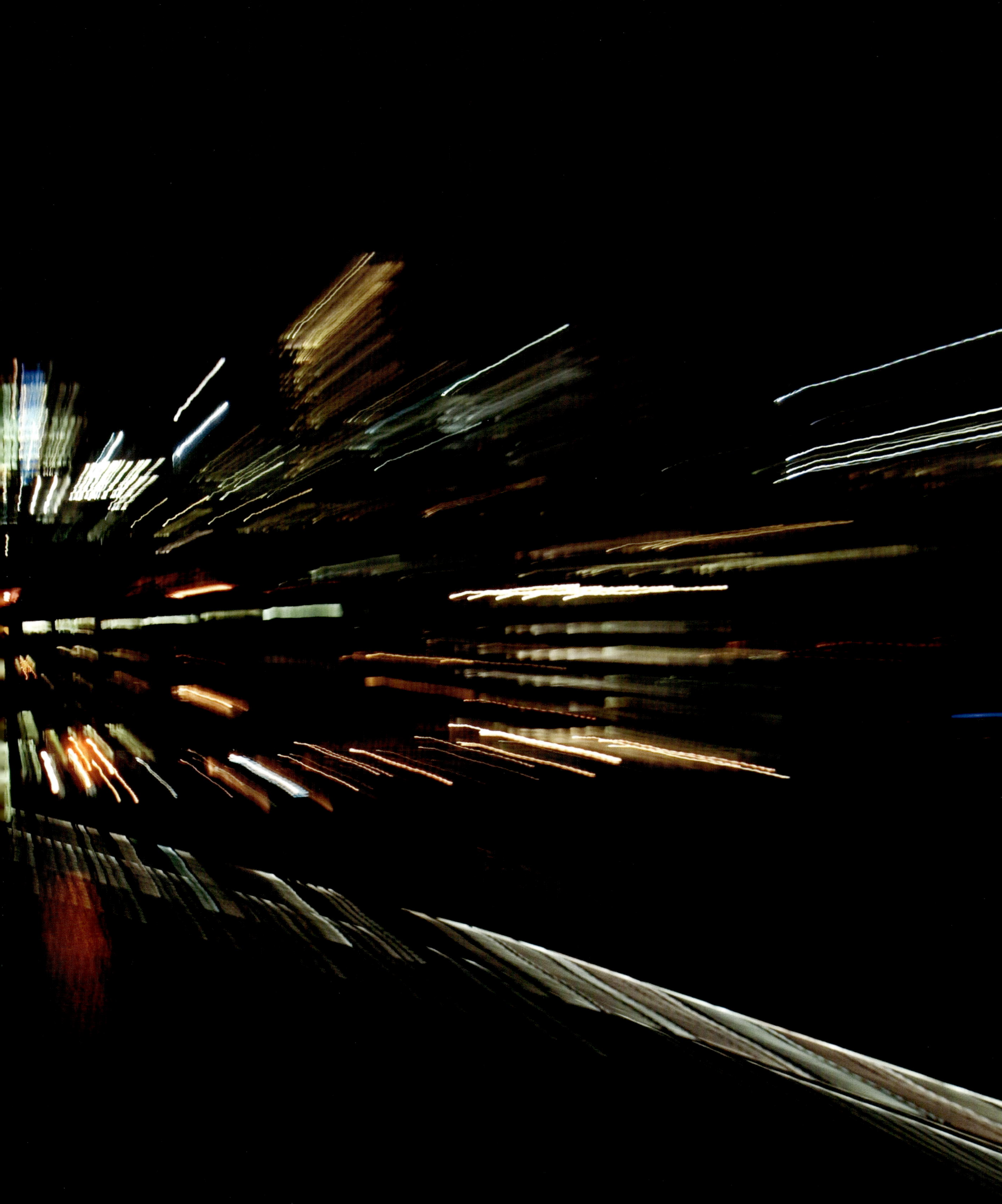

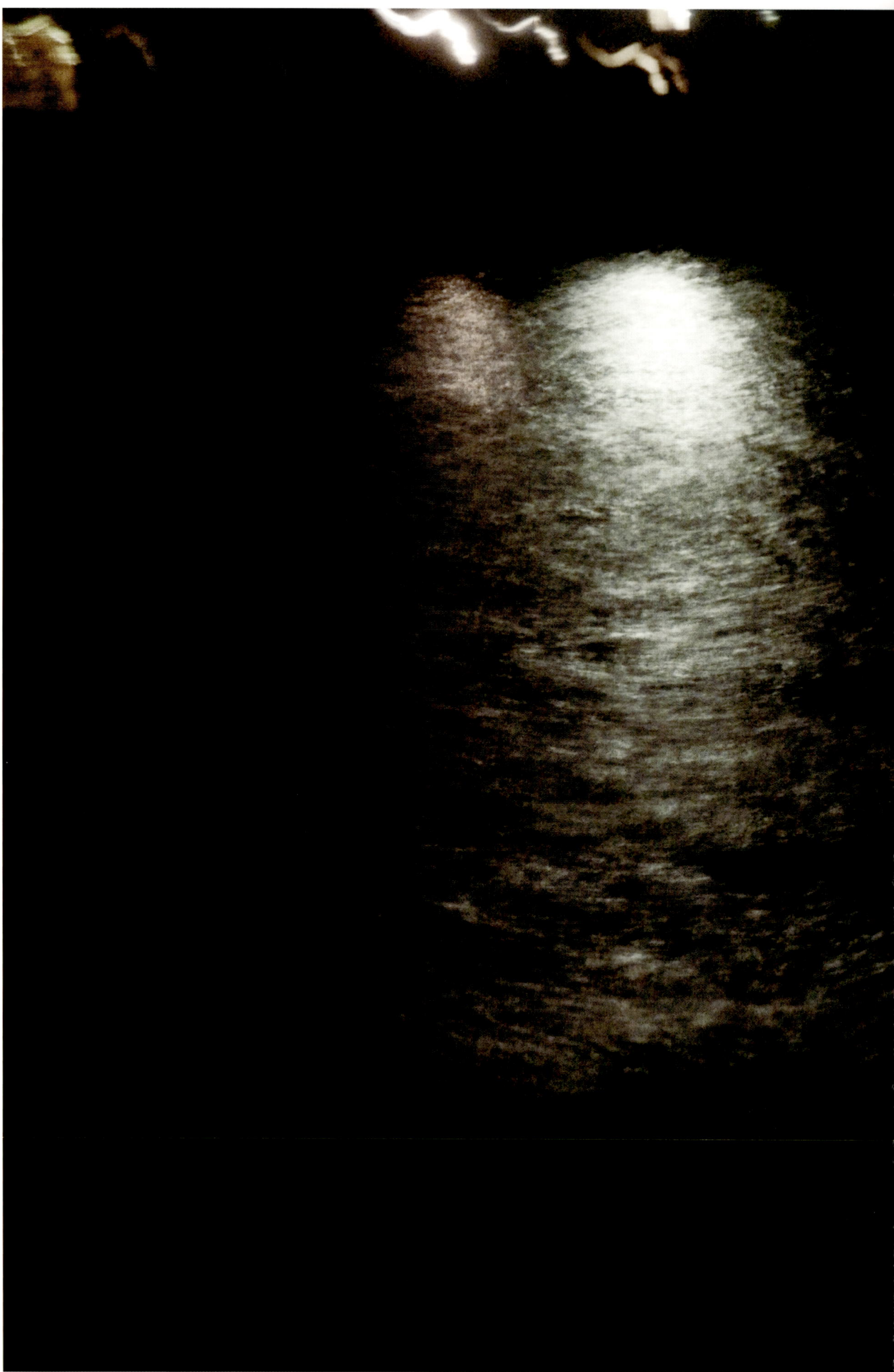

Above and opposite The Millennium Bridge

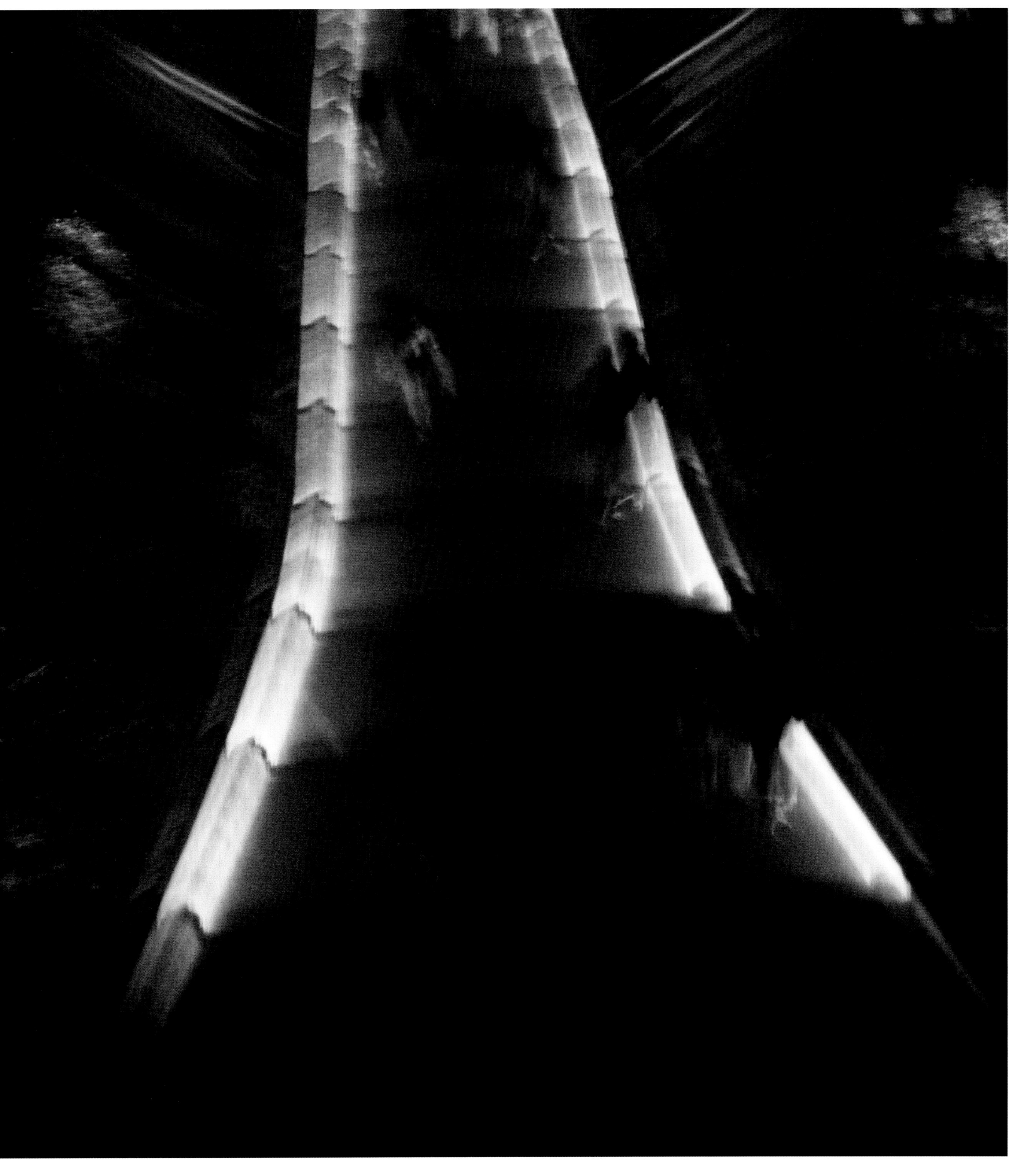

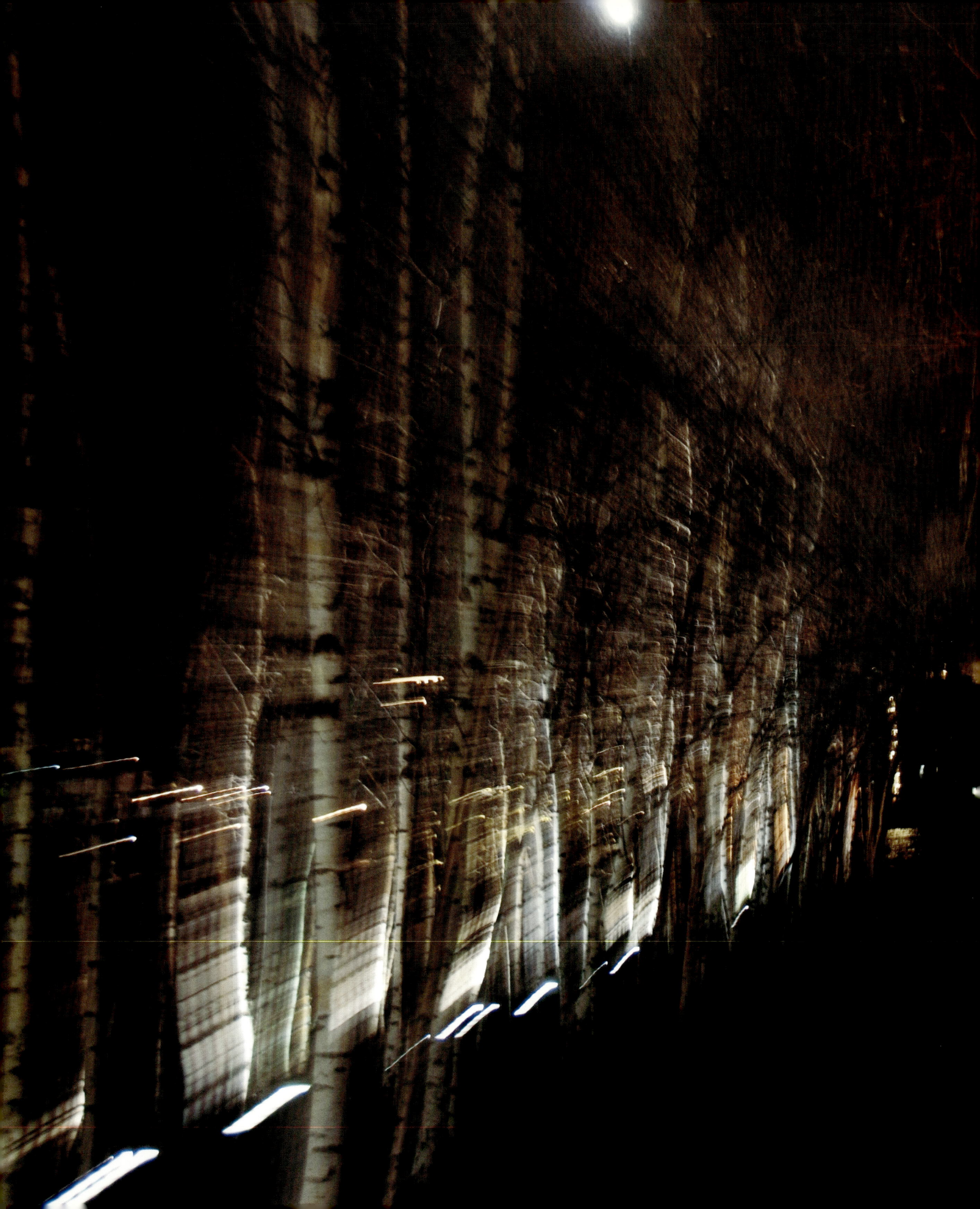

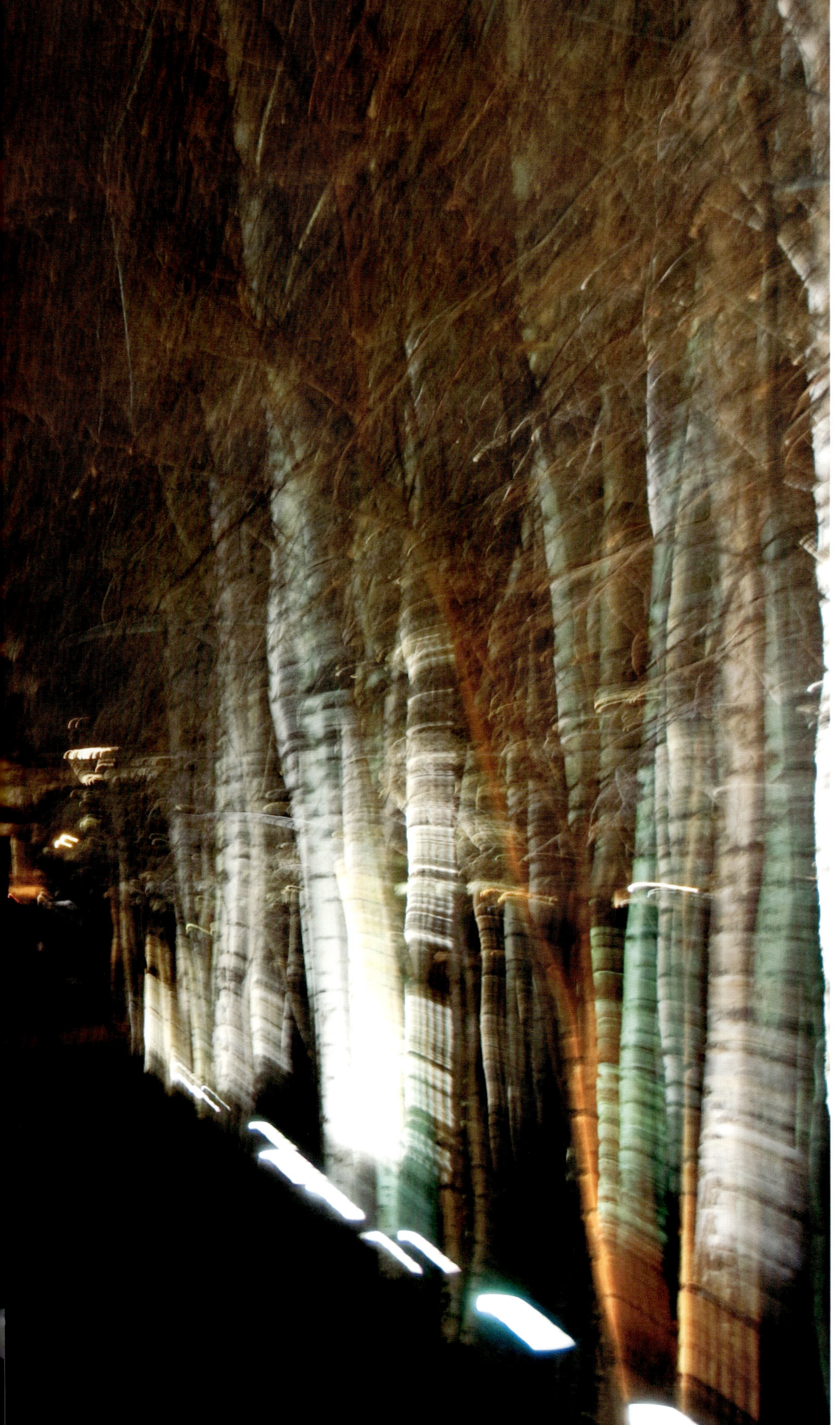

Silver birch trees at Tate Modern

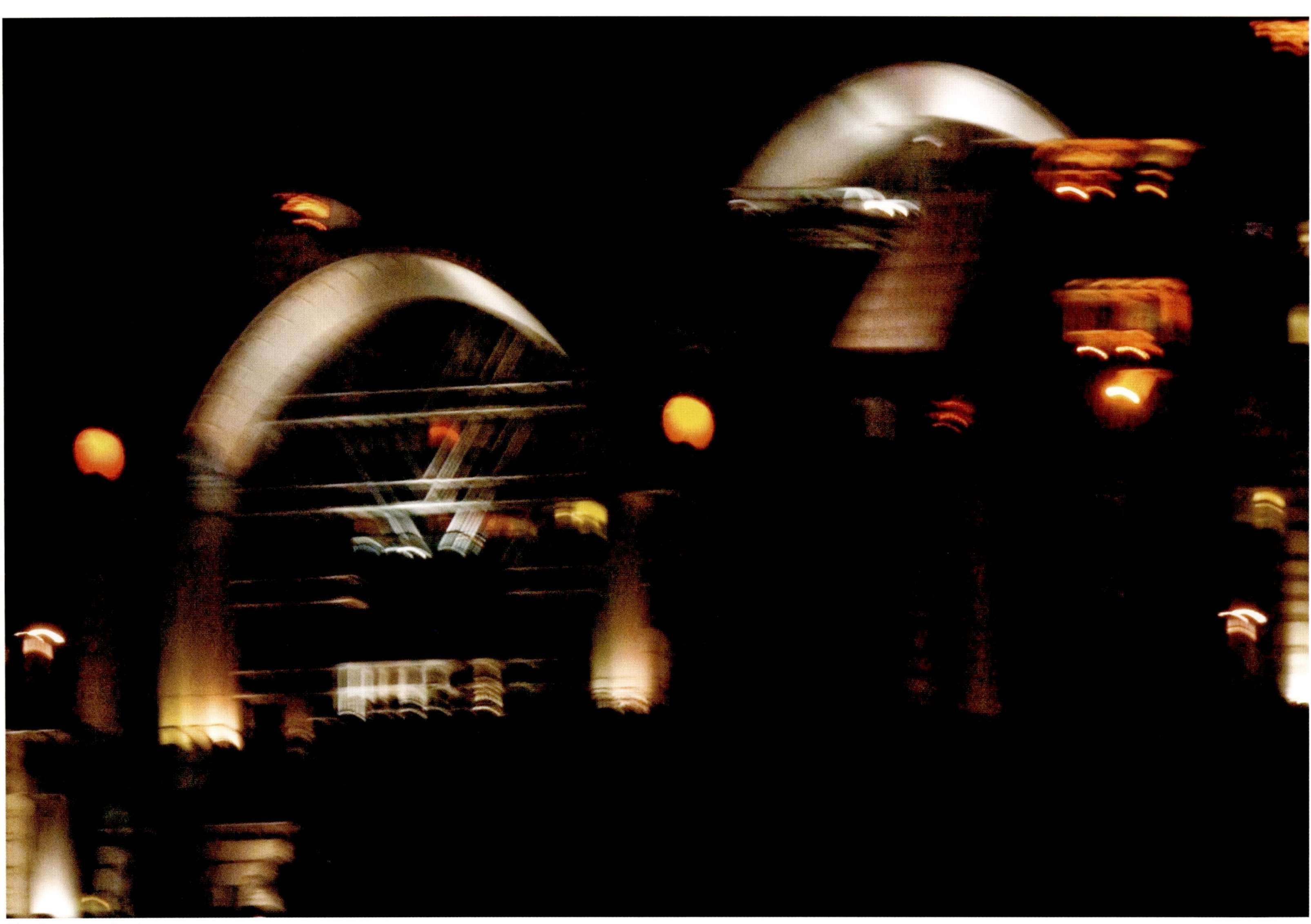

Charing Cross Station

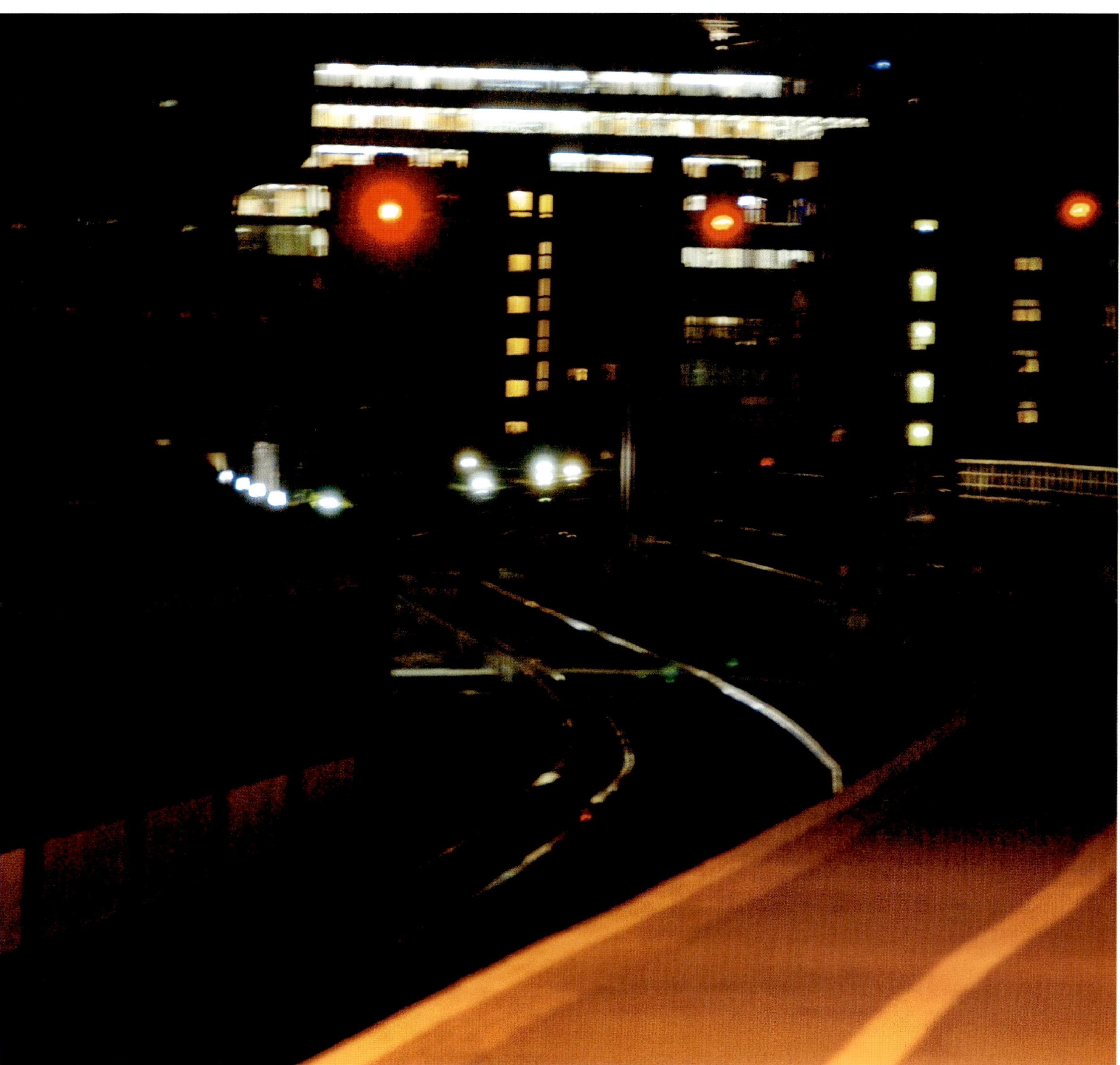

Blackfriars Station

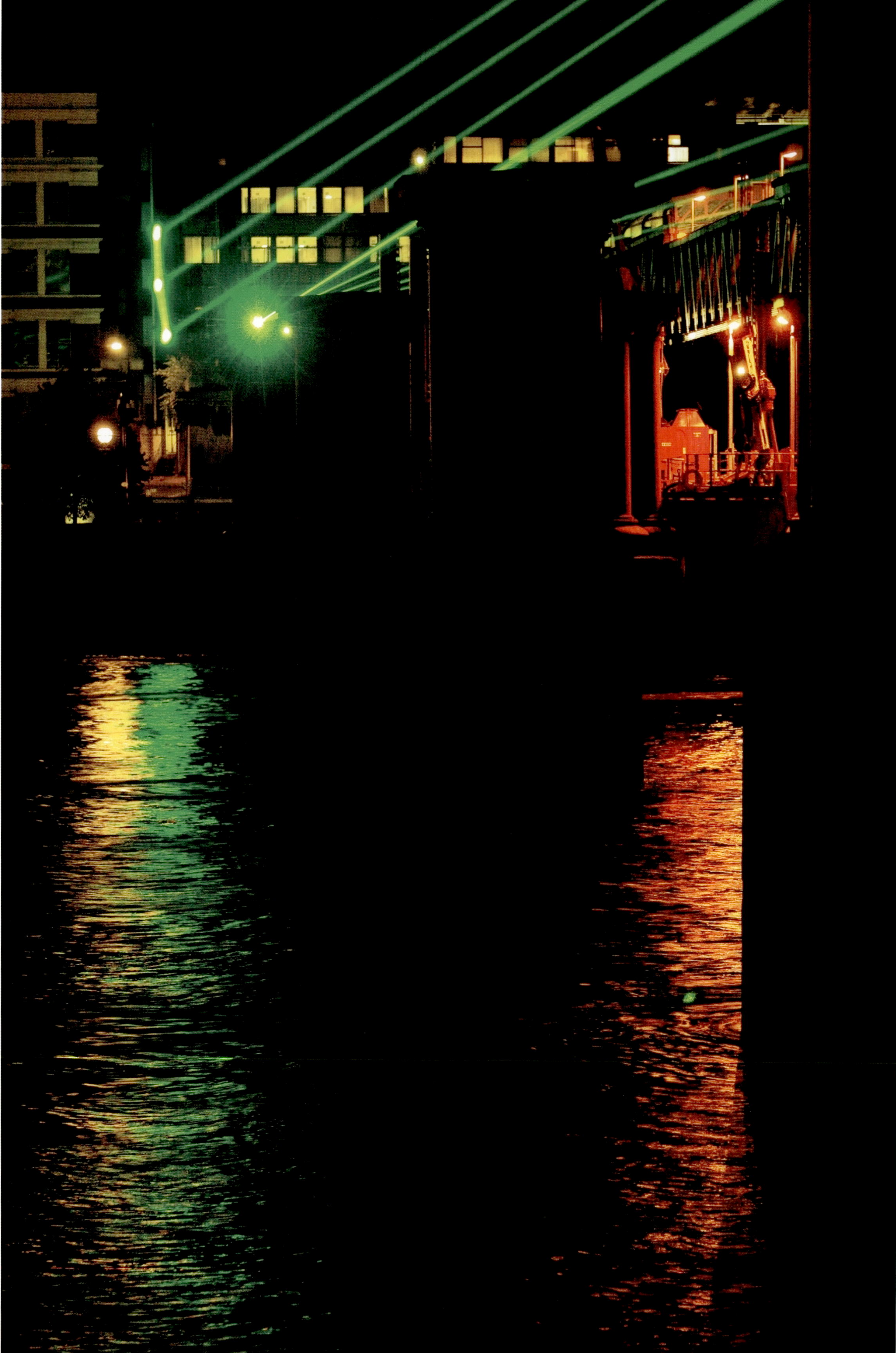

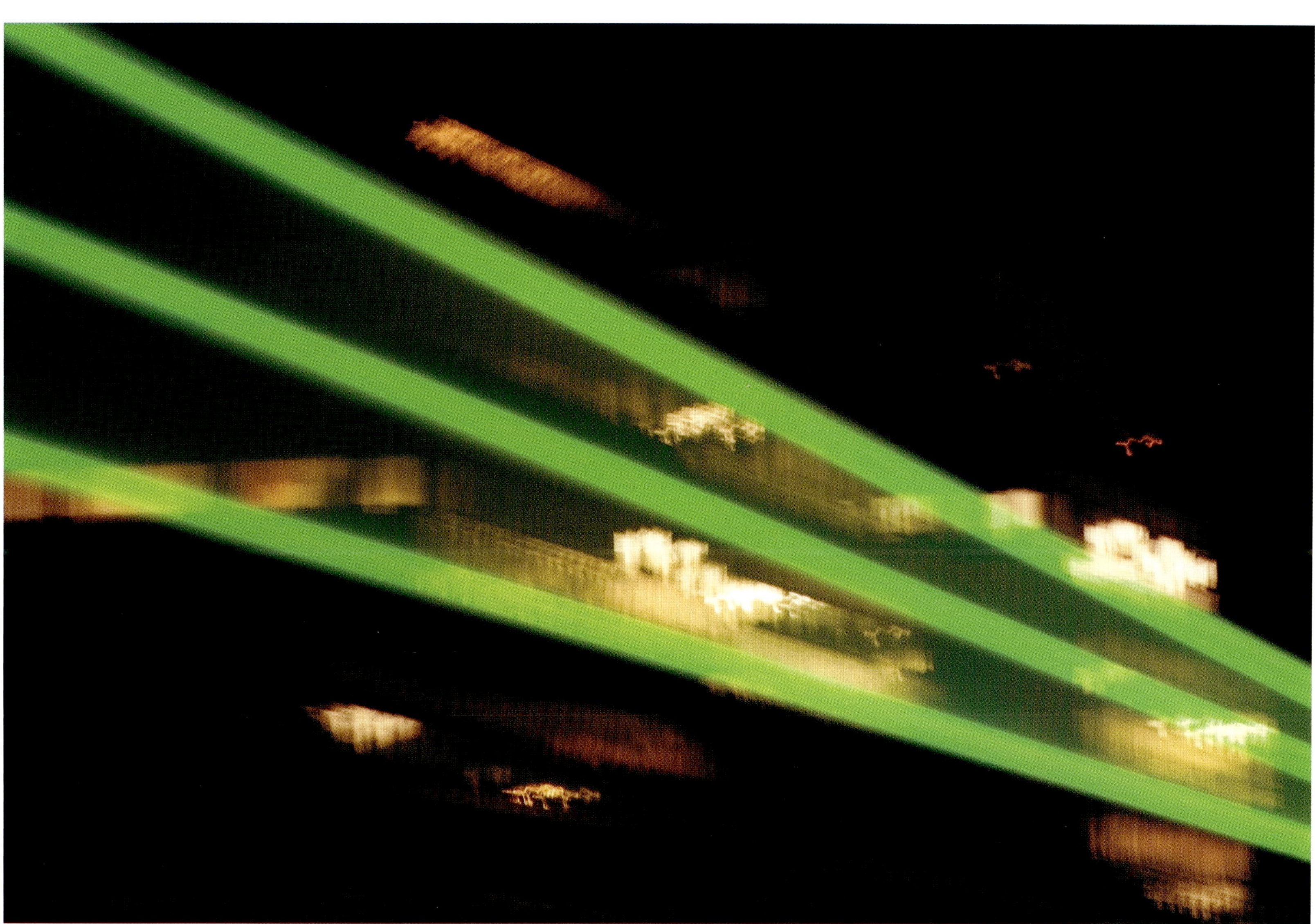

Above and left
Green laser installation alongside Blackfriars Railway Bridge

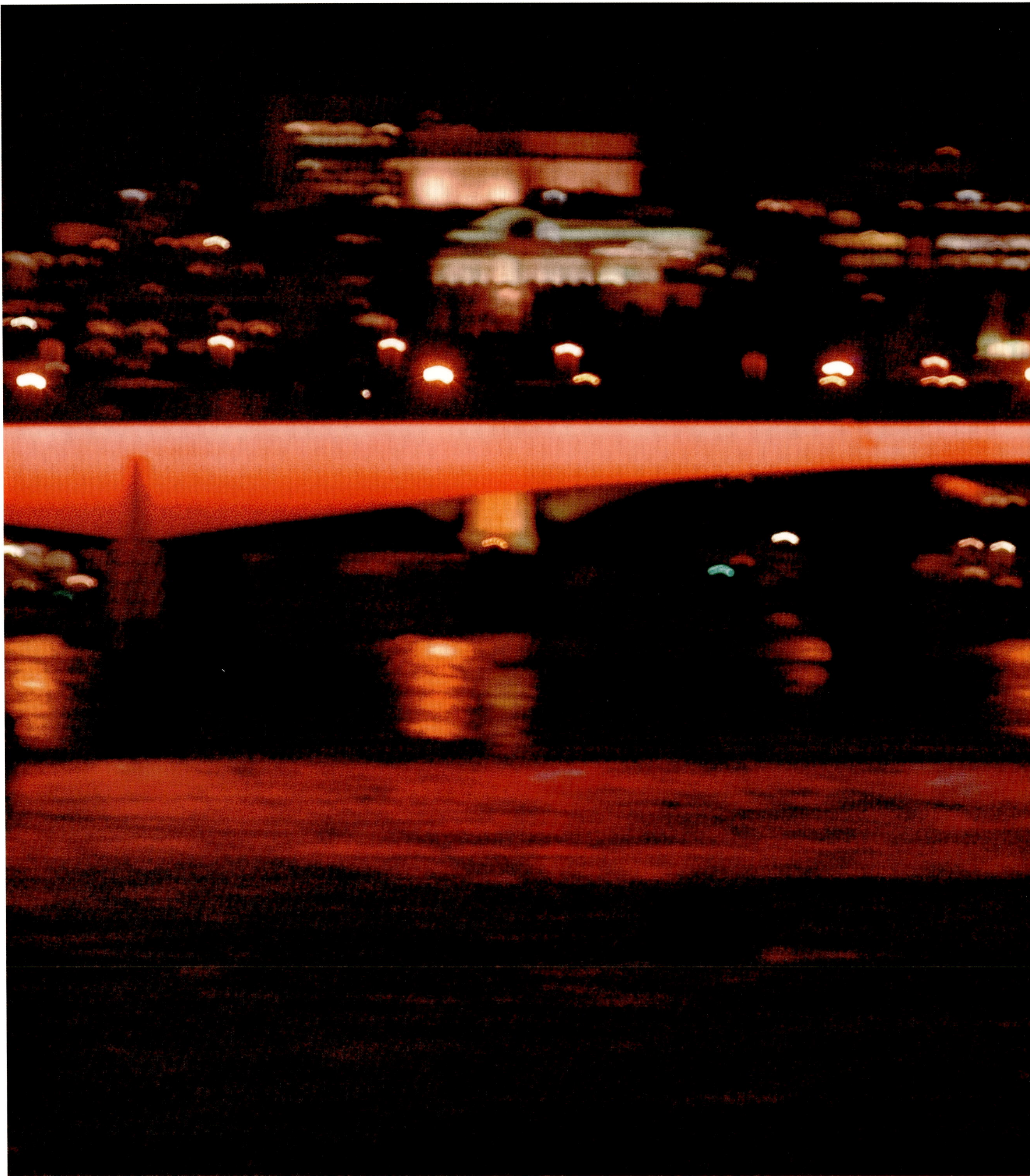

London Bridge

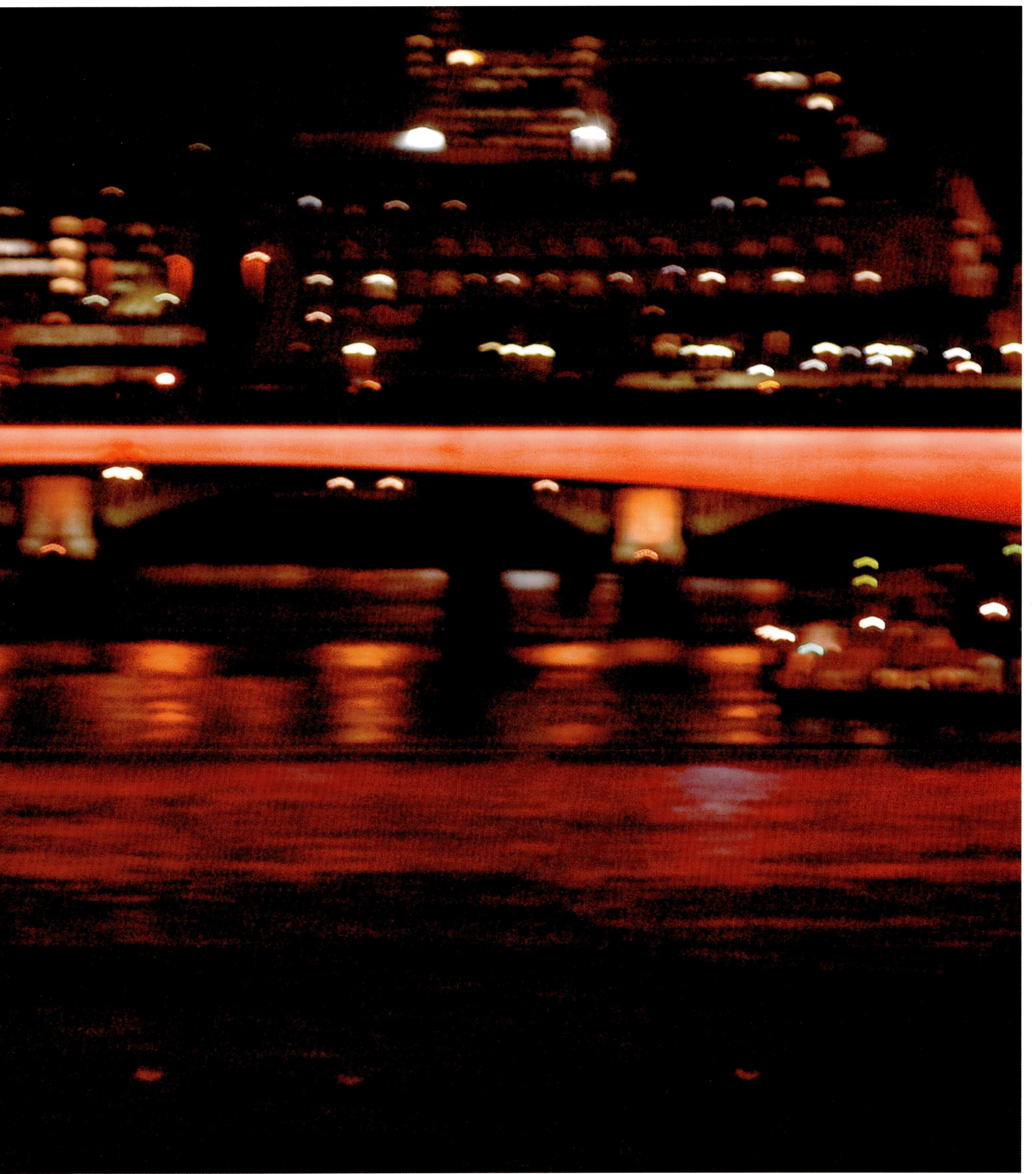

Page 106 London Bridge and the Telecom Tower
Page 107 The Oxo Tower

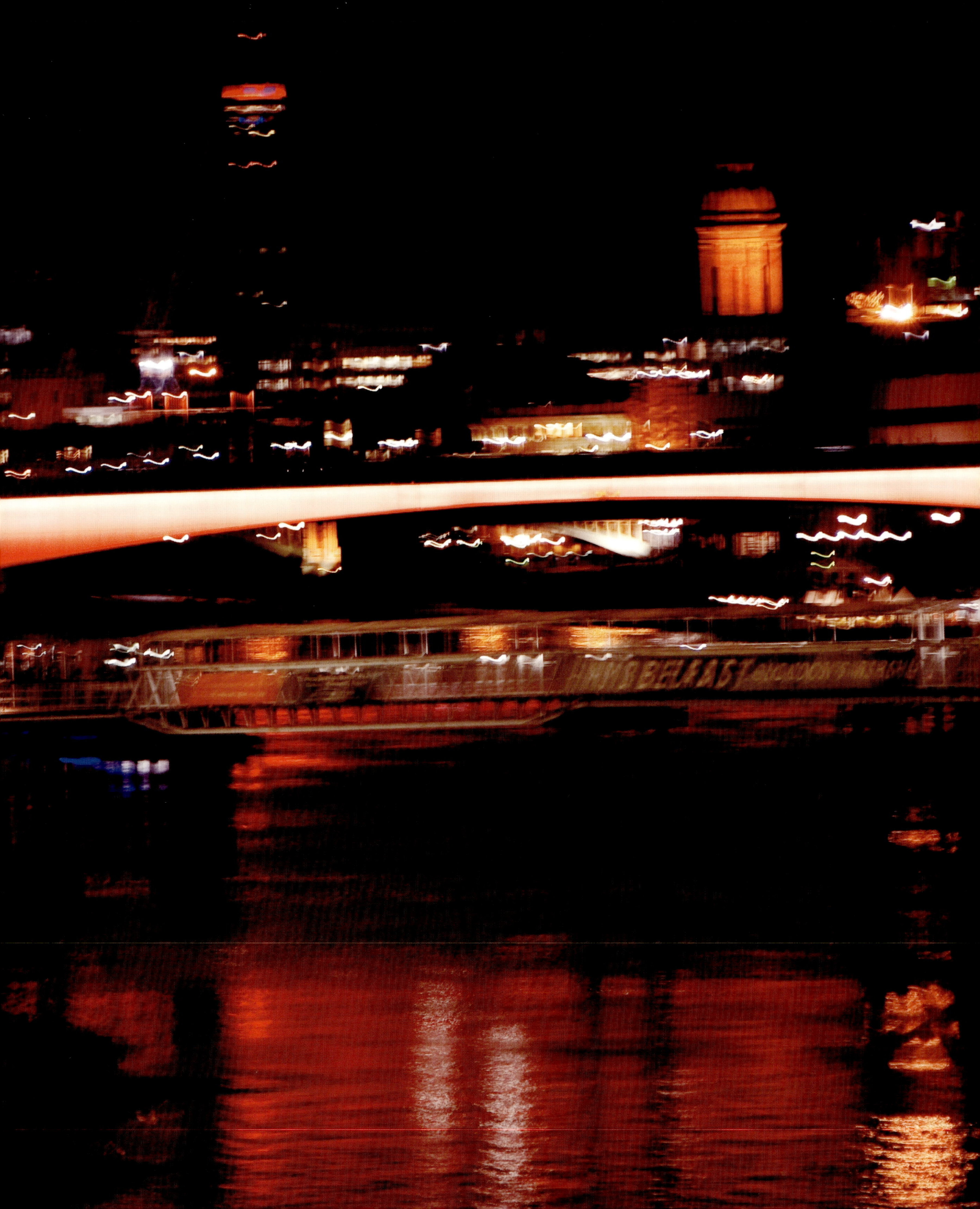
BELFAST

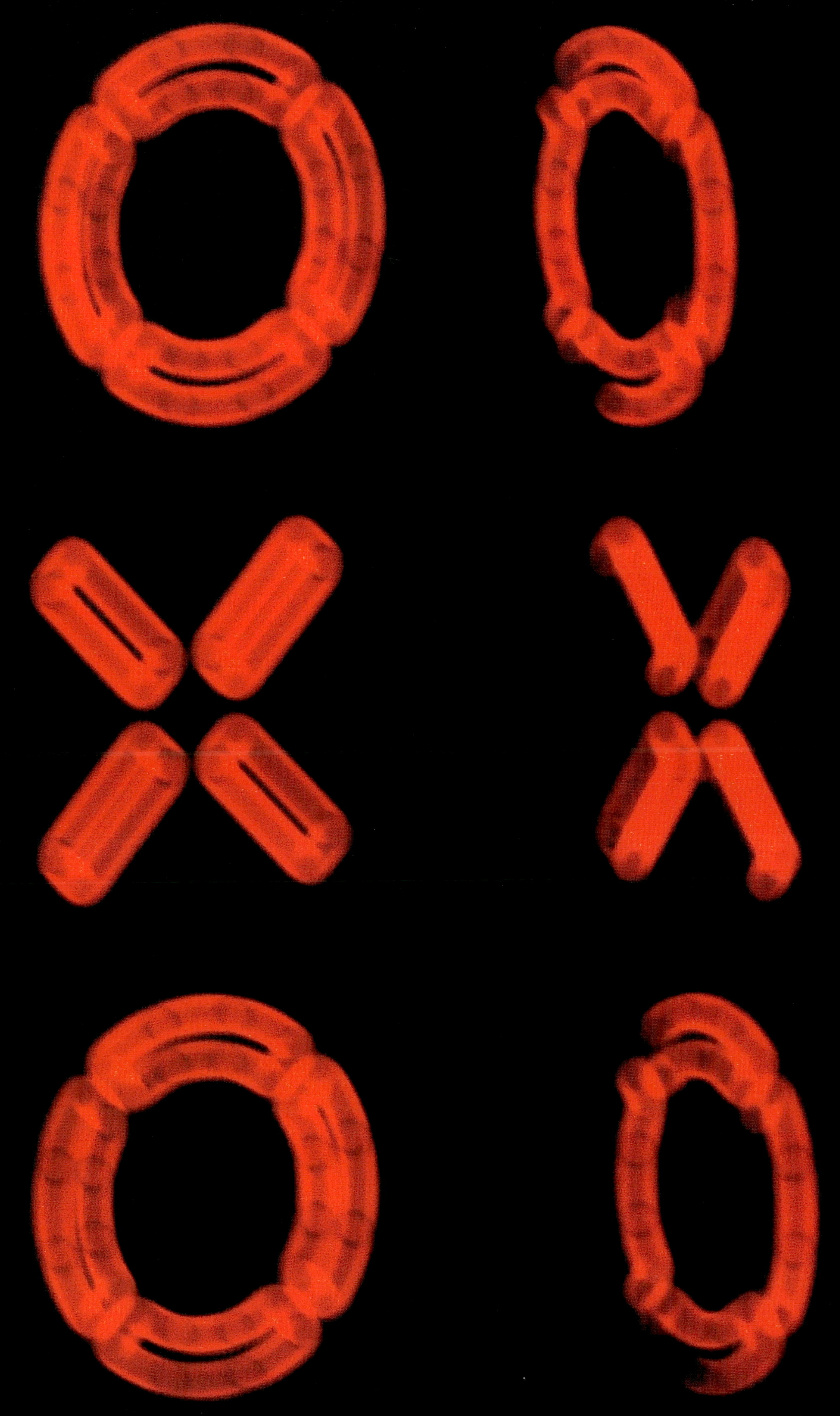

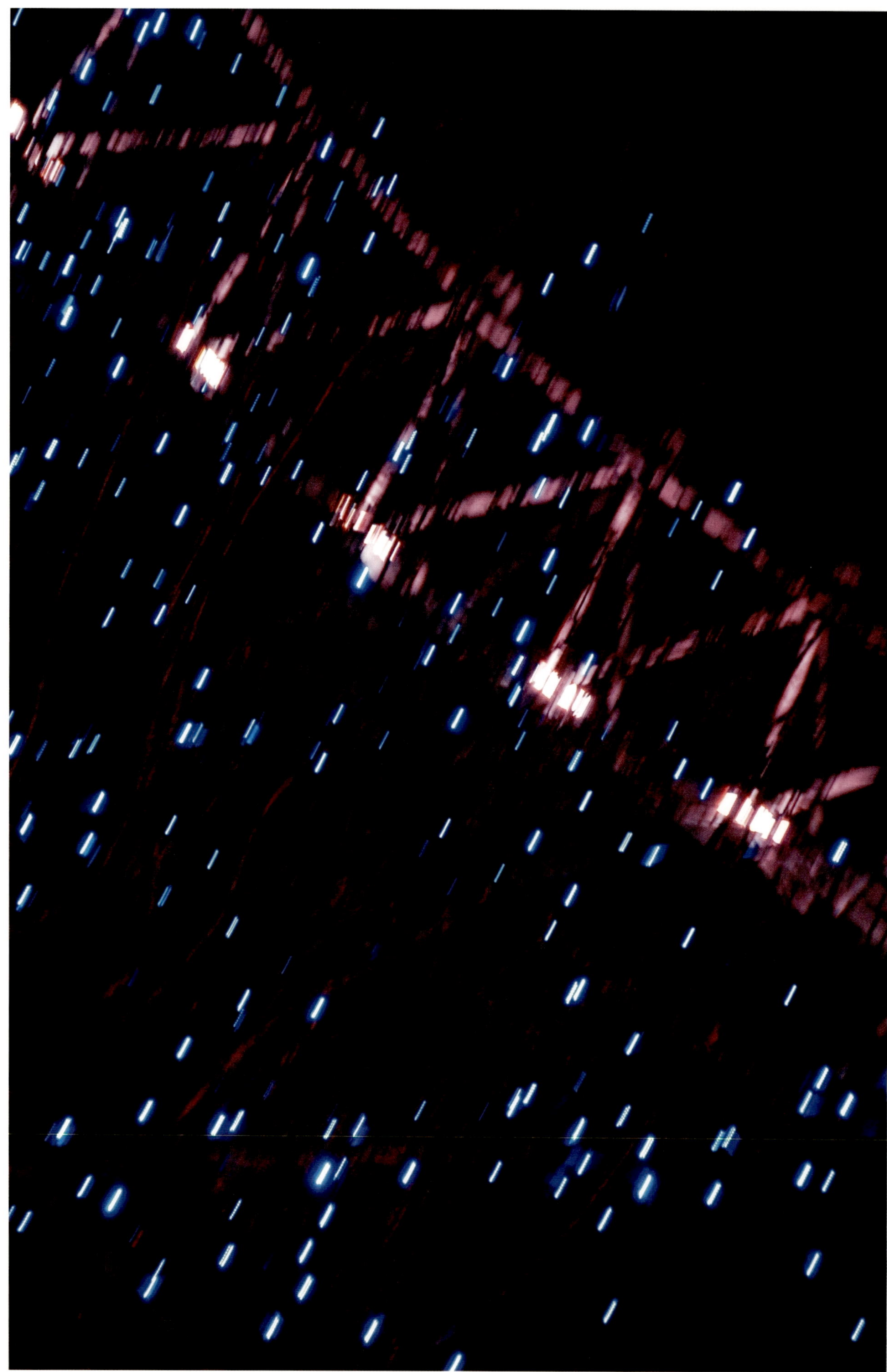

The London Eye

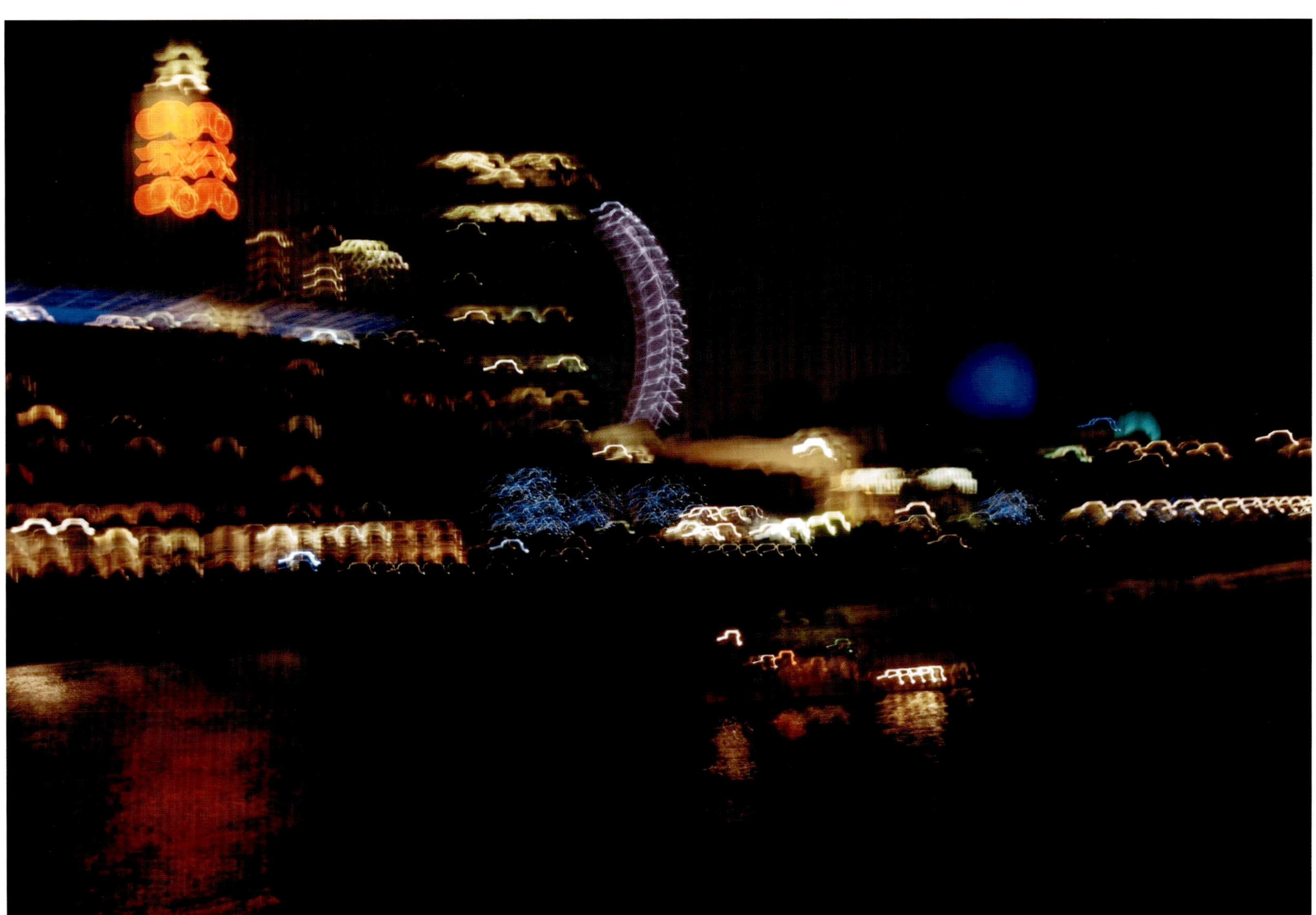

The Oxo Tower, the National Theatre and the London Eye

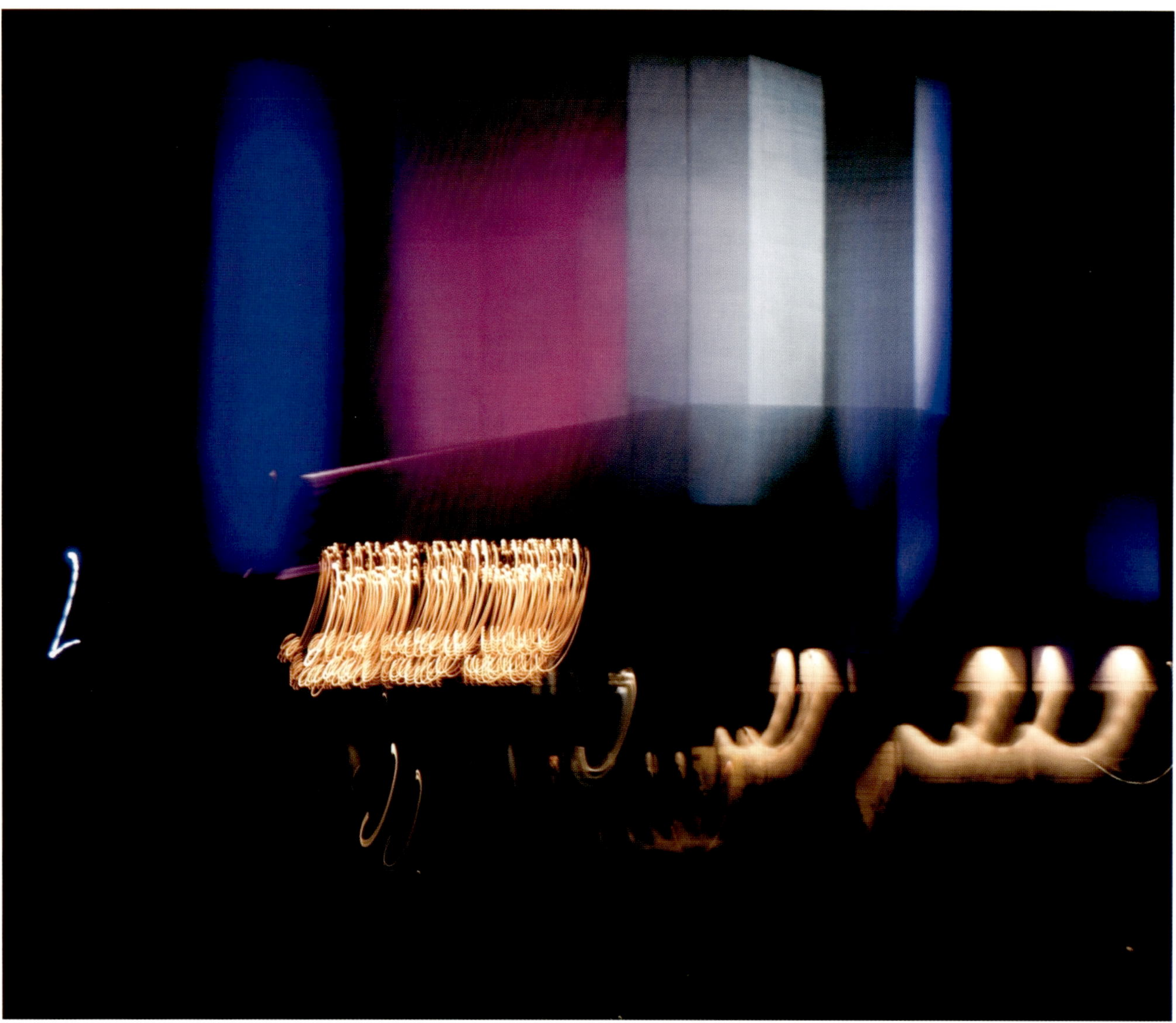

Above and opposite
The National Theatre

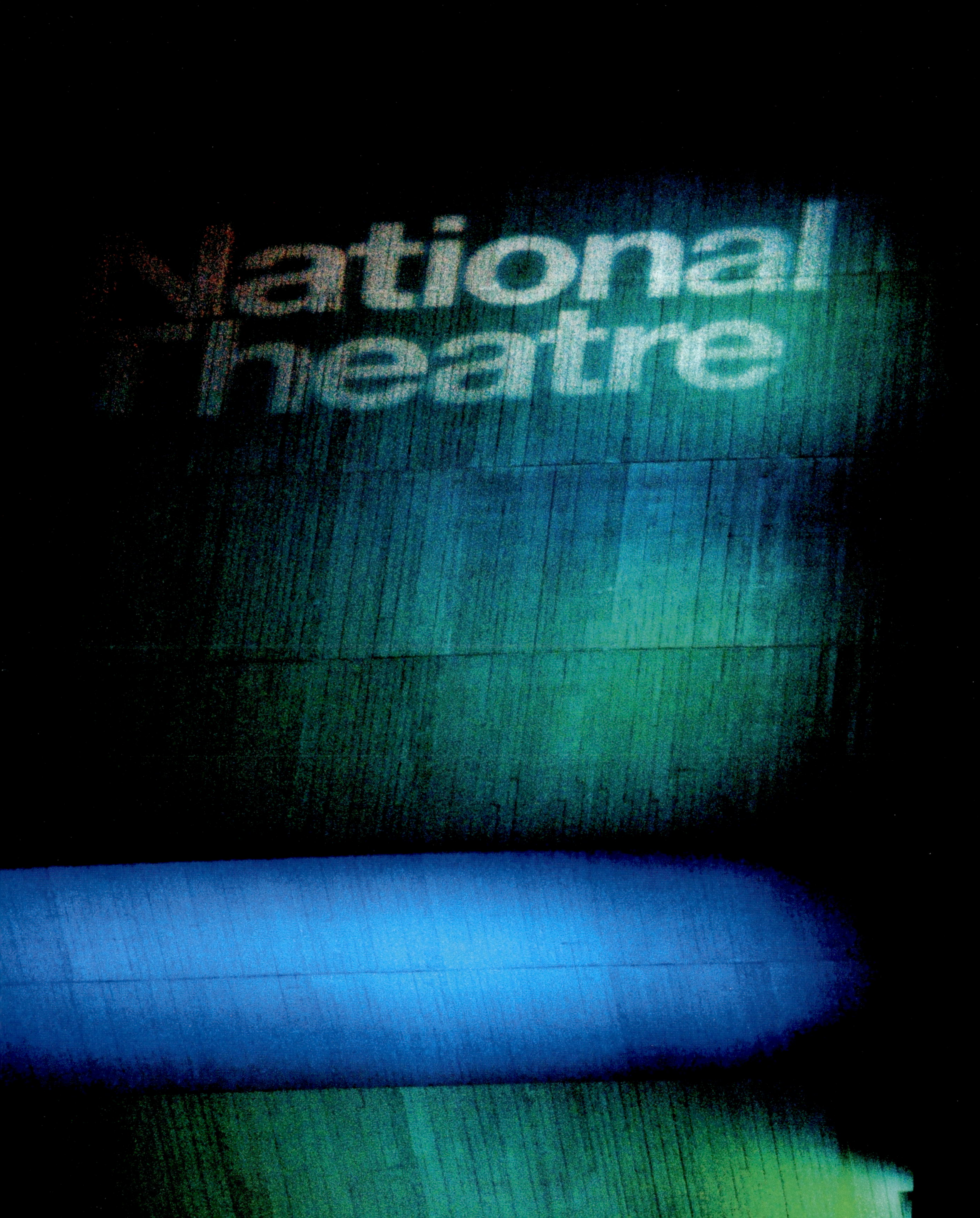
National
Theatre

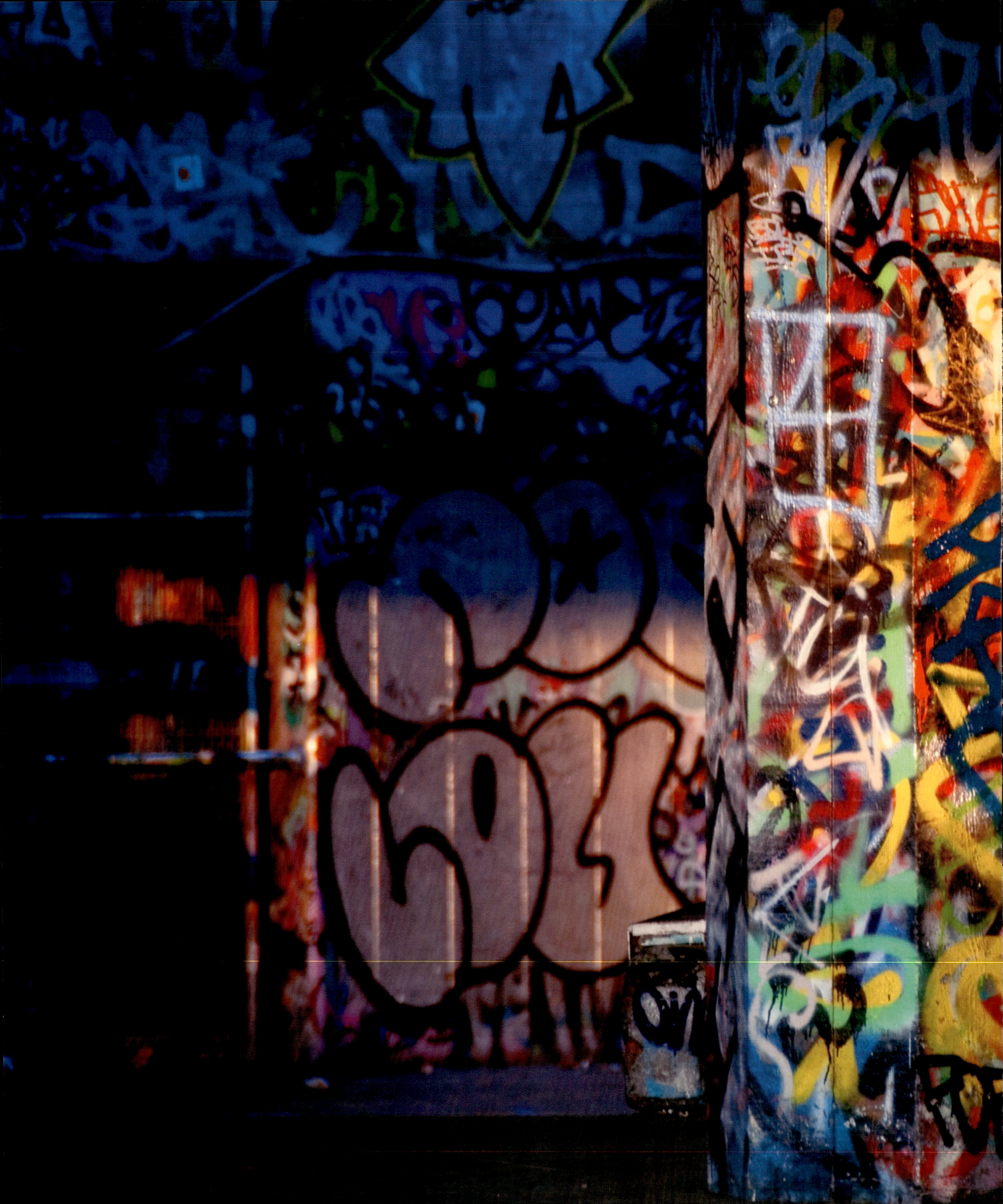

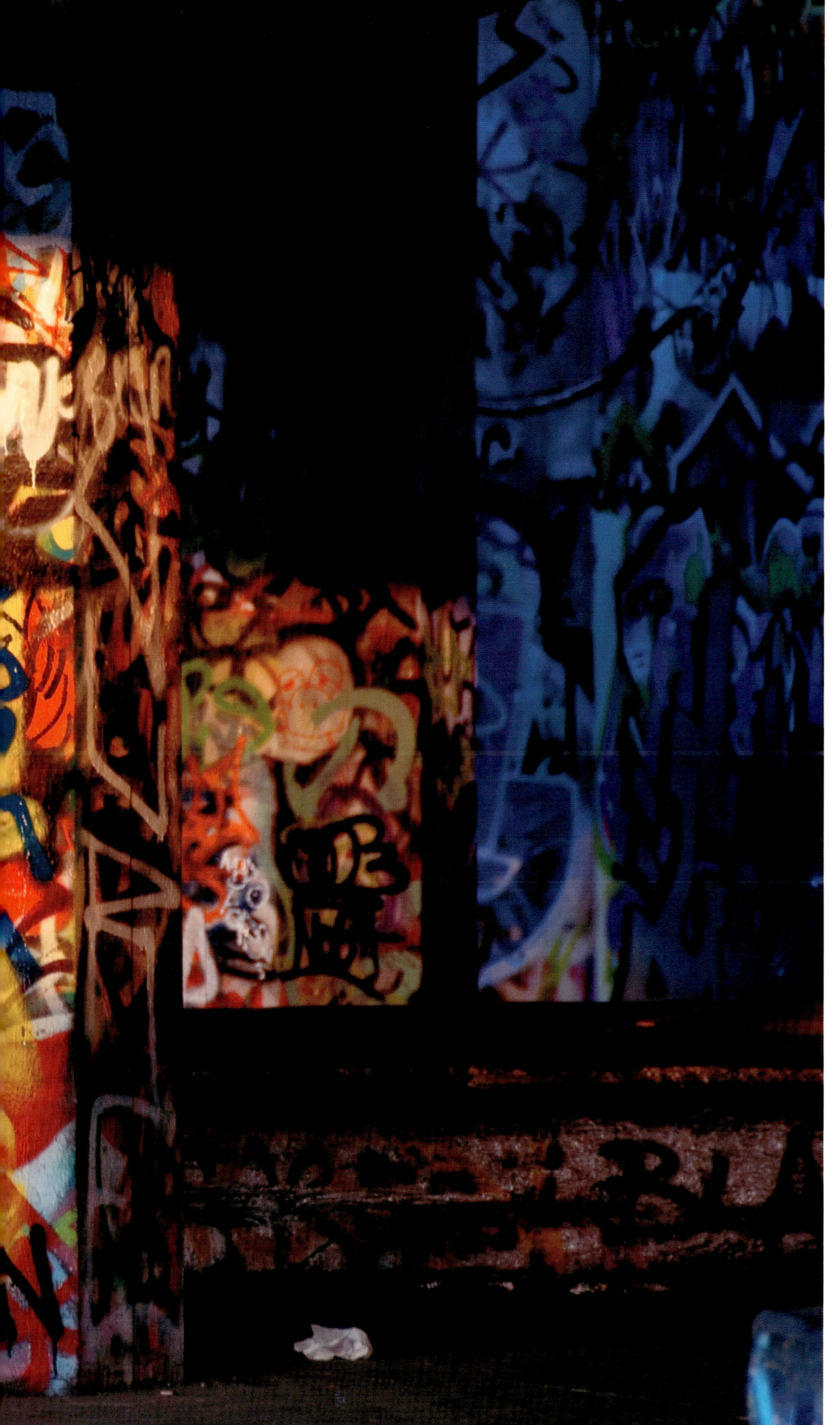

Graffiti on the South Bank

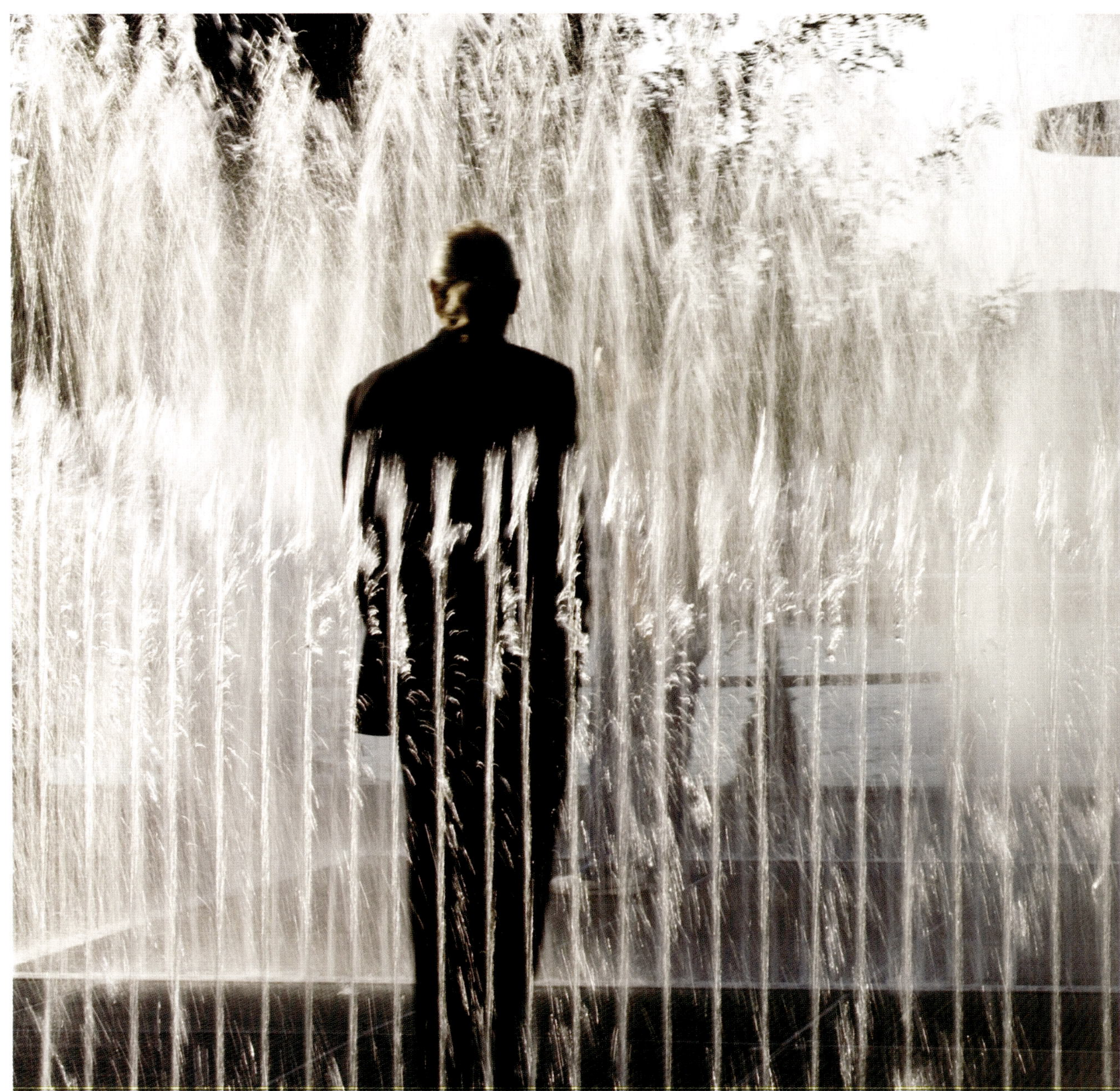

Fountain at the Festival Hall

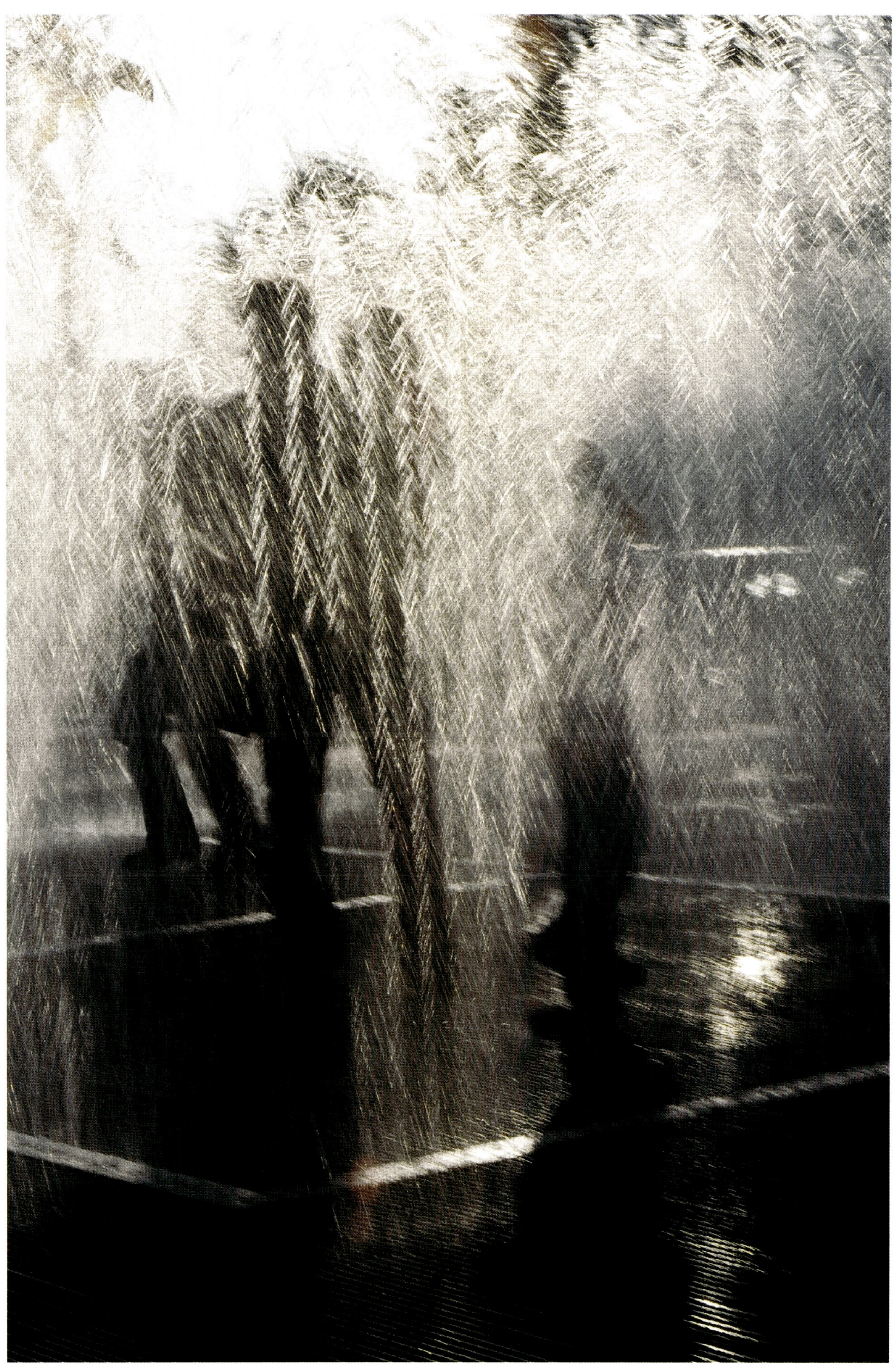

Scots football fans celebrating a win, in the Festival Hall fountains

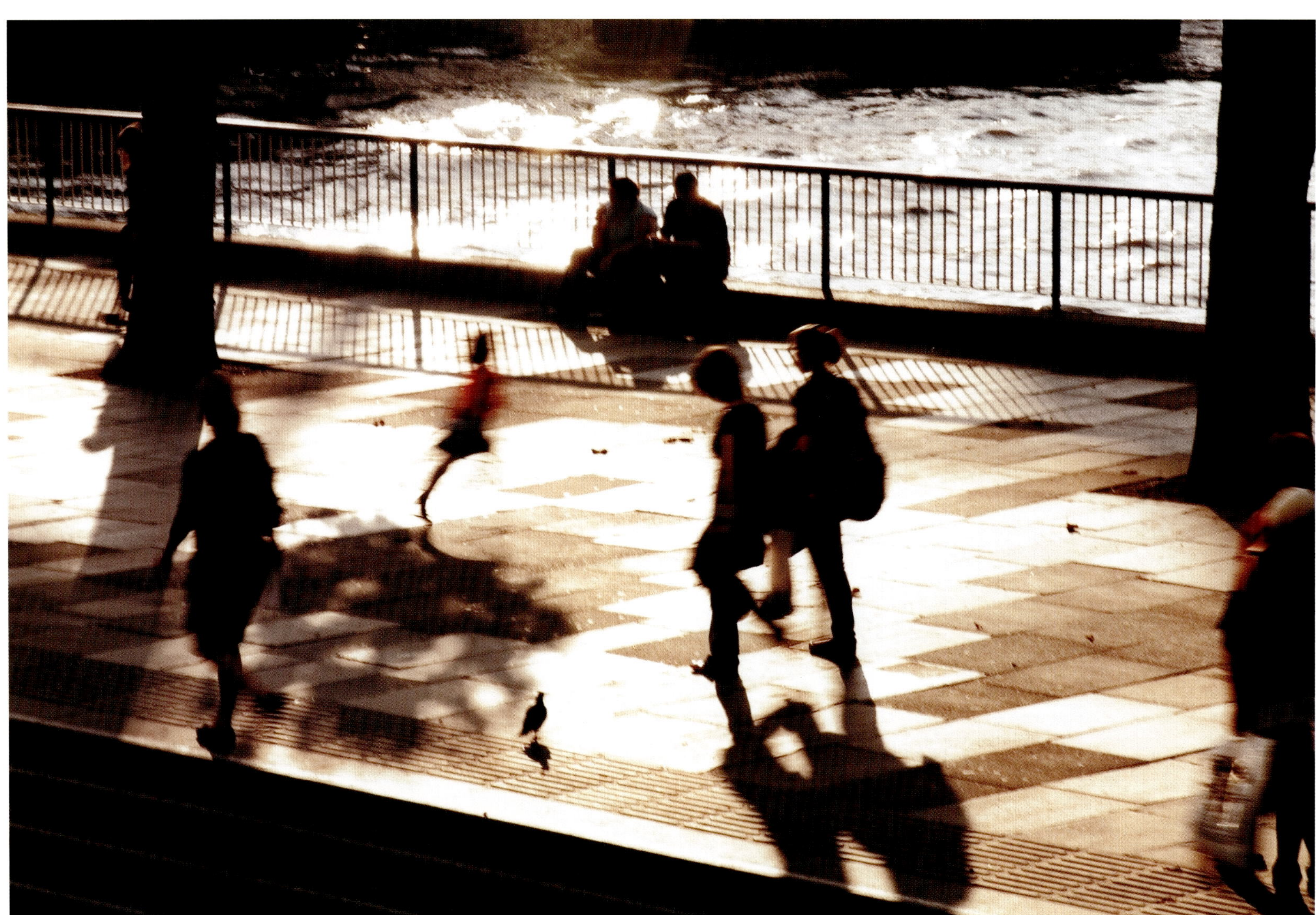

Above and opposite
On the South Bank

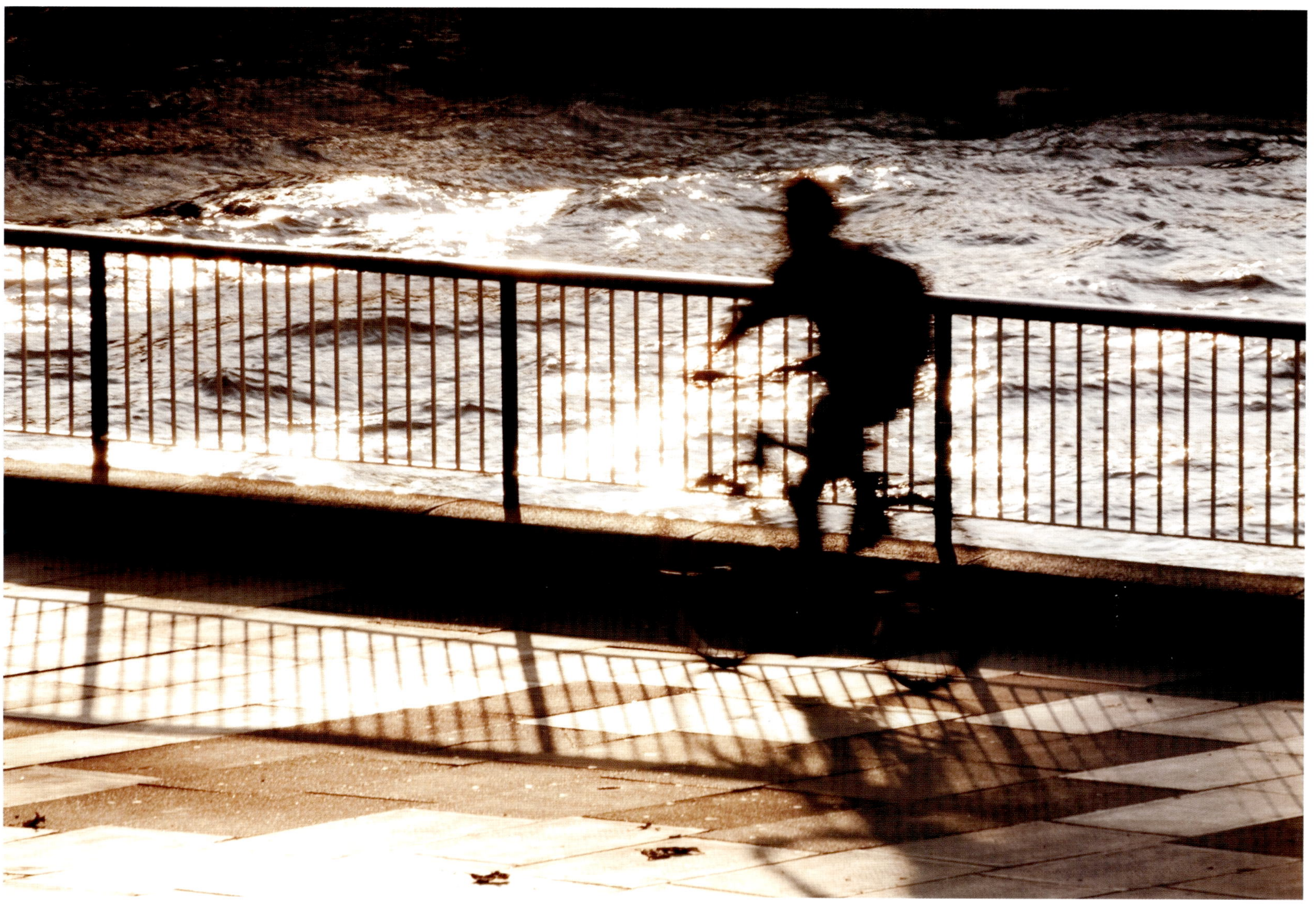

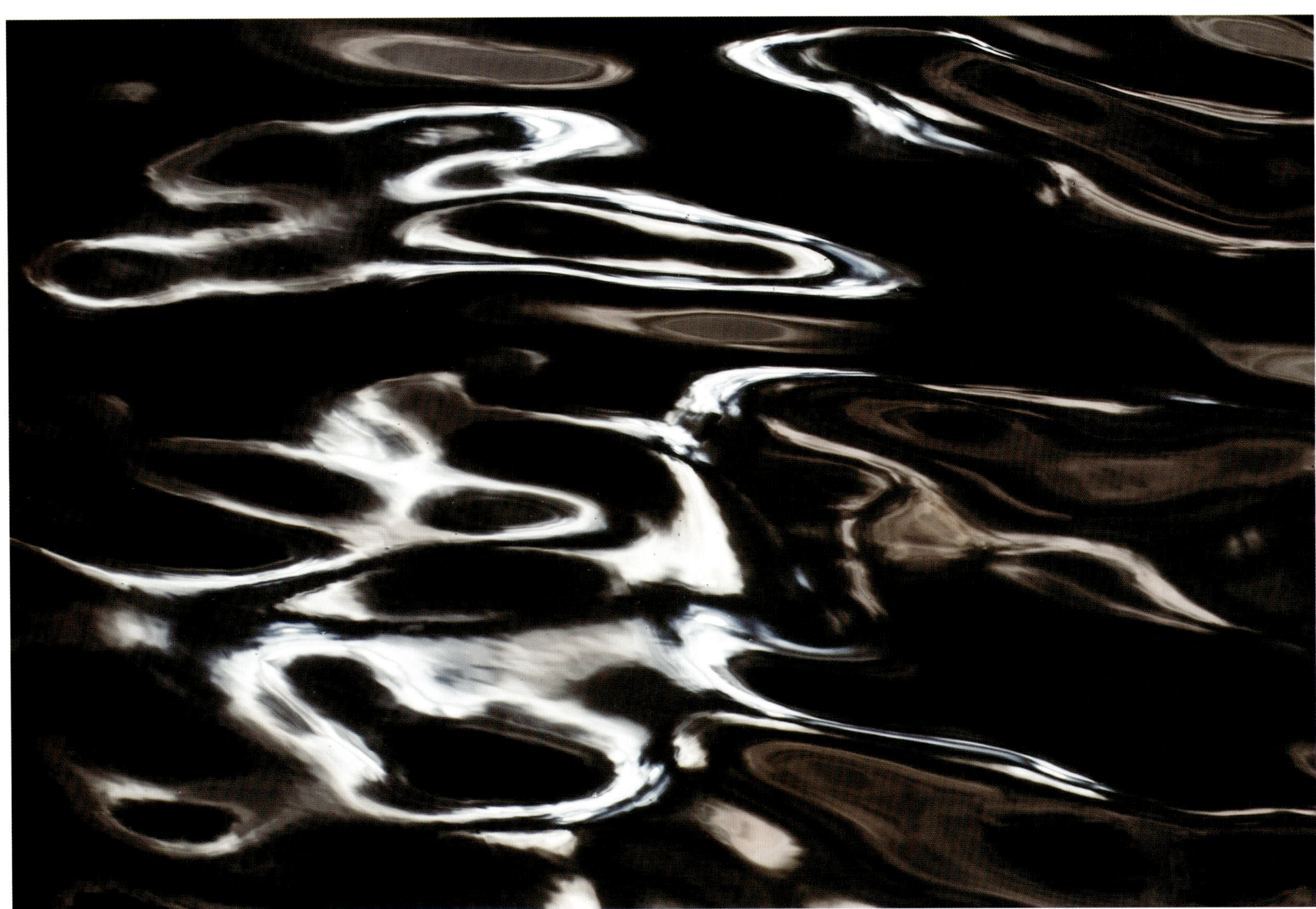

Satin-like water reflections

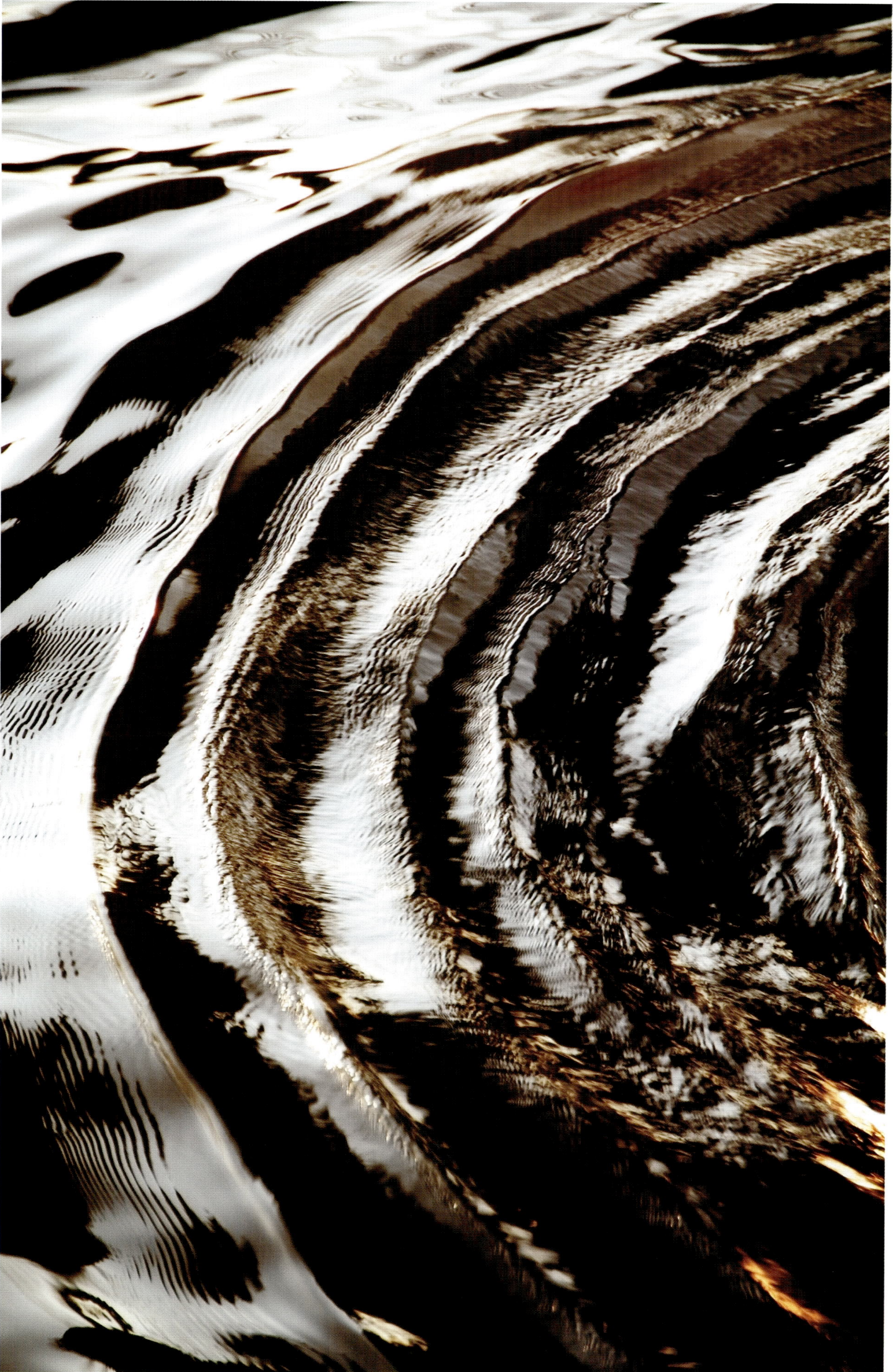

Above The Thames ebb tide

Pages 120–121 The London Eye

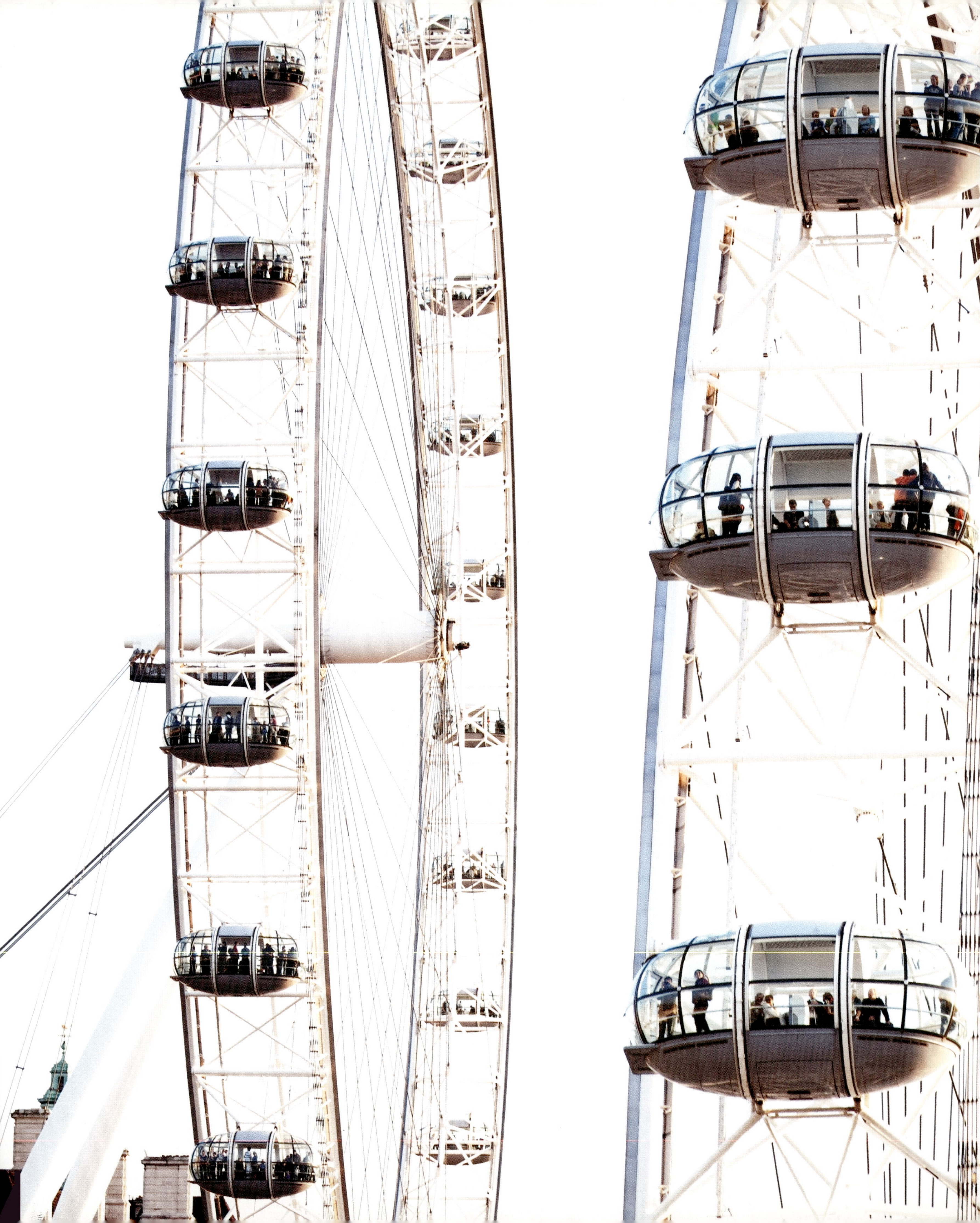

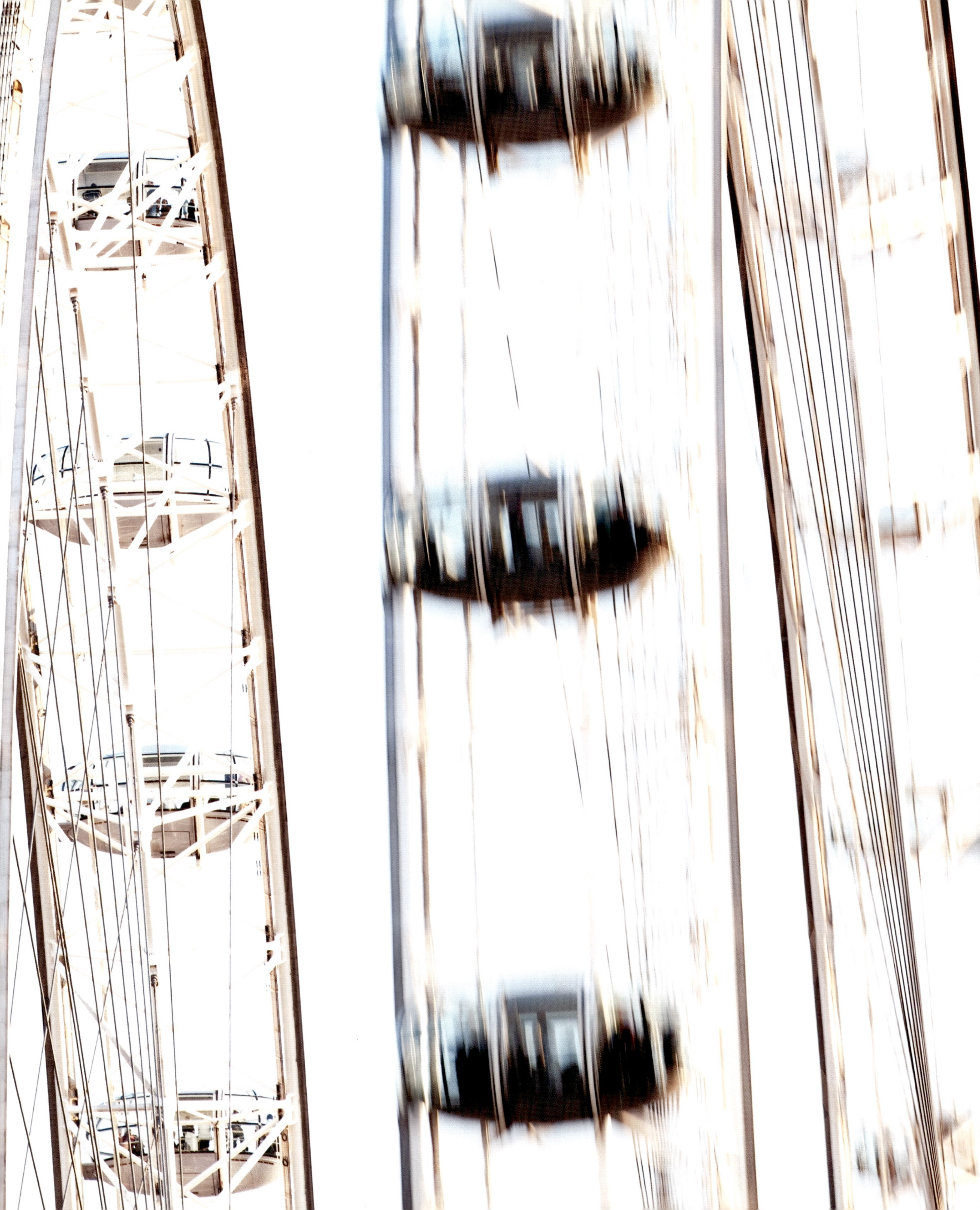

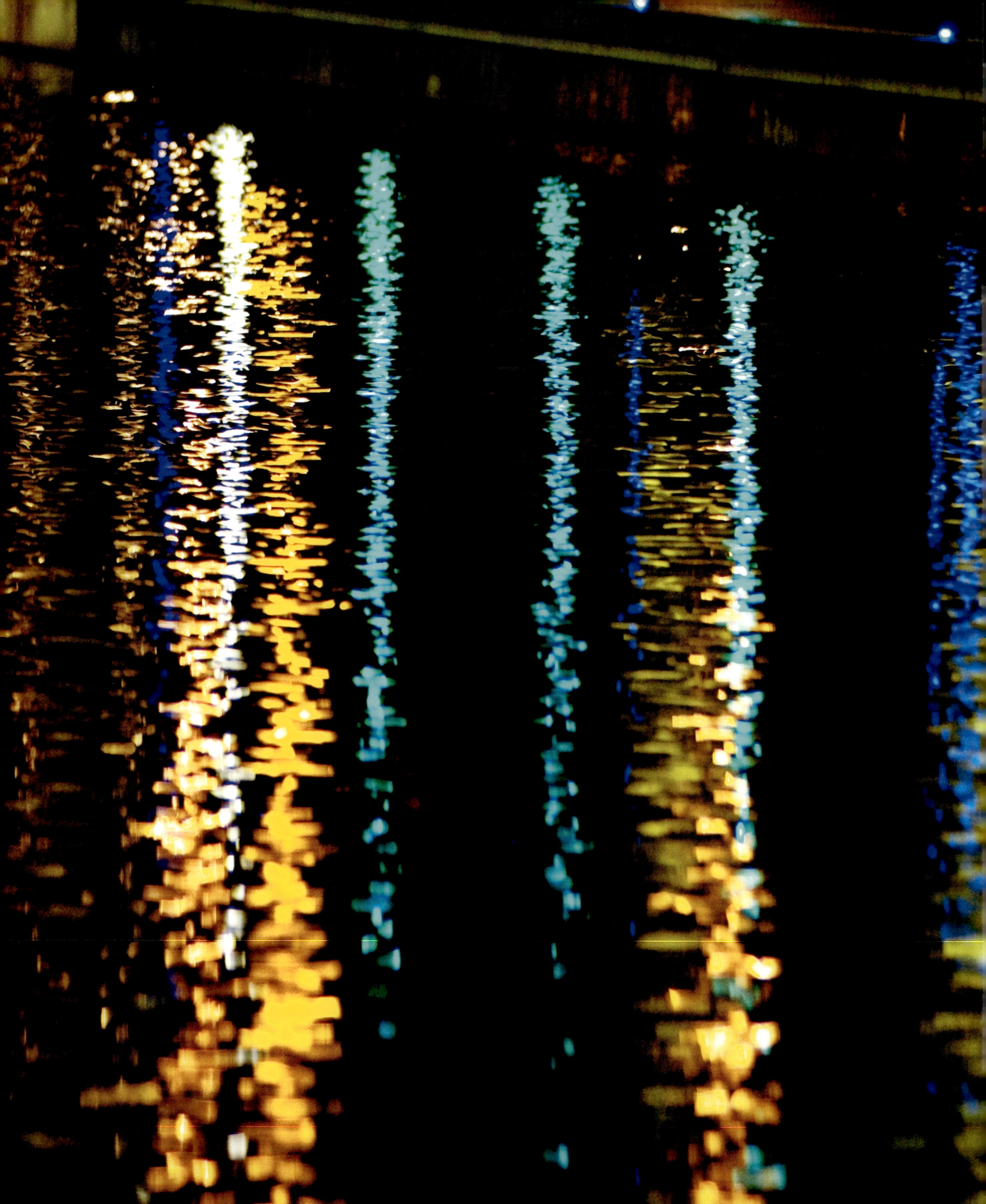

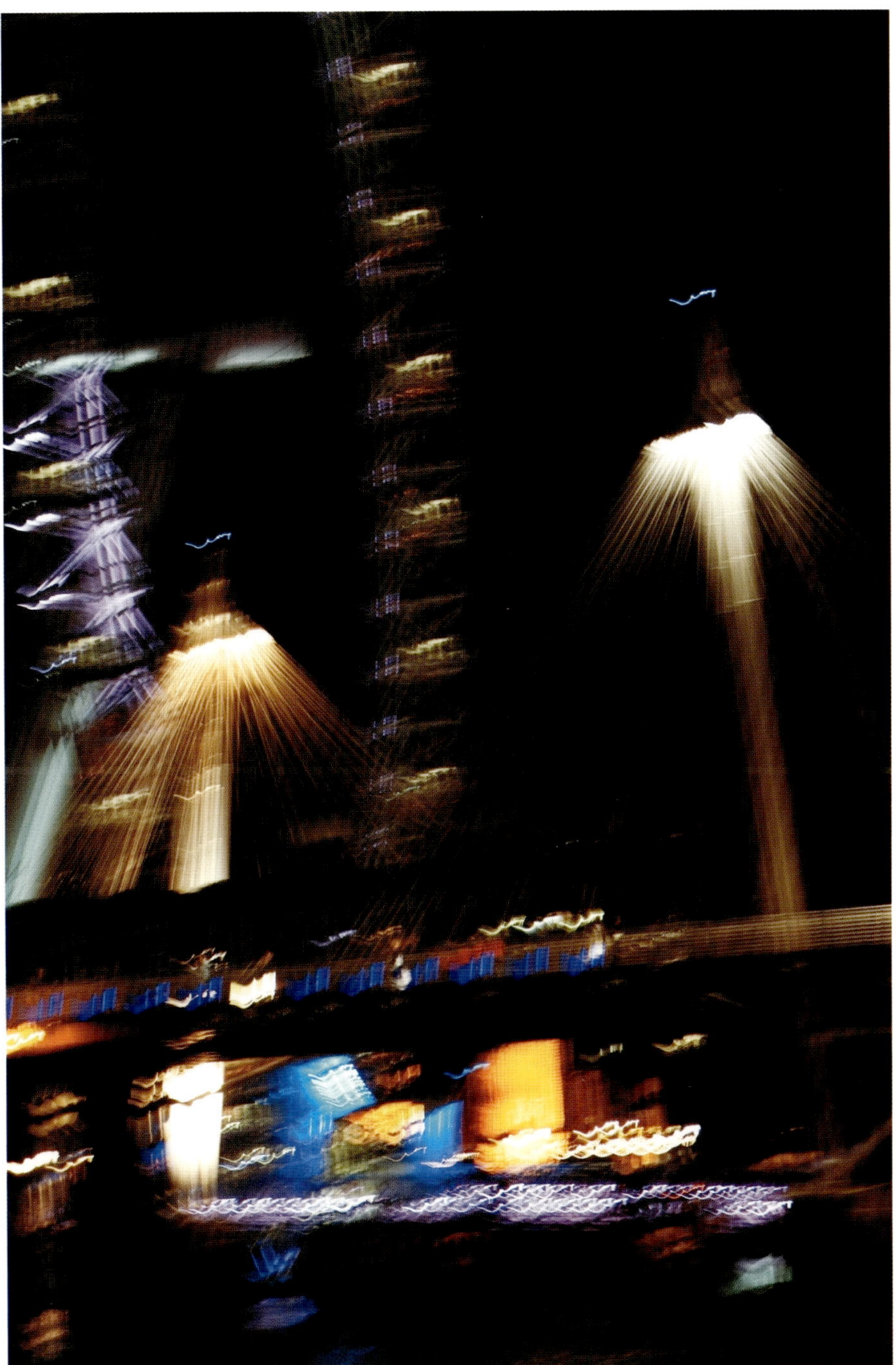

Above The London Eye and Hungerford foot and rail bridges
Left Reflections in the water

Hungerford foot and rail bridges

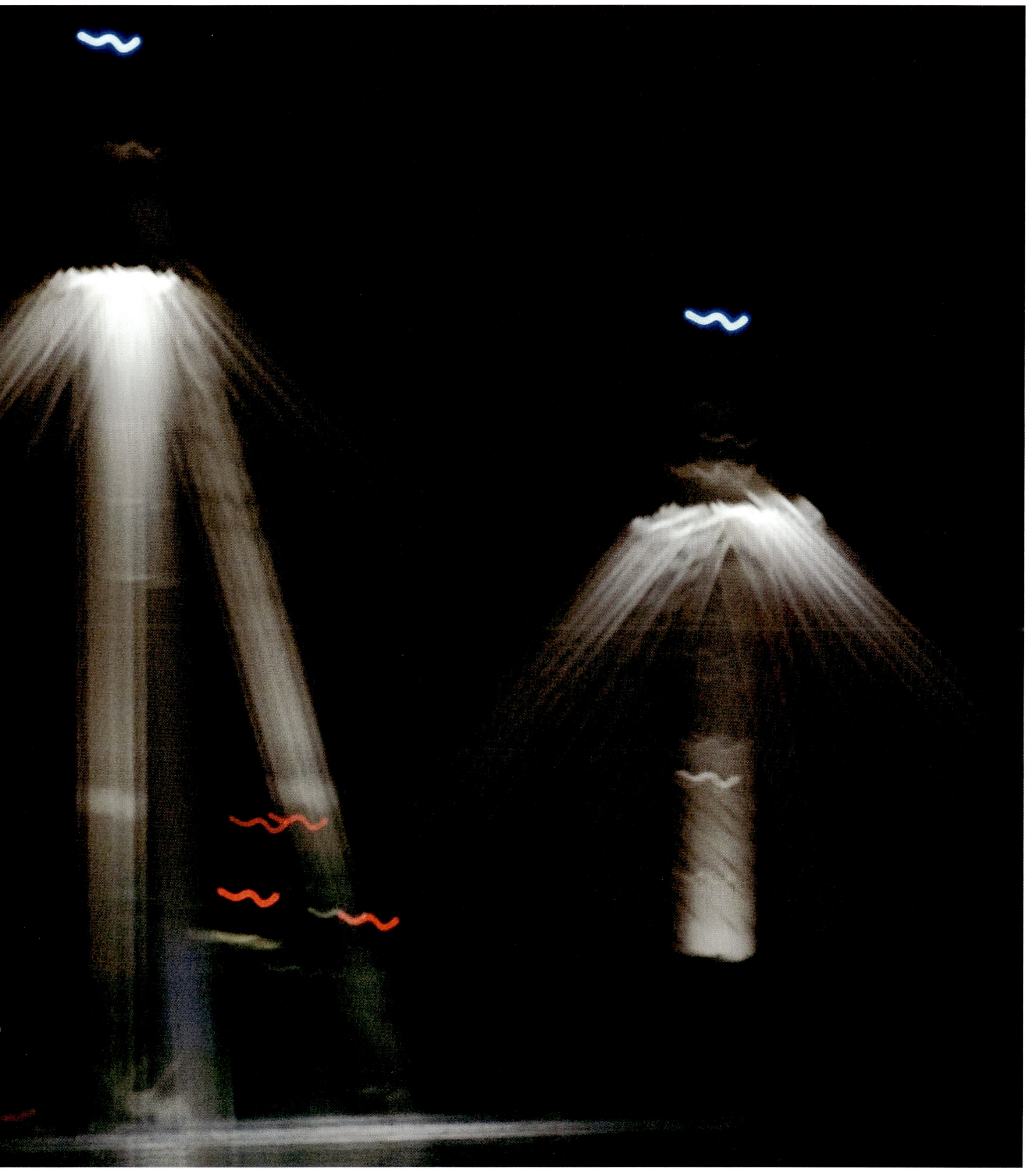

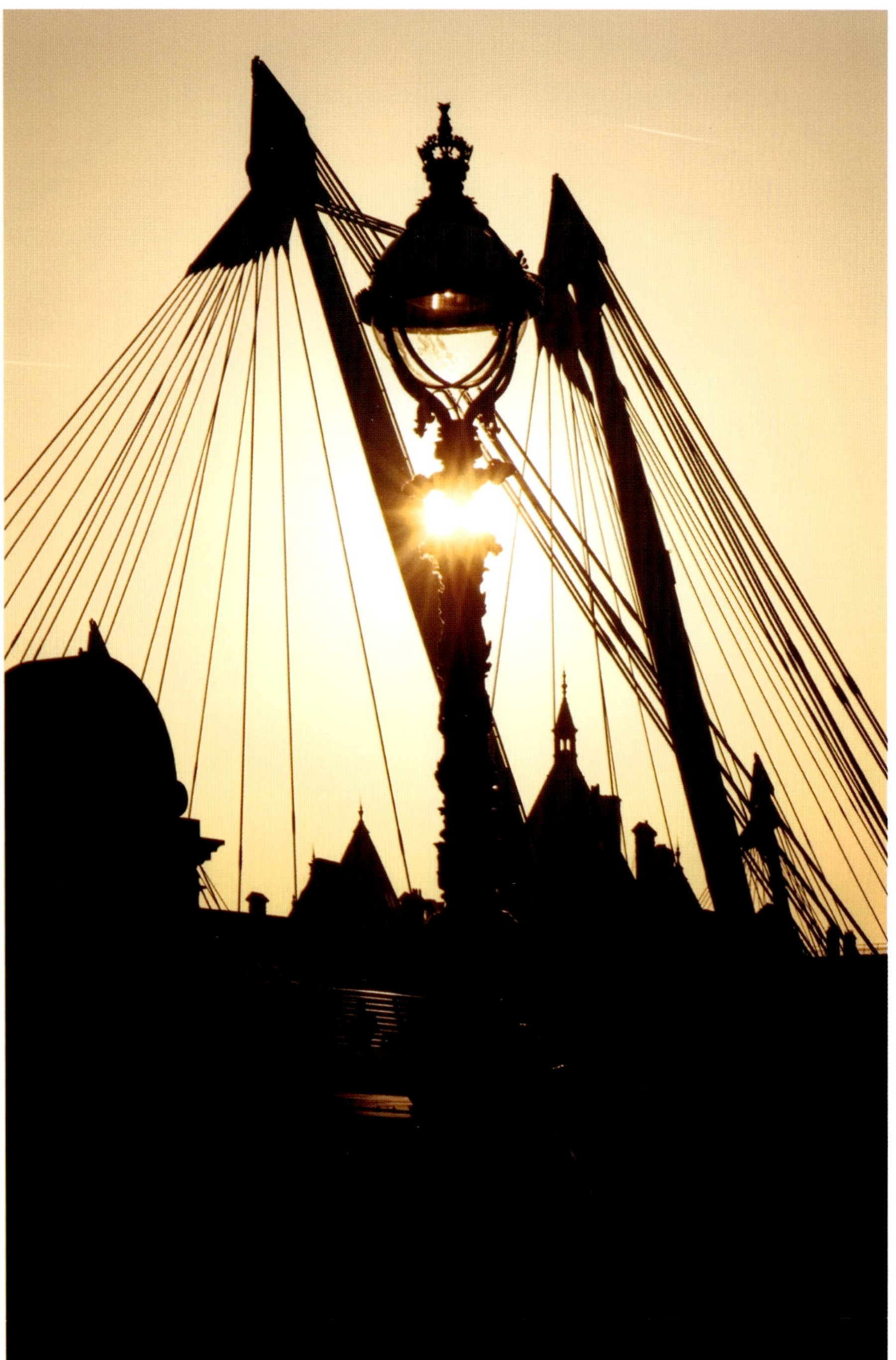

Hungerford foot and rail bridges

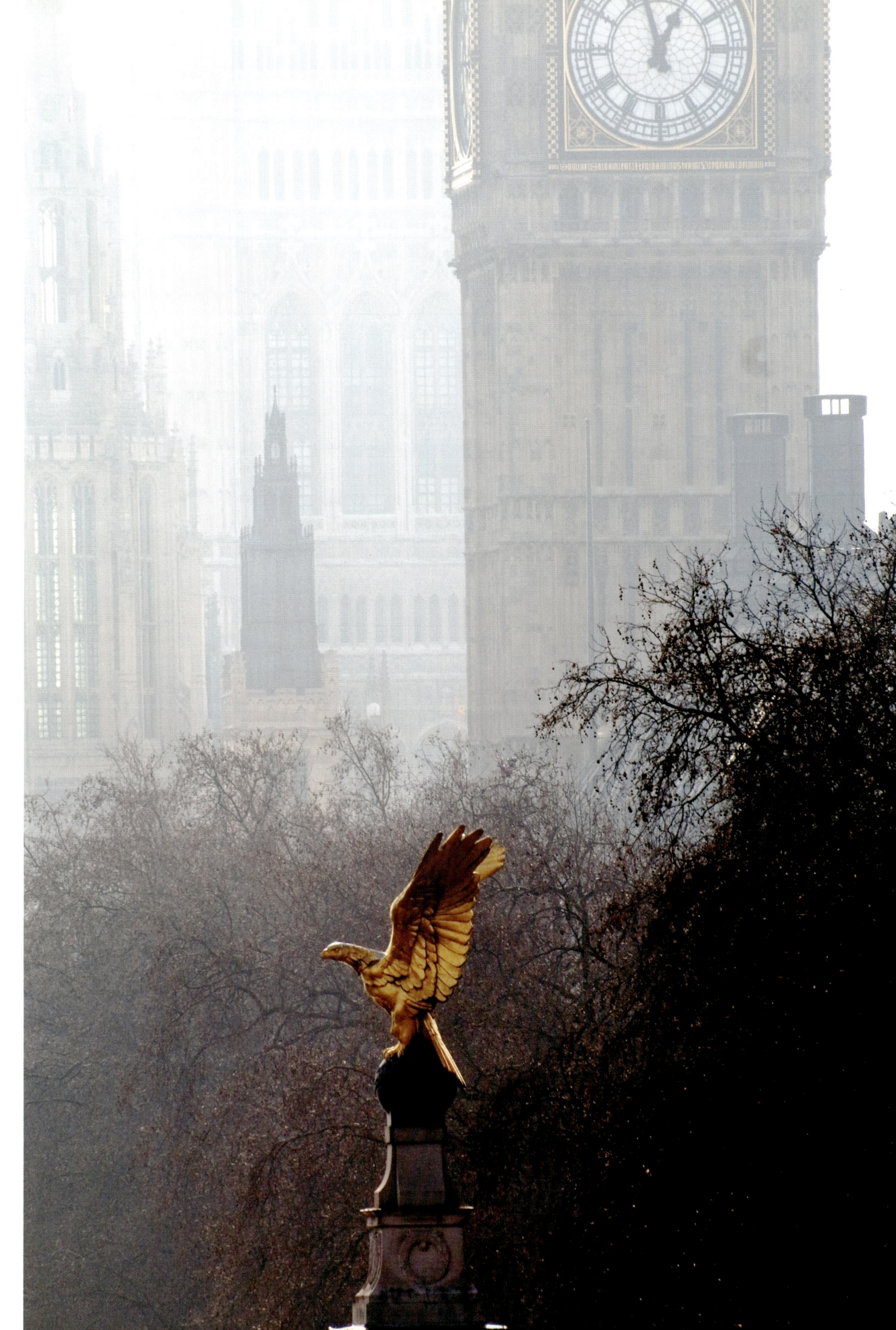

Golden Eagle sculpture by William Reid Dick, a memorial to the fallen airmen of the First World War

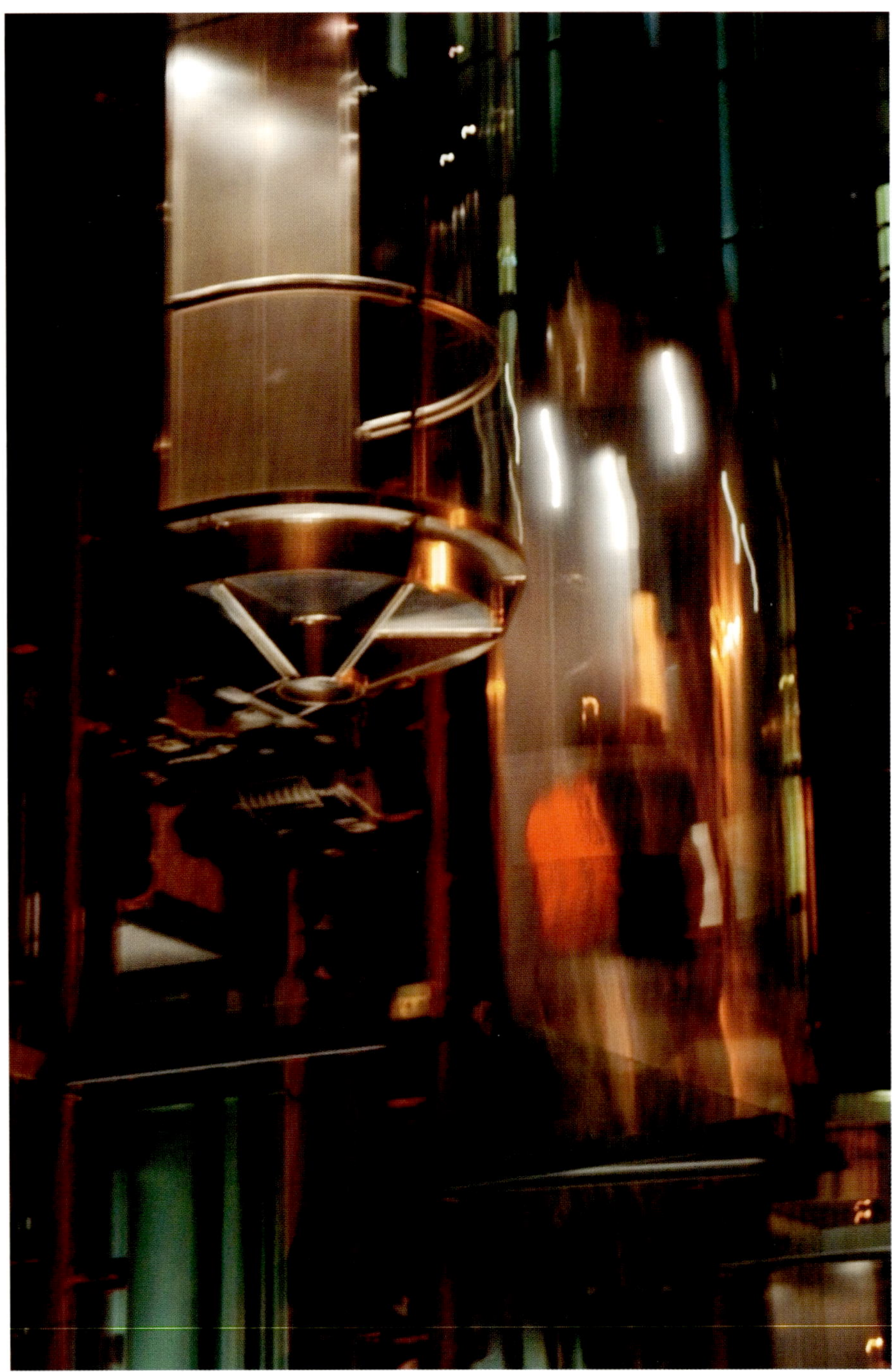

Exterior lifts of the Channel 4 Building, designed by Richard Rogers

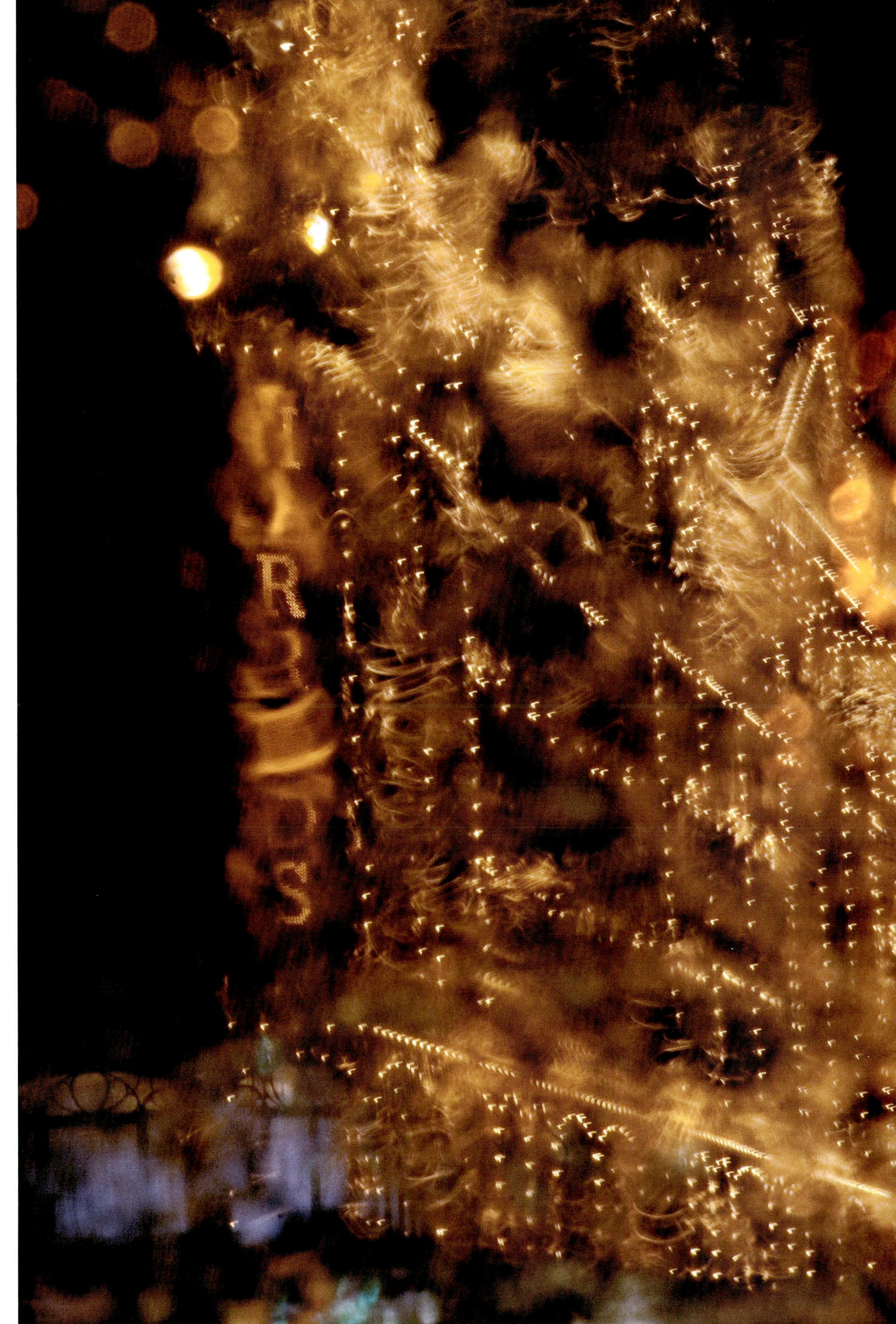

Harrods in the rain

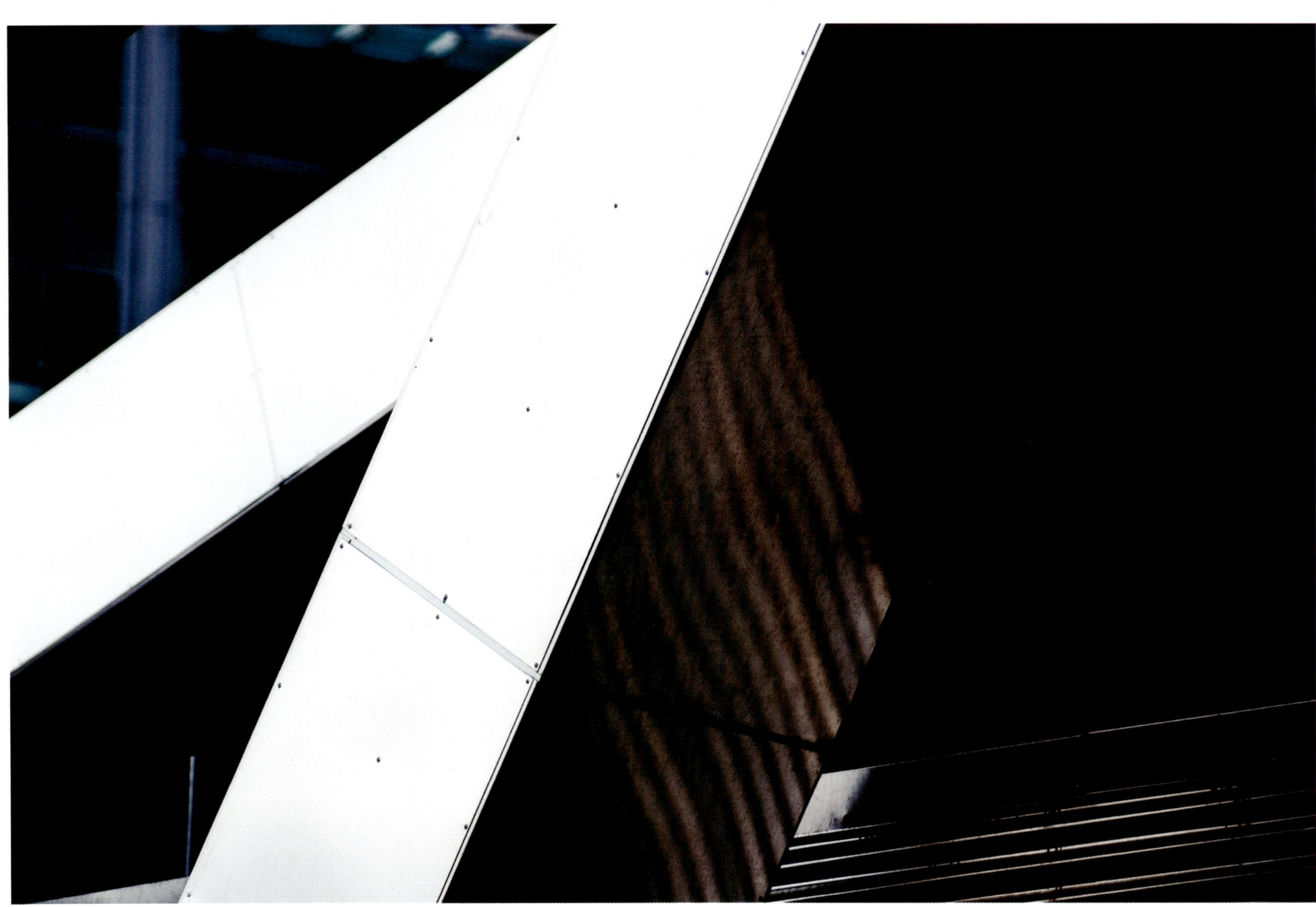

Vauxhall Bus Station

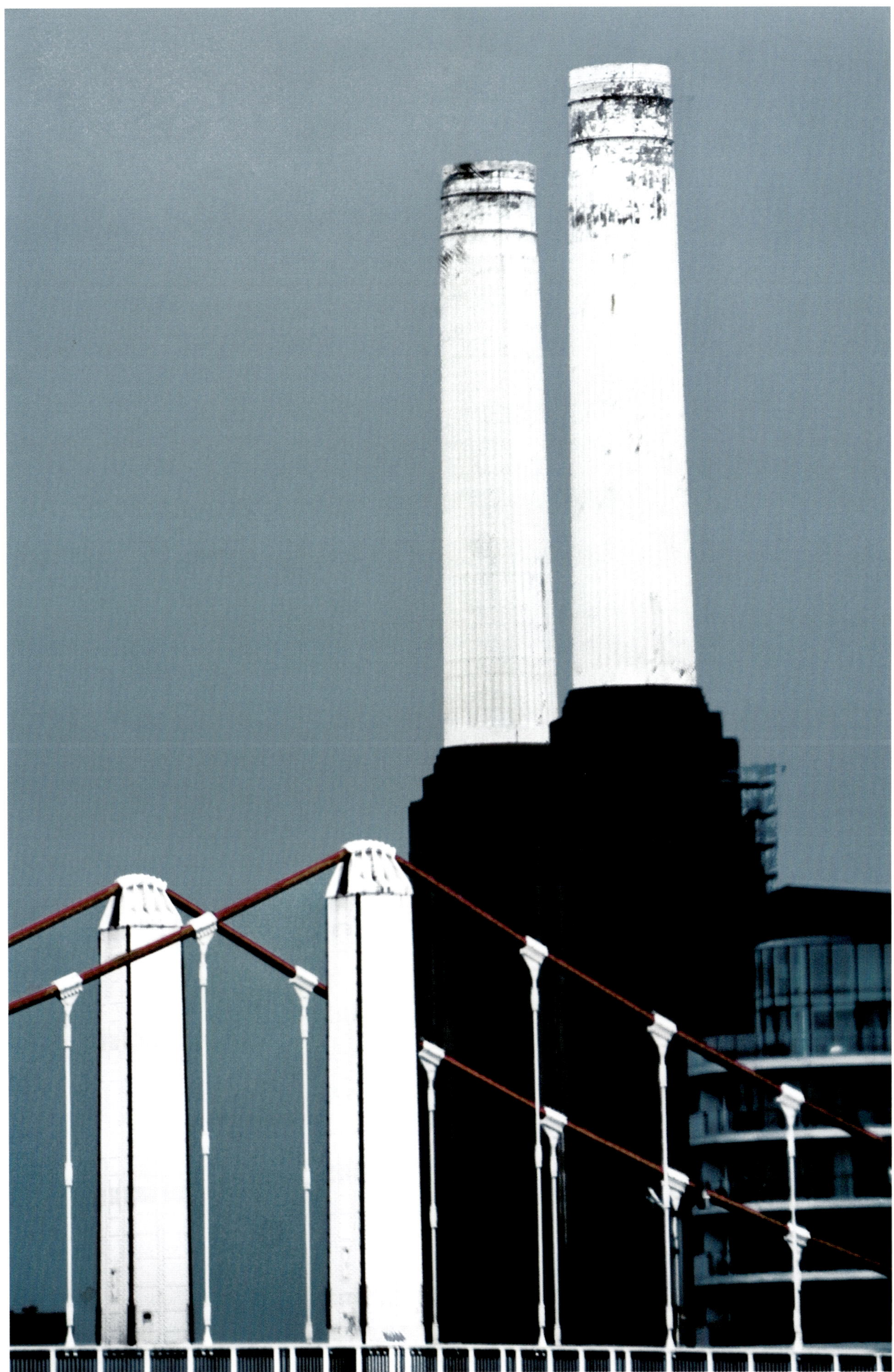

Battersea Power Station

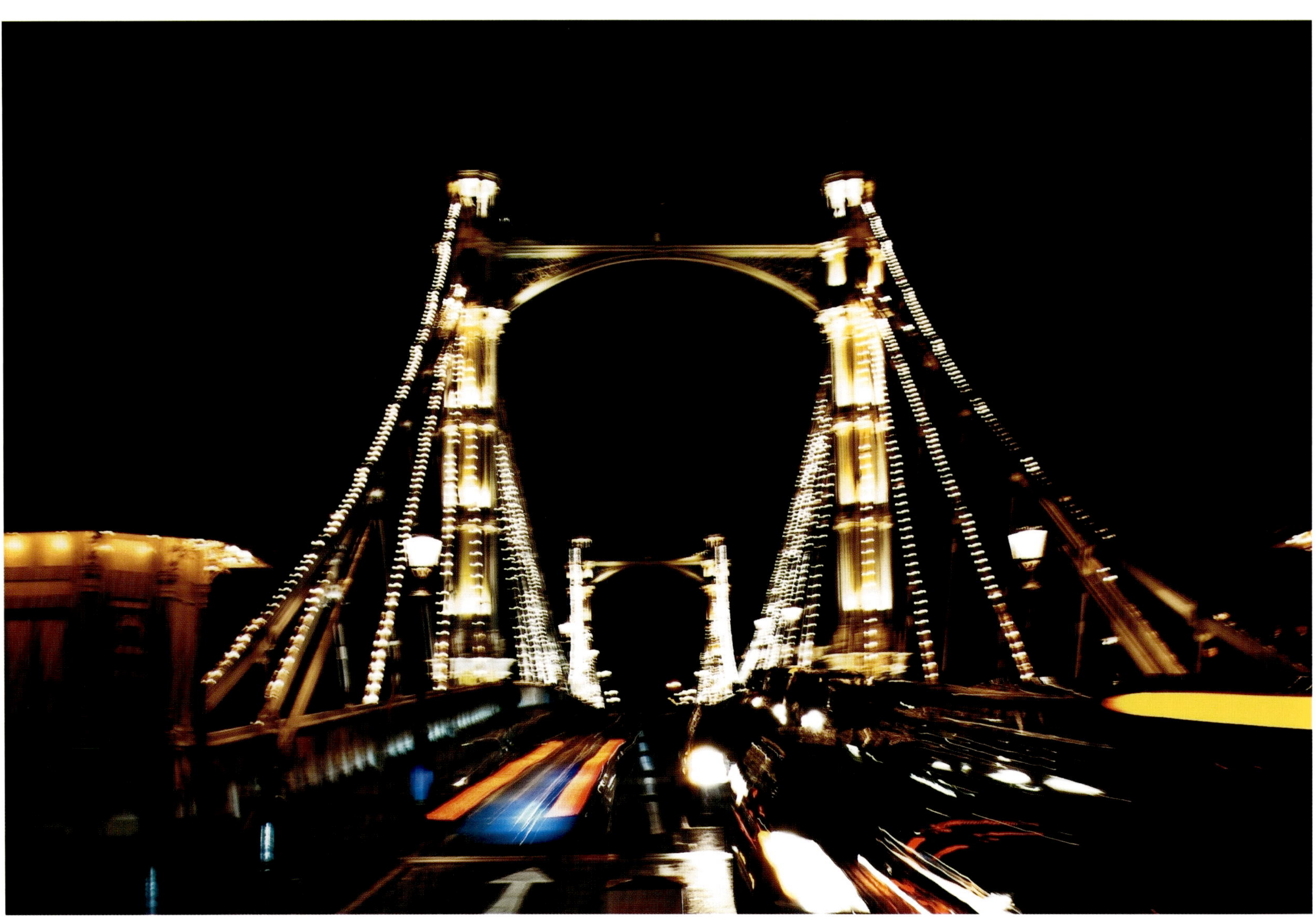

Albert Bridge

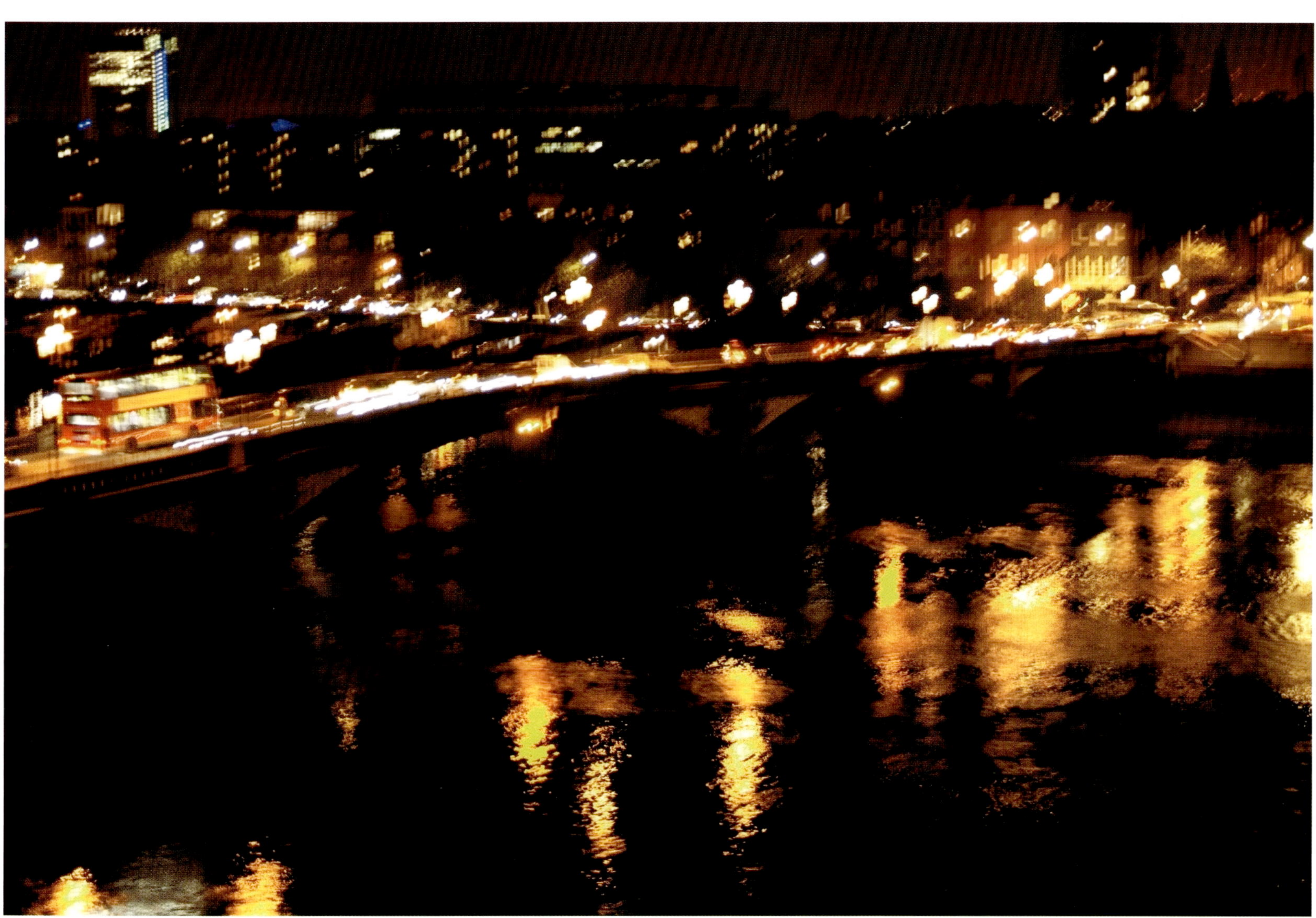

Battersea Bridge

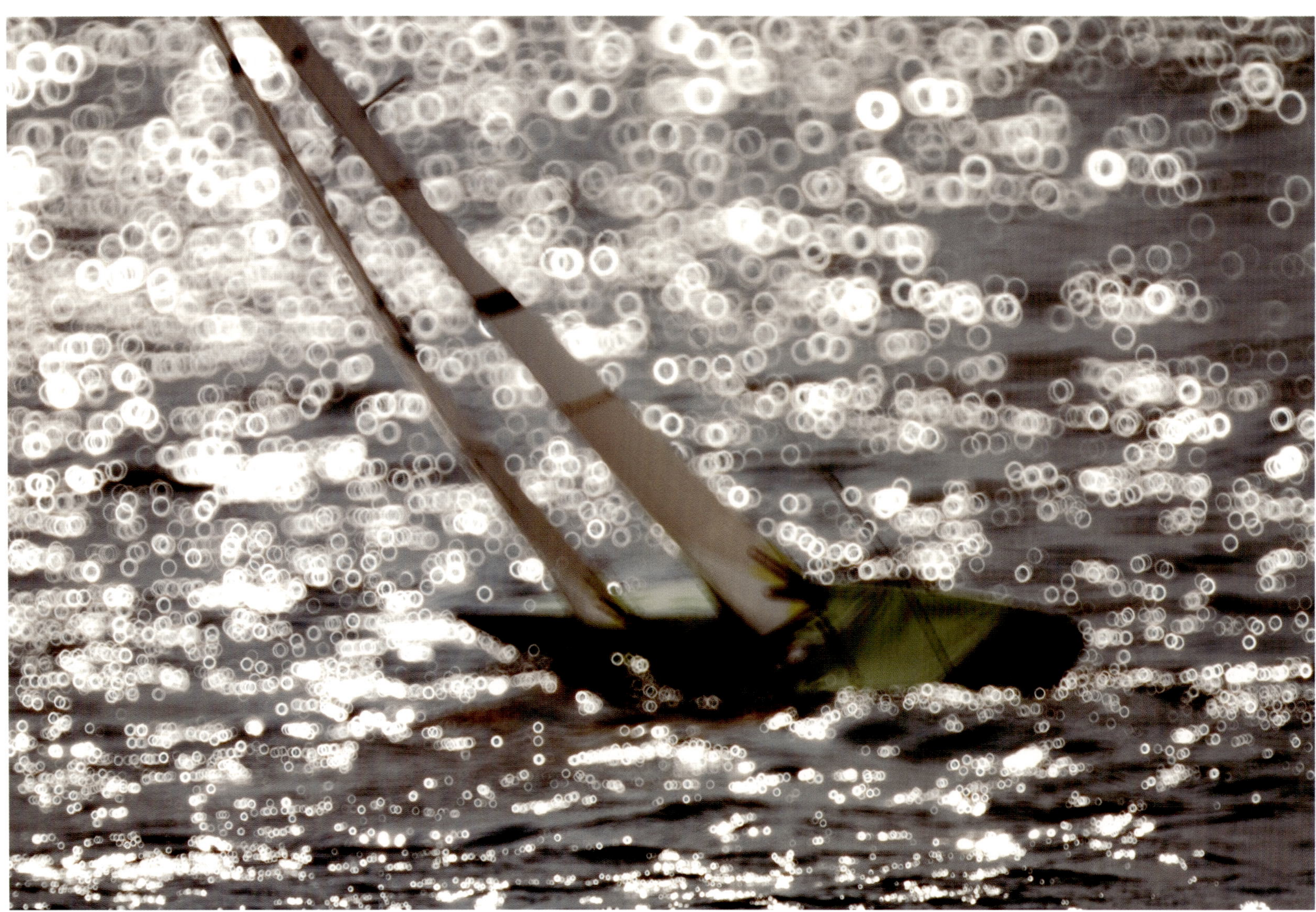

Above and opposite
Model sailing boats on the Round Pond, Kensington Gardens

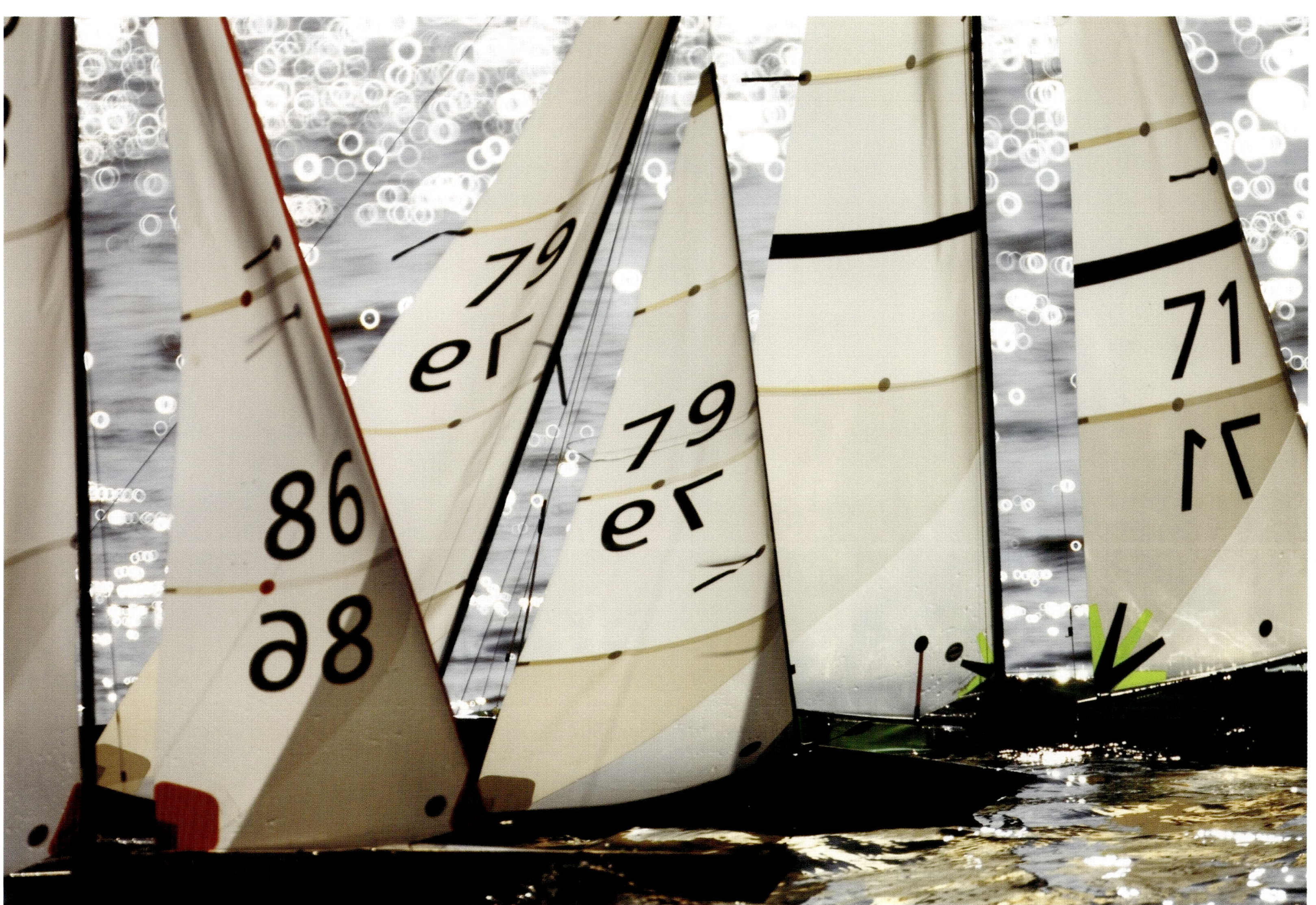

Pages 136 –137 Bumper cars on Hampstead Heath

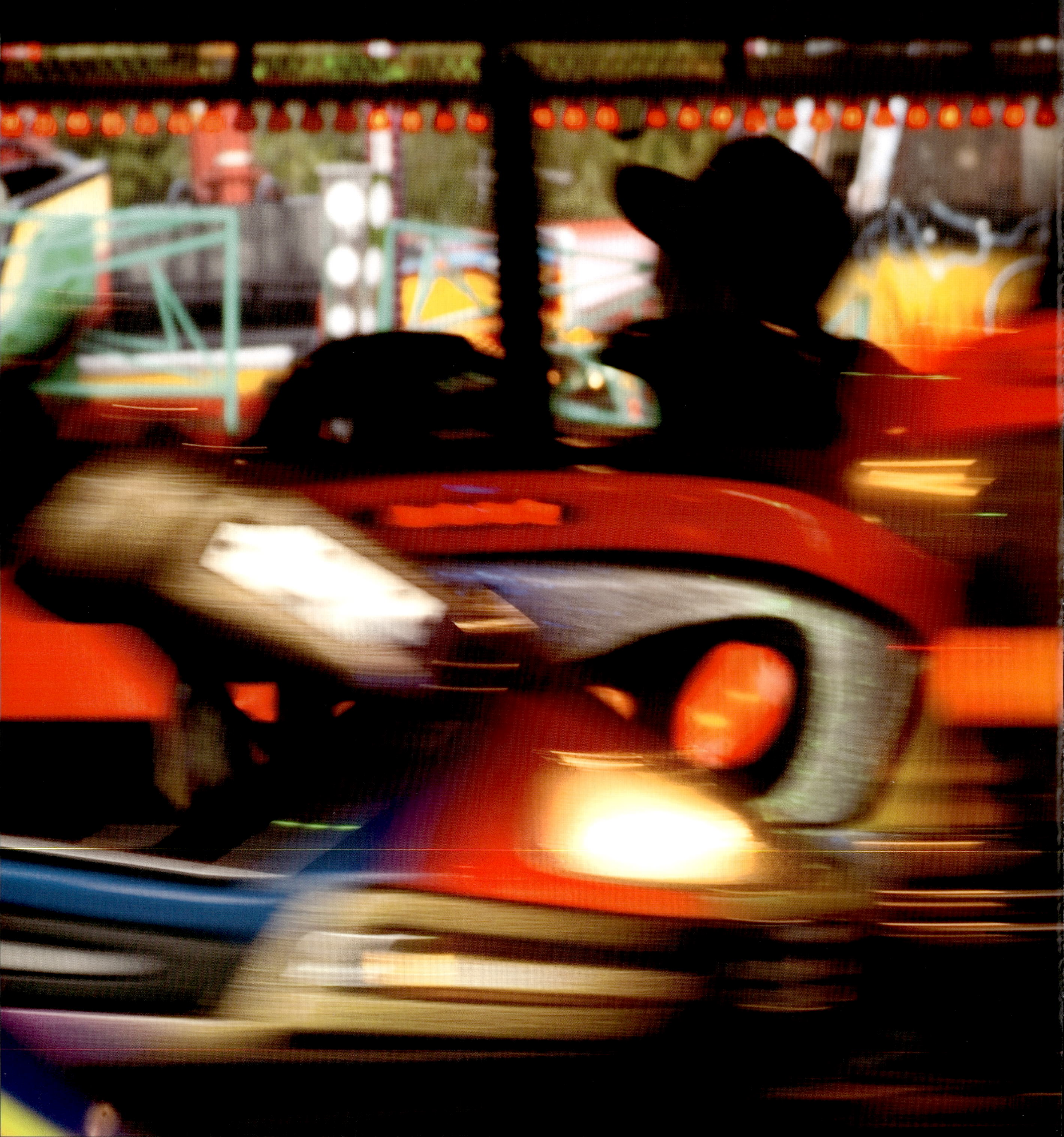

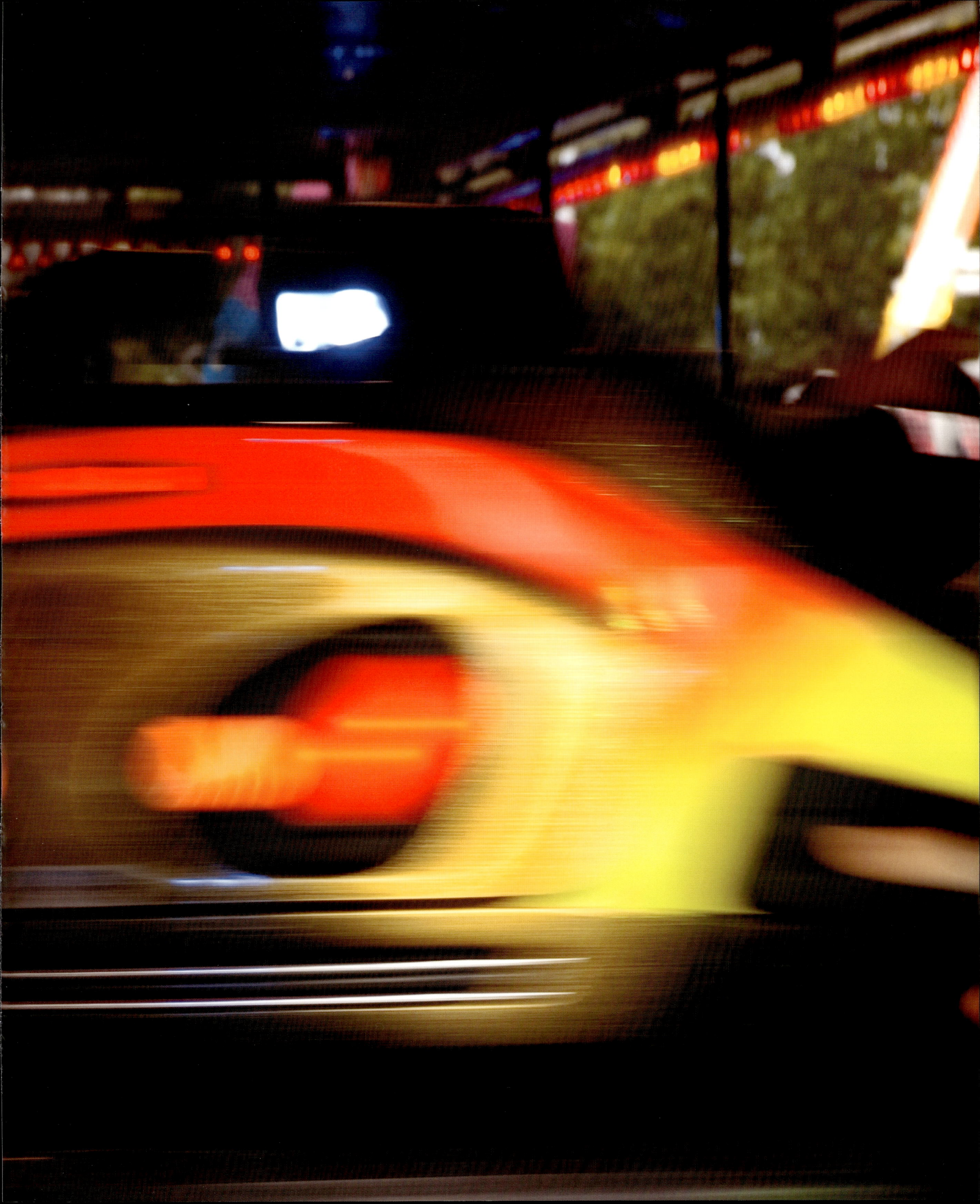

Photographic information

All the pictures in this book are digital, and except where stated I used hand-held Nikons. The only filters used were UV filters. I used a raw and a jpeg file for each photograph. The colour space used was Adobe RGB.

1

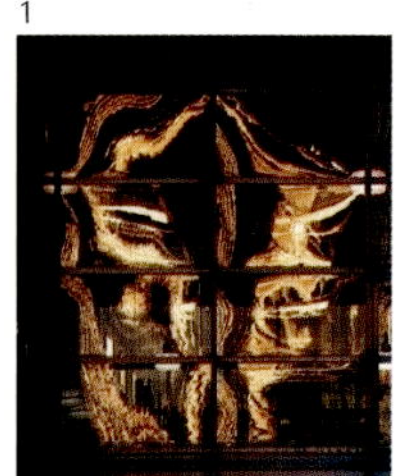

Sunset reflected through windows on Canary Wharf's South Colonnade
21/04/09, 8.35 p.m.
Nikon D300, lens 70–300
ISO 400, 1/250 sec, f5.6

2–3

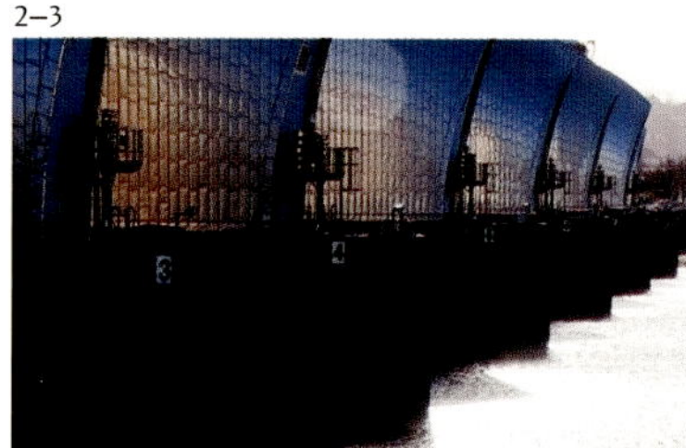

The Thames Barrier
30/1/08
Nikon D300, lens 18–200
ISO 200, 1/60 sec, f22

4–5

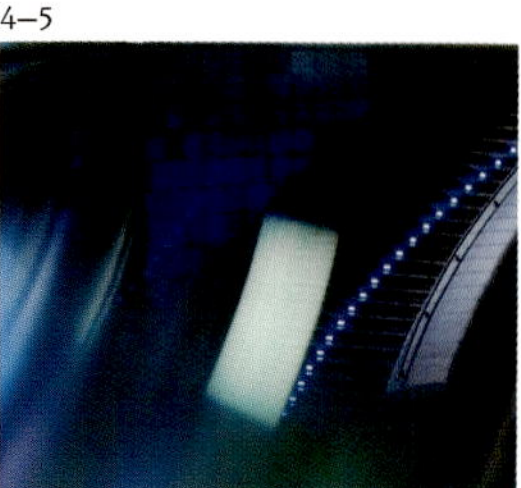

Paddington Basin at night
Nikon D70, lens 80–200
ISO 1600, 1/30 sec, f2.8

6

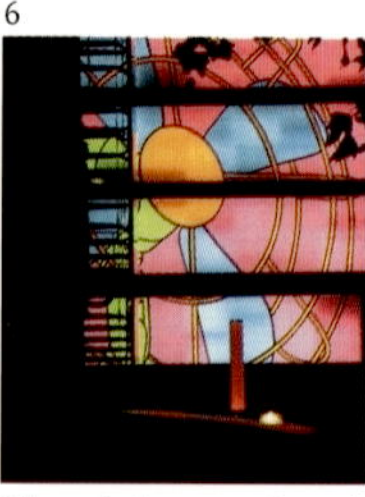

Mural, Euston Road (since demolished)
04/08/07, 9.20 p.m.
Canon G7
ISO 1600, 1/125 sec, f4

10a

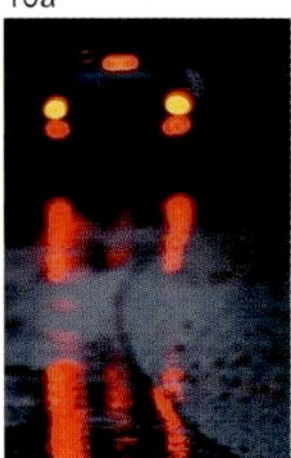

Elgin Crescent in a thunderstorm: car lights reflected
17/10/04, 5.30 p.m.
Nikon D70, lens 80–200
ISO 400, 1/125 sec, f2.8

10b

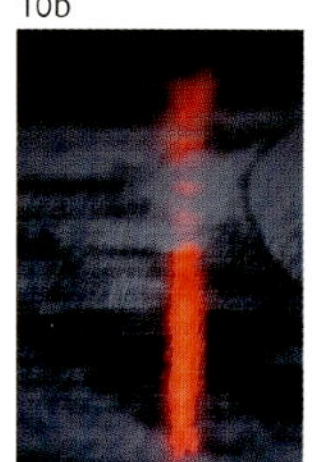

Elgin Crescent in a thunderstorm: traffic light reflections
17/10/04, 5.32 p.m.
Nikon D70, lens 80–200
ISO 400, 1/125 sec, f2.8

11

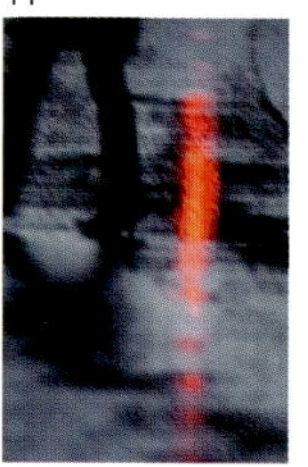

Elgin Crescent in a thunderstorm: traffic light reflections
17/10/04, 5.35 p.m.
Nikon D70, lens 80–200
ISO 400, 1/25 sec, f2.8

12–13

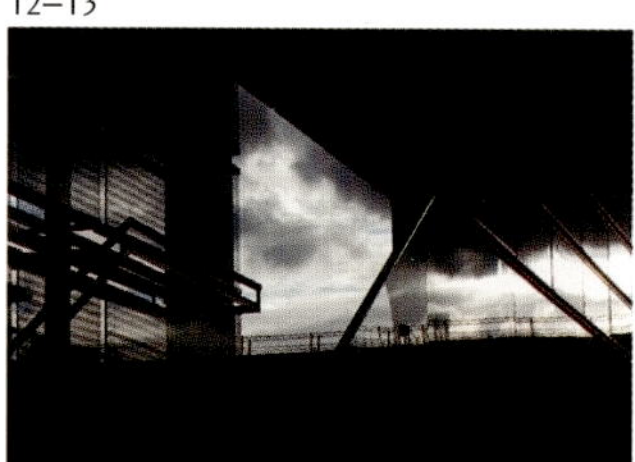

Paddington Basin footbridge & offices
25/02/05, 4.55 p.m.
Nikon D70, lens 80–200
ISO 400, 1/400 sec, f10

14

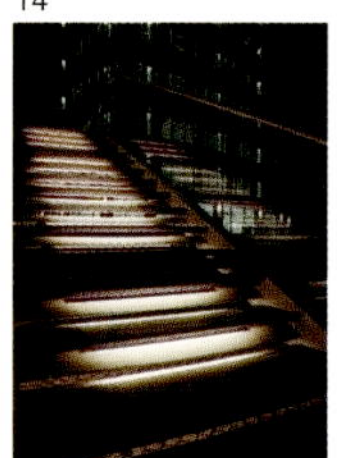

Paddington Basin footbridge & steps
25/02/05 7.30 p.m.
Nikon D70, lens 18–70
ISO 400, 1/50 sec, f3.5

14–15

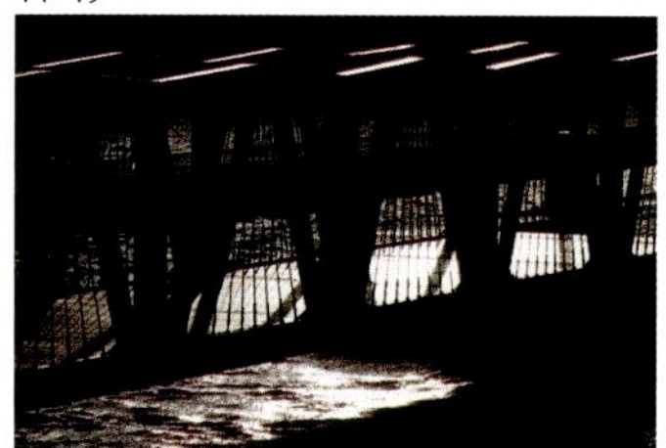

Paddington Basin Rolling Bridge
12/02/05, 4.30 p.m.
Nikon D70, lens 80–200
ISO 200, 1/1000 sec, f8

16

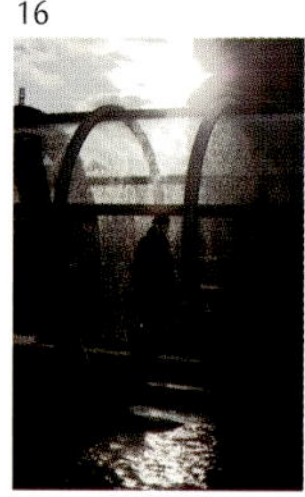

Paddington Basin Helix Bridge
12/02/05, 4.35 p.m.
Nikon D70, lens 28–105
ISO 200, 1/800 sec, f14

17

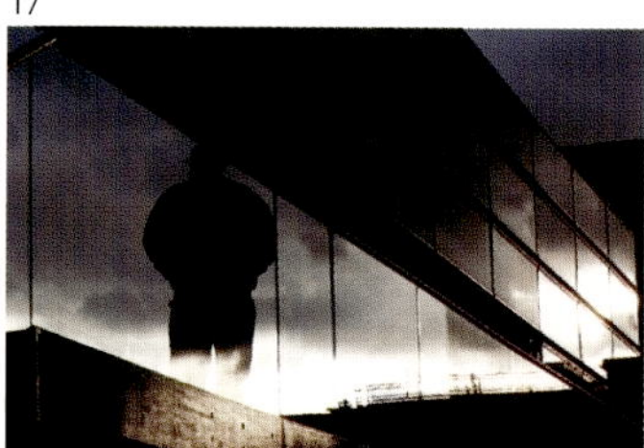

Crossing the Paddington Basin footbridge as a storm approaches
12/02/05, 4.50 p.m.
Nikon D70, lens 80–200
ISO 200, 1/250 sec, f8

18

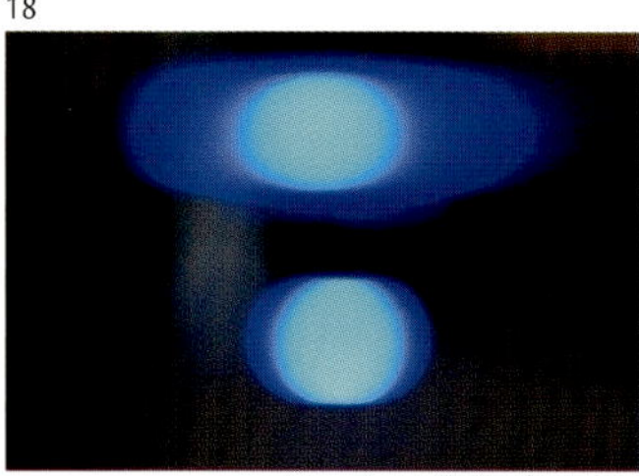

Blue lights on the Paddington Basin footbridge
25/02/05, 7.15 p.m.
Nikon D70, lens 80–200
ISO 1600, 1/20 sec, f2.8

19

Building security lights reflected in Paddington Basin
25/02/05, 7.20 p.m.
Nikon D70, lens 80–200
ISO 1600, 1/13 sec, f2.8

20–21

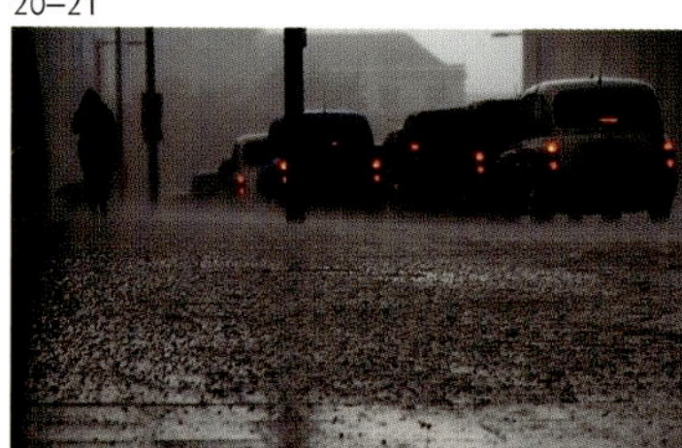

Taxis on Bishop's Bridge Road, queuing for Paddington Station
07/07/09, 5.15 p.m.
Nikon D200, lens 18–200
ISO 200, 1/250 sec, f8

22

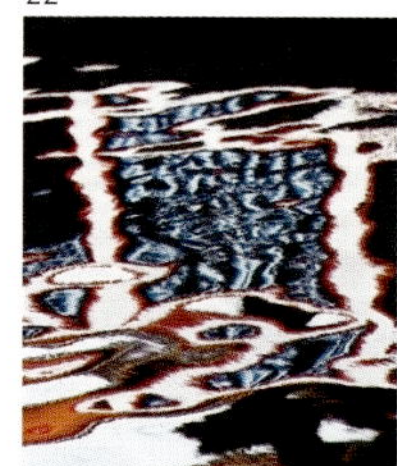

Reflections in the Regent's Canal at Little Venice
26/02/05, 11.20 a.m.
Nikon D70, lens 80–200
ISO 400, 1/320 sec, f4.5

23

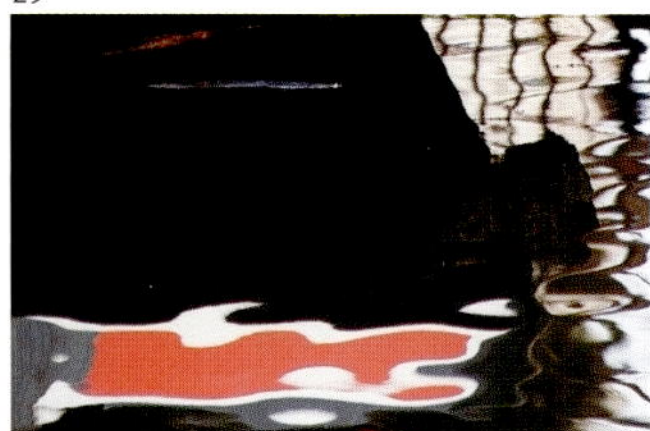

Reflections in the Regent's Canal
26/02/05, 11.30 a.m.
Nikon D70, lens 80–200
ISO 400, 1/250 sec, f4

24

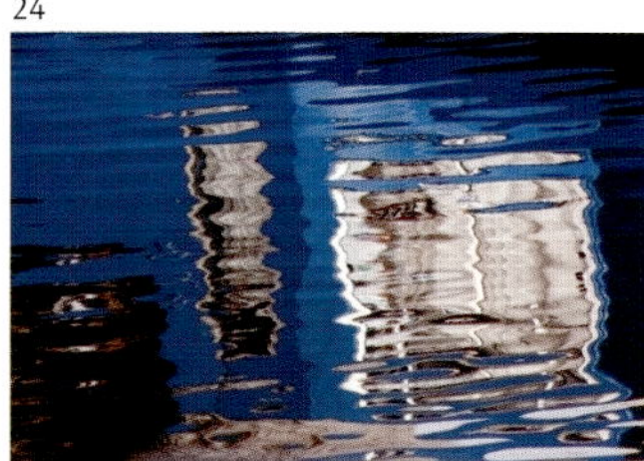

Reflections in the Regent's Canal
26/02/05, 11.35 a.m.
Nikon D70, lens 80–200
ISO 400, 1/500 sec, f5.6

25

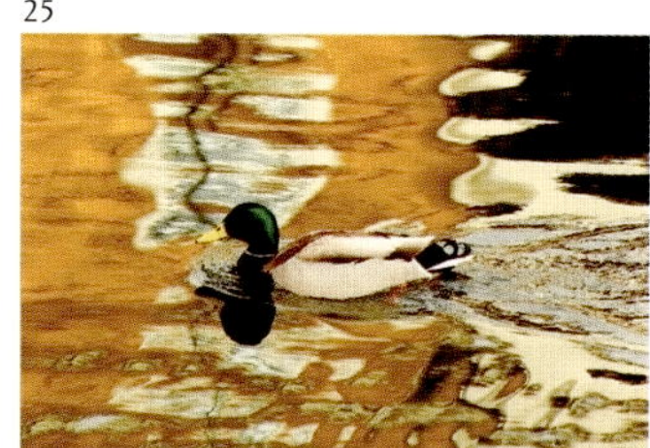

Reflections in the Regent's Canal
26/02/05, 11.30 a.m.
Nikon D70, lens 80–200
ISO 400, 1/500 sec, f5.6

26–27

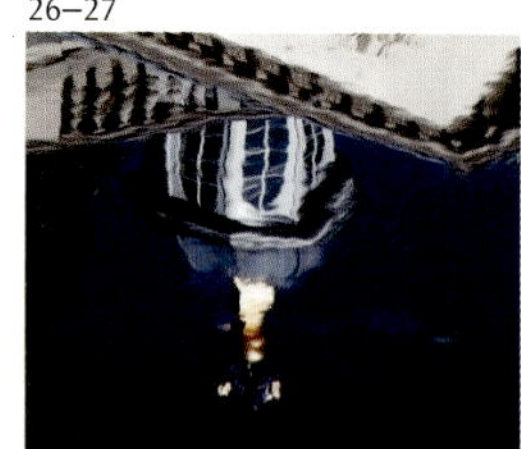

House reflection, Regent's Canal
15/07/08, 6.42 p.m.
Nikon D300, lens 18–200
ISO 200, 1/250 sec, f16

27

Metalwork of bridge over the Regent's Canal, glowing in reflected sunlight
20/09/08, 4.44 p.m.
Nikon D300, lens 18–200
ISO 200, 1/100 sec, f5.3

28

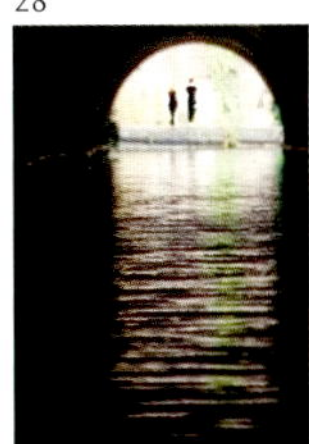

Tunnel under the Regent's Canal at Lisson Grove
20/09/08, 3.49 p.m.
Nikon D300, lens 70–300
ISO 200, 1/80 sec, f5.6

29

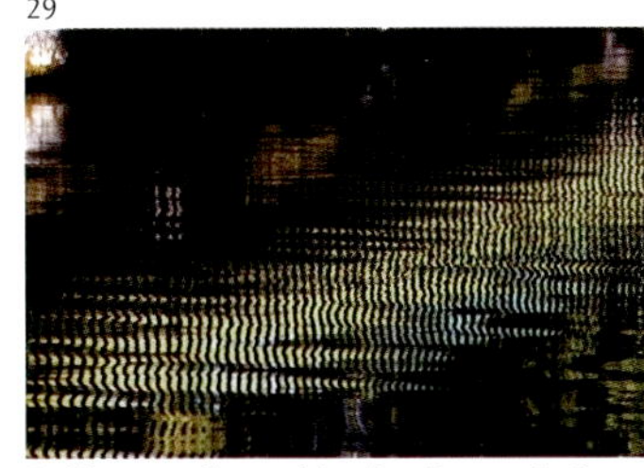

Railings reflected in the Regent's Canal
15/07/08, 6.38 p.m.
Nikon D300, lens 70–300
ISO 200, 1/250 sec, f18

30

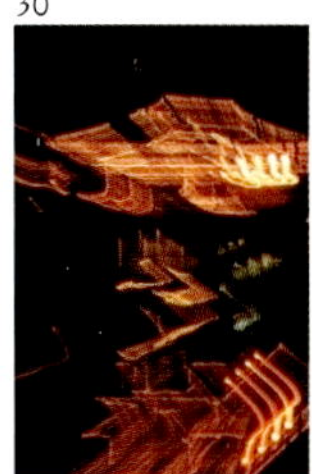

Chinese restaurant
22/10/08, 7.45 p.m.
Nikon D300, lens 18–200
ISO 1600, 1.6 sec, f5

30–31

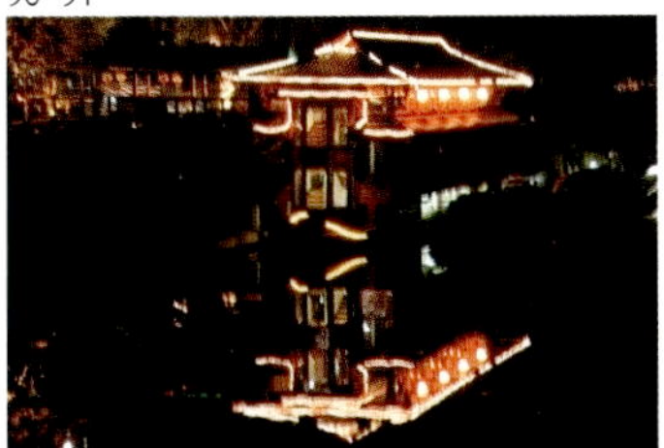

Chinese restaurant on the Regent's Canal, near Regent's Park
22/10/08, 7.40 p.m.
Nikon D300, lens 18–200
ISO 1600, 1.6 sec, f5

32–33

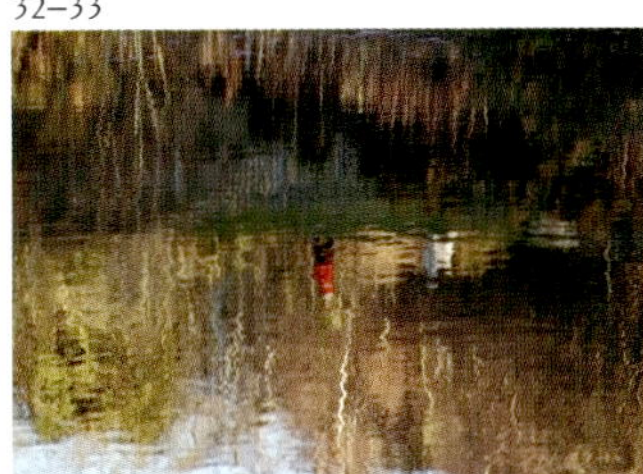

Viaduct Pond on Hampstead Heath
09/02/06, 10.15 a.m.
Nikon D70, lens 28–105
ISO 1000, 1/125 sec, f5.6

34

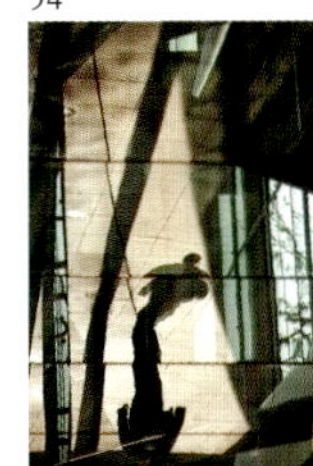

Reflection in a glass canopy over the pavement in the Euston Road
22/04/08, 3.45 p.m.
Nikon D200, lens 18–200
ISO 400, 1/500 sec, f5.6

35

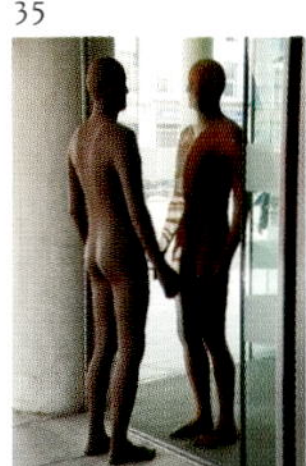

Reflection, by Antony Gormley, in Euston Road
22/04/08, 3.30 p.m.
Nikon D200, lens 18–200
ISO 400, 1/125 sec, f4.8

36

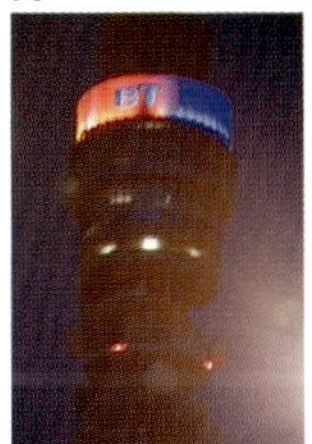

The Telecom Tower
15/07/08 11.16 p.m
Nikon D300, lens 70–300
ISO 1600, 1/5 sec, f5

37

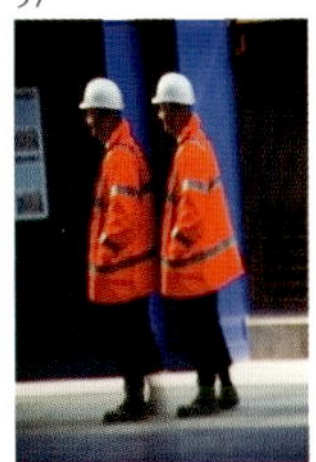

A site worker reflected in a window on a Euston Road site
22/04/08, 3.49 p.m.
Nikon D200, lens 18–200
ISO 400, 1/125 sec, f6.3

38

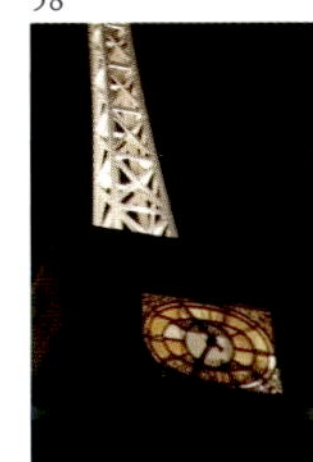

BBC Broadcasting House, Portland Place
27/02/09, 7.52 p.m.
Nikon D200, lens 18–200
ISO 800, 1/30 sec, f5.6

39

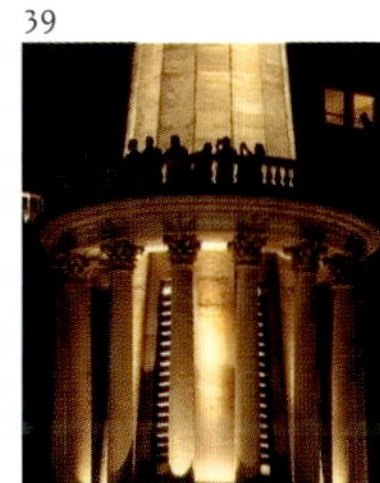

All Souls Church, Langham Place
27/02/09, 8.02 p.m.
Nikon D200, lens 18–200
ISO 800, 1/6 sec, f7

40

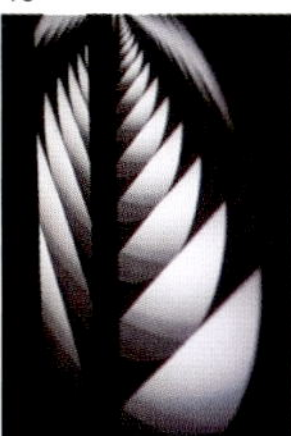

Erco Lighting, Dover Street: light pattern projected
19/09/08, 8.20 p.m.
Nikon D300, lens 18–200
ISO 800, 1/50 sec, f6.3

41

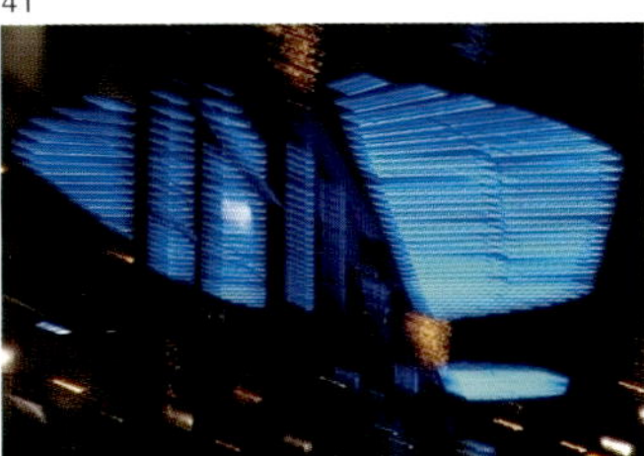

The blue-lit canopy of an Oxford Street shop
05/12/04, 8.10 p.m.
Nikon D70, lens 80–200
ISO 400, 1.2 sec, f22

42

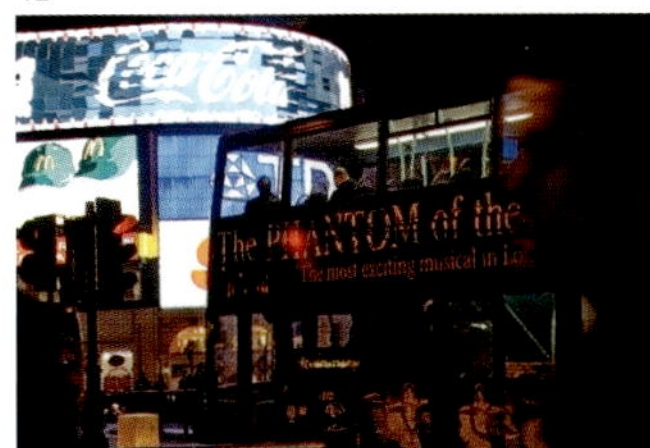

Piccadilly Circus lights
03/12/04, 7.20 p.m.
Nikon D70 lens 18 –70
ISO 800, 1/30 sec, f4.5

43

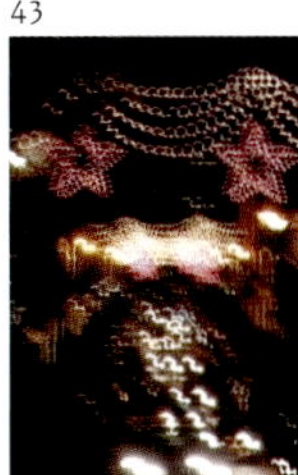

Christmas lights in Bond Street
05/12/04, 7.20 p.m.
Nikon D70, lens 80–200
ISO 400, 1.3 sec, f16

44

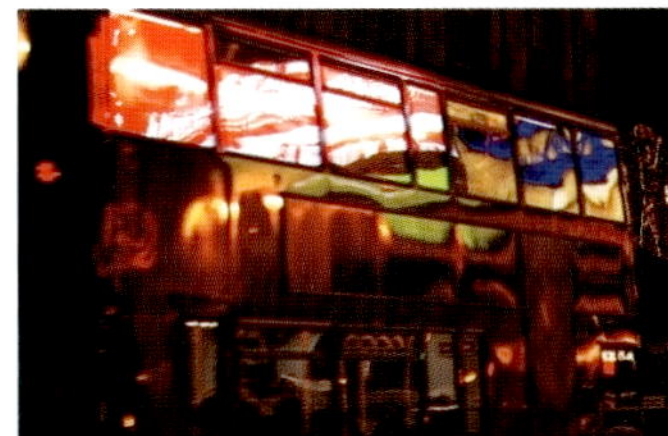

Lights reflected in a double-decker bus
03/12/04, 7.10 p.m.
Nikon D70, lens 80–200
ISO 800, 1/40 sec, f4

45

Burlington Gardens Christmas lighting
05/12/04, 6.58 p.m.
Nikon D70, lens 80–200
ISO 400, 1 sec, f8

46

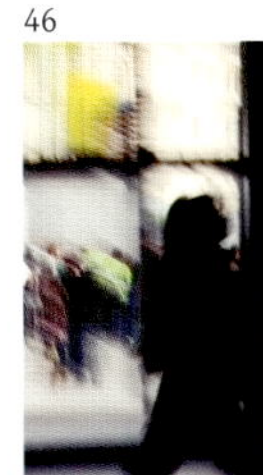

Fourth plinth, Trafalgar Square
15/03/09, 4 p.m.
Canon Powershot G7
ISO 400, 1/5 sec, f8

46–47

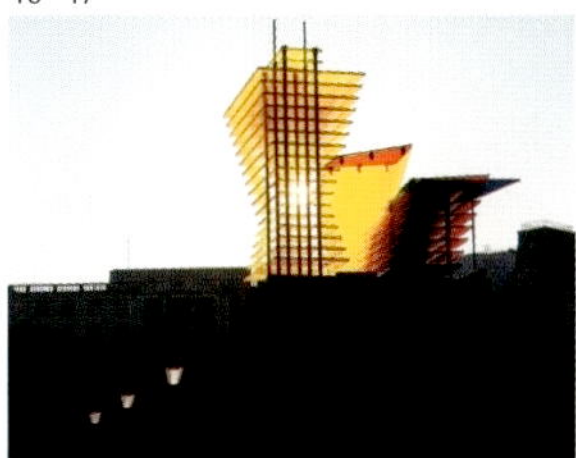

Fourth plinth, Trafalgar Square
14/04/08, 6.33 a.m.
Nikon D200, lens 18–200
ISO 100, 1/1000 sec, f8

48

Fountain in Trafalgar Square
12/01/05, 7.20 p.m.
Nikon D70, lens 80–200
ISO 200, 1/3 sec, f4.5

49

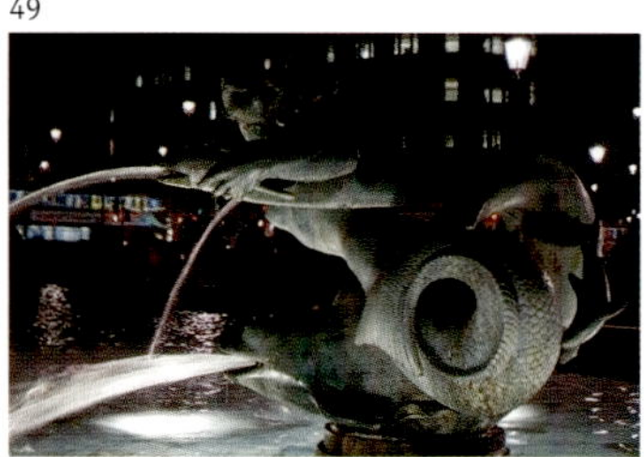

Fountain in Trafalgar Square
12/01/05, 7.15 p.m.
Nikon D70, lens 18–70
ISO 1600, 1/20 sec, f4.5

50–51

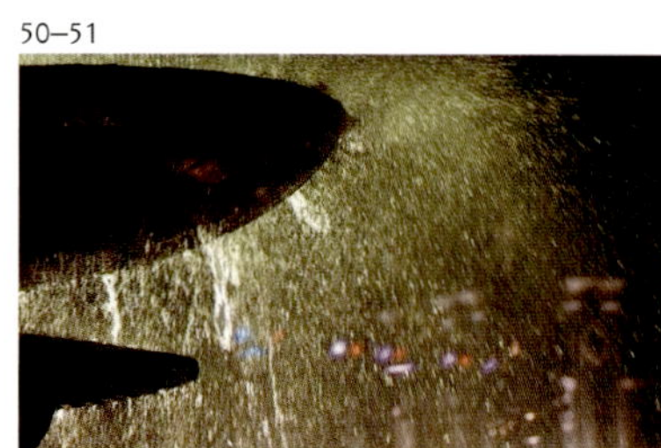

Fountain in Trafalgar Square
12/01/05, 7.10 p.m.
Nikon D70, lens 80–200
ISO 800, 1/125 sec, f2.8

52

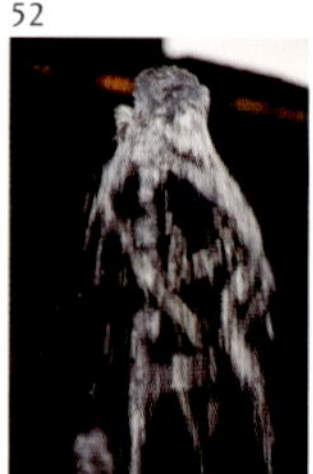

Fountain in the courtyard
at Somerset House
30/05/08, 8.15 p.m.
Nikon D200, lens 18–200
ISO 200, 1/30 sec, f5.6

53

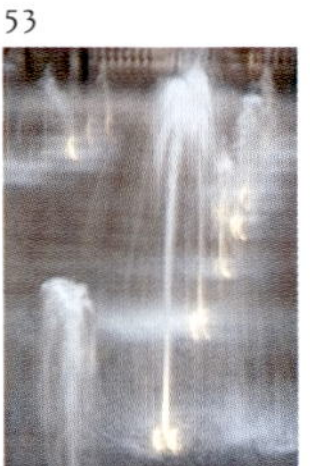

Fountain in the courtyard
at Somerset House
30/05/08, 8.06 p.m.
Nikon D200, lens 18–200
ISO 200, 1/6 sec, f5.3

54

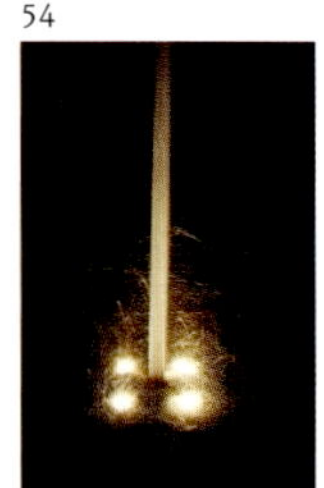

Fountain in the courtyard at
Somerset House
30/05/08, 8.25 p.m.
Nikon D200, lens 18–200
ISO 200, 1/15 sec, f5.6

55

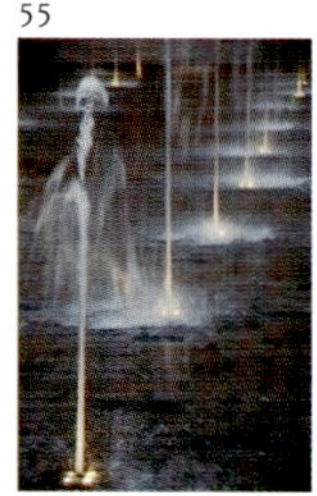

Fountains in the courtyard at
Somerset House
30/05/08, 8.05 p.m.
Nikon D200, lens 18–200
ISO 200, 1/125 sec, f5.3

56

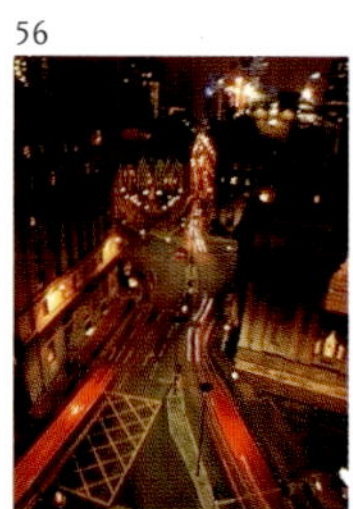

The Mansion House and Royal
Exchange, in the City of London
20/02/07, 9.45 p.m.
Canon Powershot G7
ISO 1600, 1 sec, f5.6

57

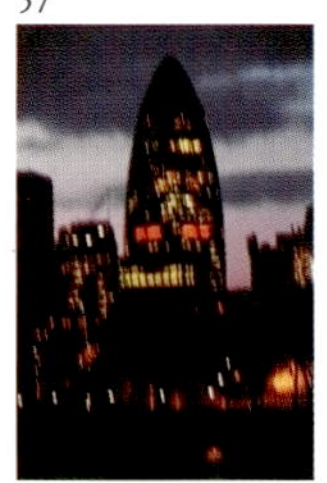

The Gherkin: Swiss Re
Building, 30 St Mary Axe
09/04/08, 7.10 p.m.
Nikon D20, lens 18–200
ISO 800, 1/6 sec, f5.3

58

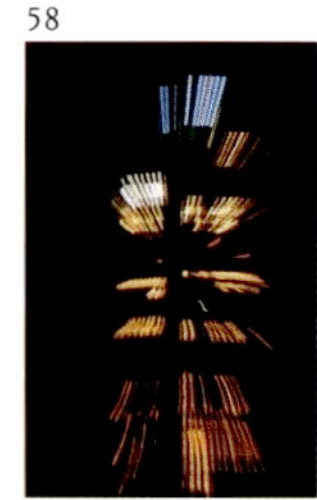

Tower 42:
the NatWest Tower
10/05/08, 8.45 p.m.
Nikon D200 , lens 18–200
ISO 800, 1/8 sec, f4.8

59

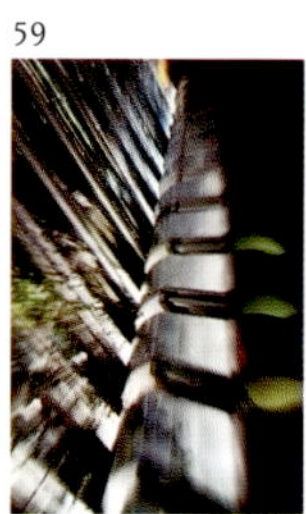

The Lloyds Building
10/05/08, 8.34 p.m.
Nikon D200, lens 18–200
ISO 800, 1/5 sec, f4.5

60

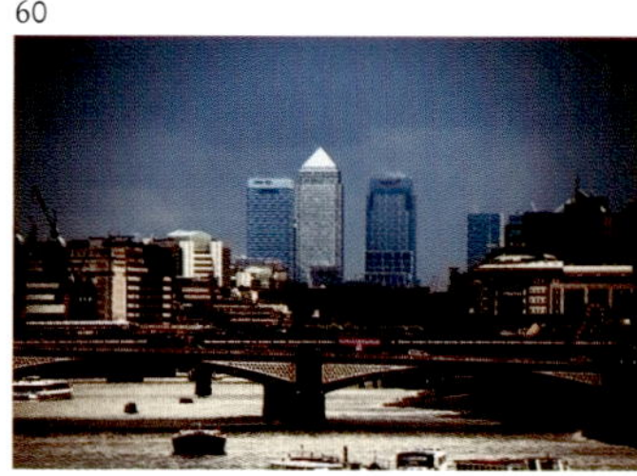

Canary Wharf from Waterloo Bridge
13/04/08, 10.50 a.m.
Nikon D200, lens 18–200
ISO 200, 1/500 sec, f5.6

61

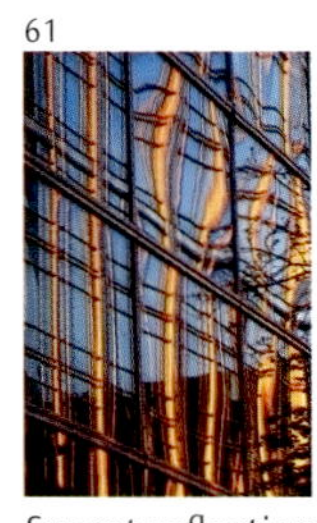

Sunset reflections in the windows of a
Canary Wharf office block
21/04/09, 8.40 p.m.
Nikon D300, lens 18–200
ISO 400, 1/125 sec, f4.8

62

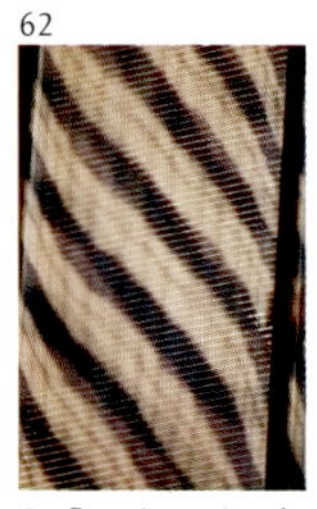

Reflections in the windows of a
Canary Wharf office block
21/04/09, 8.37 p.m.
Nikon D300, lens 70–300
ISO 400, 1/50 sec, f5.6

63

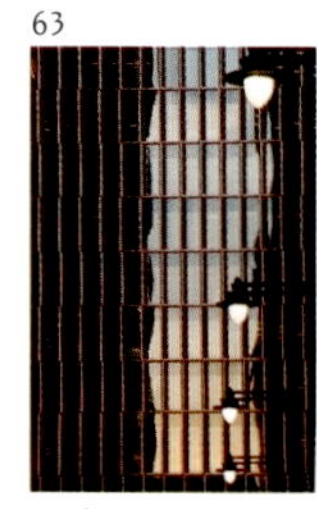

Reflections in the windows of a
Canary Wharf office block
21/04/09, 8.45 p.m.
Nikon D300, lens 18–200
ISO 400, 1/400 sec, f6.3

64

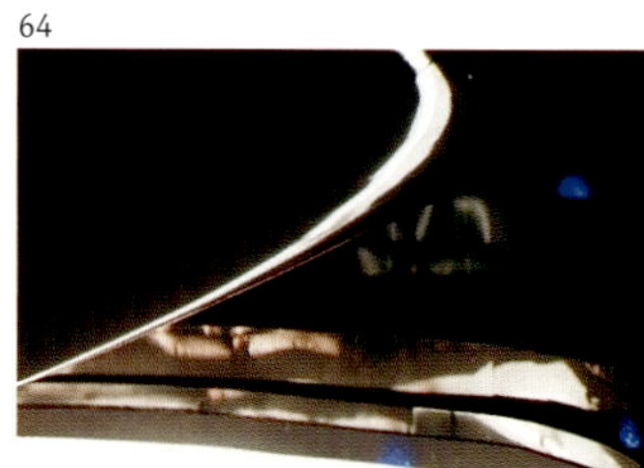

Big Blue sculpture by Ron Arad,
outside Canary Wharf Tower
21/04/09, 8.56 p.m.
Nikon D300, lens 70–300
ISO 400, 1/20 sec, f9

65

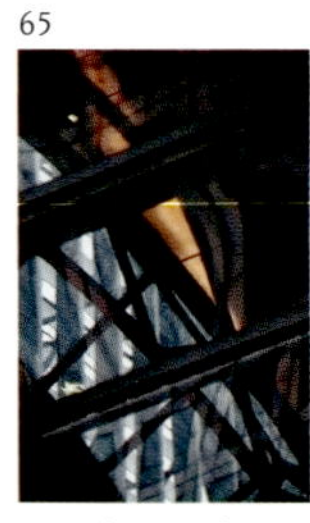

Window reflections in the North
Colonnade, Canary Wharf
21/04/09, 9.20 p.m.
Nikon D300, lens 18–200
ISO 400, 1/20 sec, f5.6

66–67

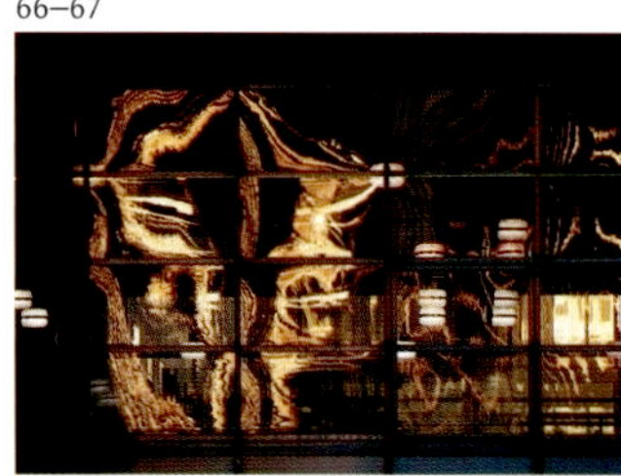

Sunset reflected through windows on
Canary Wharf's South Colonnade
21/04/09, 8.35 p.m.
Nikon D300, lens 70–300
ISO 400, 1/250 sec, f5.6

68

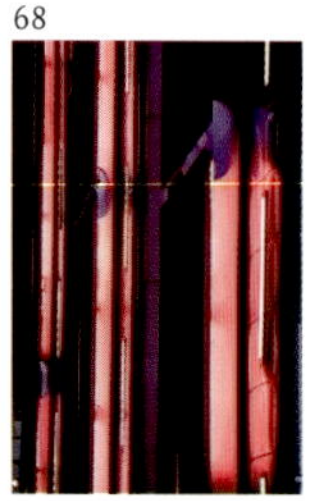

Ceiling lighting for a Canary Wharf
pedestrian crossing
21/04/09, 9.08 p.m.
Nikon D300, lens 18–200
ISO 400, 1/20 sec, f5.6

69

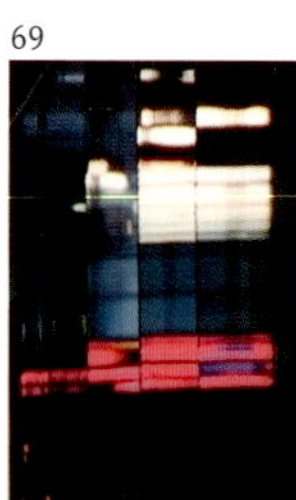

Lighting reflected in a North
Colonnade office block
21/04/09, 9.06 p.m.
Nikon D300, lens 18–200
ISO 400, 1/20 sec, f5.6

70

South Colonnade, Canary Wharf
21/04/09, 8.47 p.m.
Nikon D300, lens 18–200
ISO 800, 1/80 sec, f5.3

71

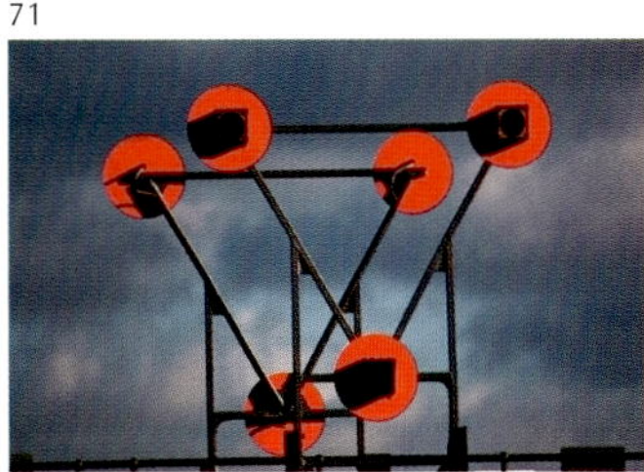

Thames Barrier signs: 'Closed for Navigation'
06/02/08, 1.45 p.m.
Nikon D300 , mirror lens 500
ISO 200, 1/250 sec, f8

72–73

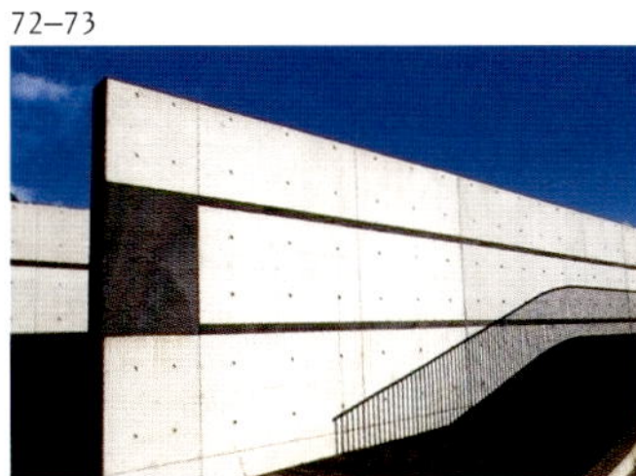

White walls and railing shadows, Thames Barrier Park
06/02/08, 1.56 p.m.
Nikon D300, lens 18–200
ISO 200, 1/640 sec, f4

73

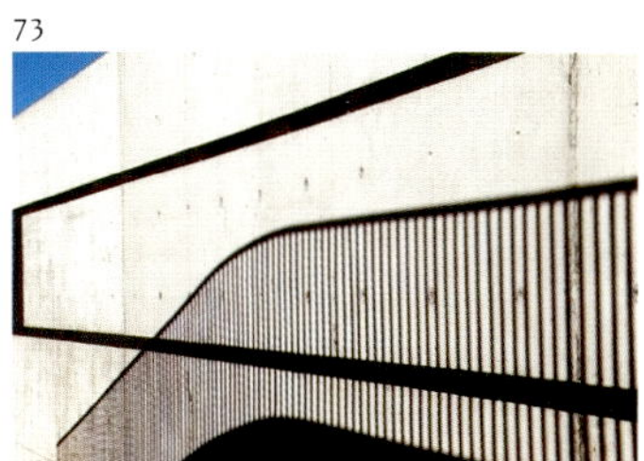

White walls and railing shadows, Thames Barrier Park
06/02/08, 2 p.m.
Nikon D300 , lens 18 –200
ISO 200, 1/640 sec, f13

74

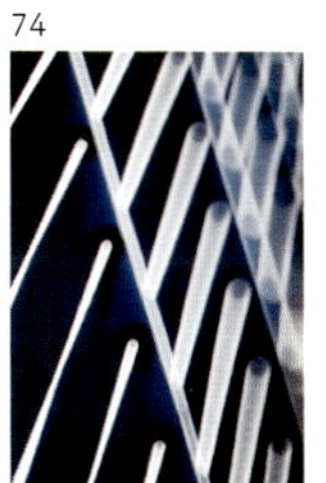
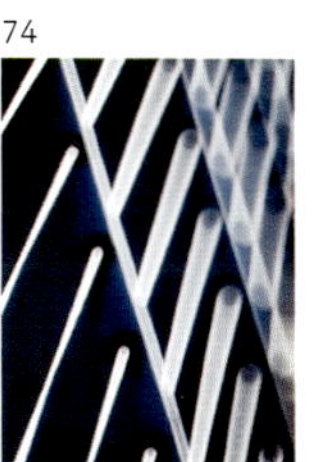

Railings, Thames Barrier Park
31/01/08, 11.51 a.m.
Nikon D300, mirror lens 500
ISO 200, 1/125 sec, f8

75

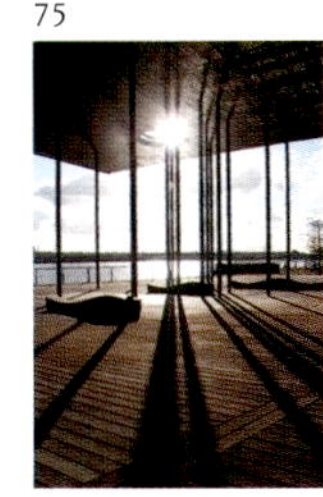

Pavilion, Thames Barrier Park
06/02/08, 2.02 p.m.
Nikon D300, lens 18–200
ISO 200, 1/400 sec, f11

76–77

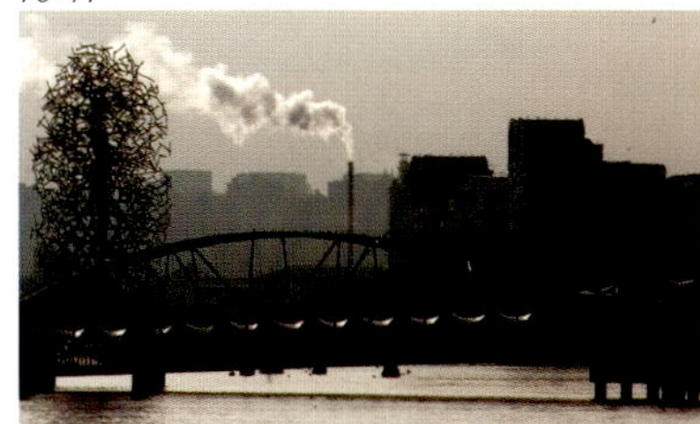

Quantum Cloud by Antony Gormley, on the end of the O2 pier
21/02/09, 9.15 a.m.
Nikon D200, lens 70–300
ISO 100, 1/125 sec, f32

78

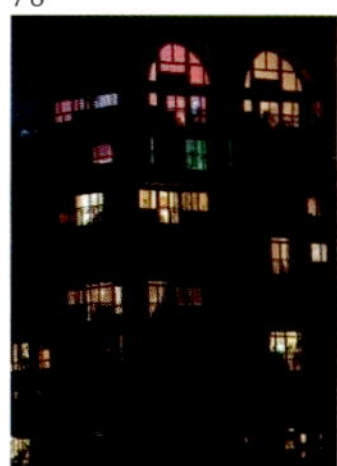

Greenwich Millennium Village housing, designed by Ralph Erskine
29/04/09, 10.36 p.m.
Nikon D300, lens 18–200
ISO 1600, 1/6 sec, f5.6

79a

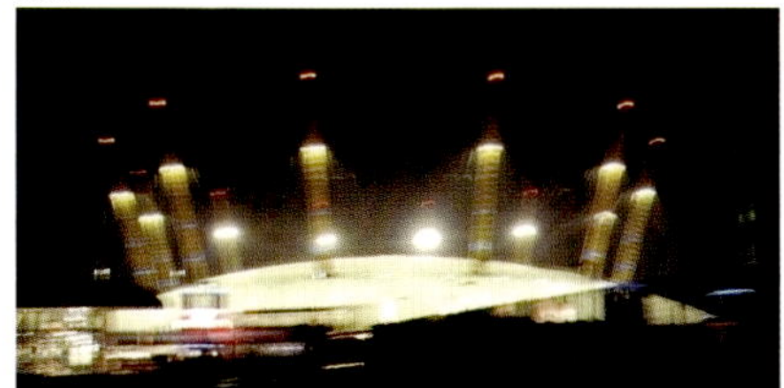

The O2 (the Dome) at night
27/01/08, 7.52 p.m.
Canon Sure Shot G7
ISO 1600, 0.8 sec, f2.8

79b

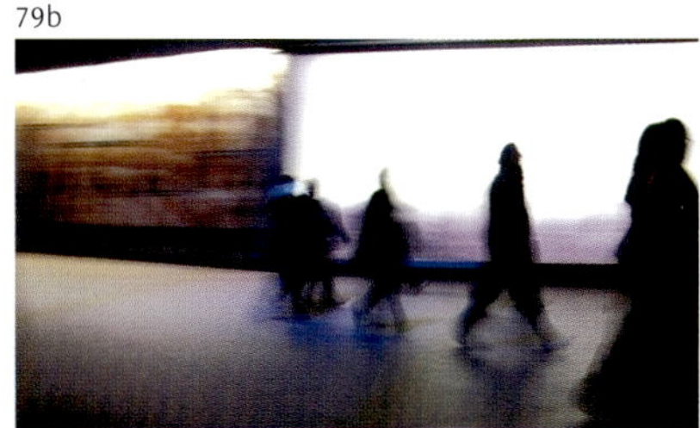

Walkway to the O2
27/01/08, 7.45 p.m.
Canon Sure Shot G7
ISO 1600, 0.4 sec, f2.8

80–81

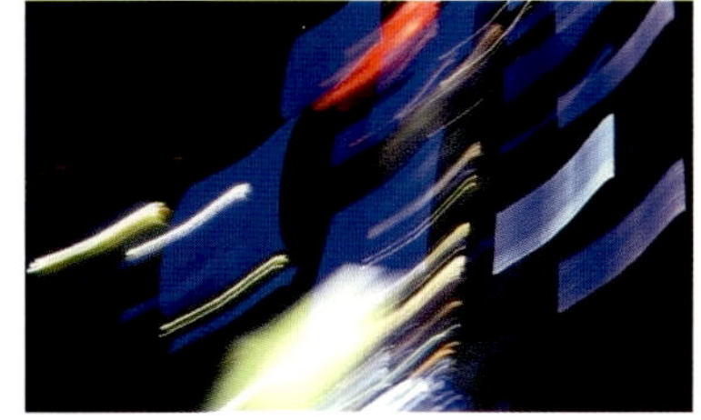

The O2 at night
27/01/08, 7.44 p.m.
Canon Sure Shot G7
ISO 1600, 0.6 sec, f2.8

82–83

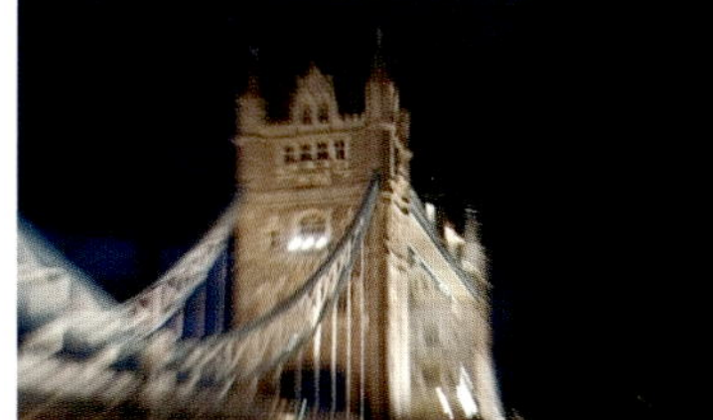

Tower Bridge
09/04/08, 7.21 p.m.
Nikon D200, lens 18–200
ISO 800, 1/10 sec, f4.5

84

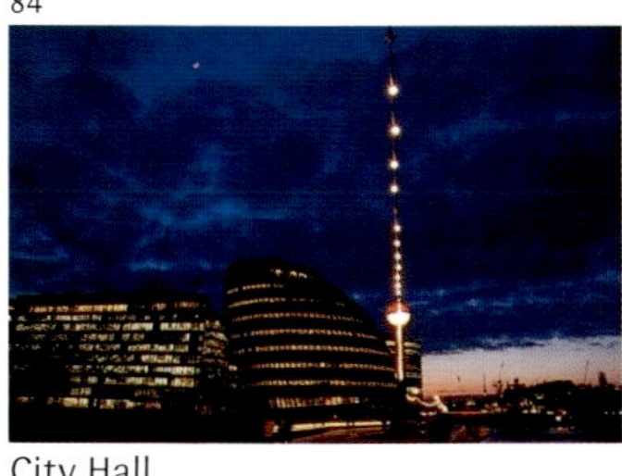

City Hall
09/04/08, 7.15 p.m.
Nikon D200, lens 18–200
ISO 800, 1/8 sec, f5.6

84–85

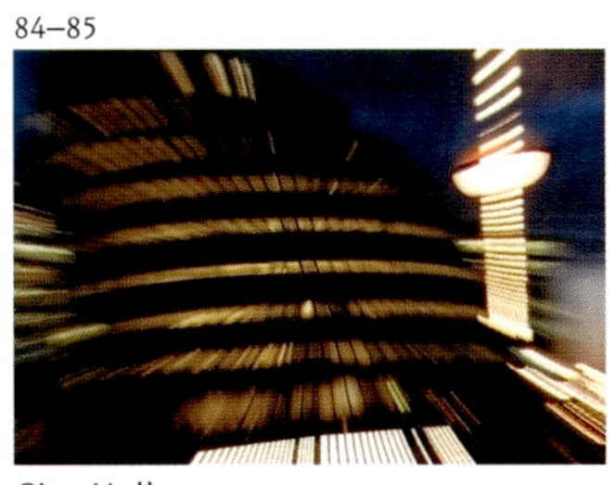

City Hall
09/04/08, 7.18 p.m.
Nikon D200, lens 18–200
ISO 800, 1/10 sec, f8

86

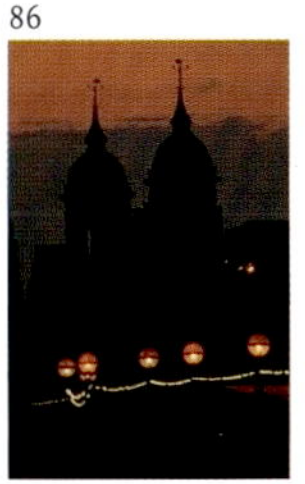

Cannon Street Station
09/04/08, 6.57 p.m.
Nikon D200, lens 18–200
ISO 800, 1/80 sec, f8

87

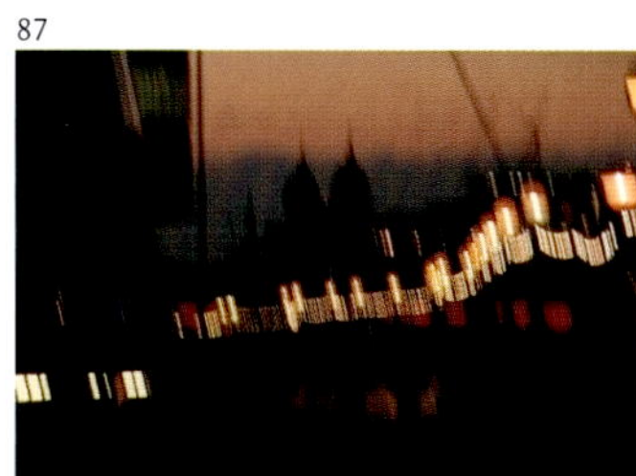

Thames Path walkway by City Hall
09/04/08, 7.06 p.m.
Nikon D200, lens 18–200
ISO 400, 1/20 sec, f10

88

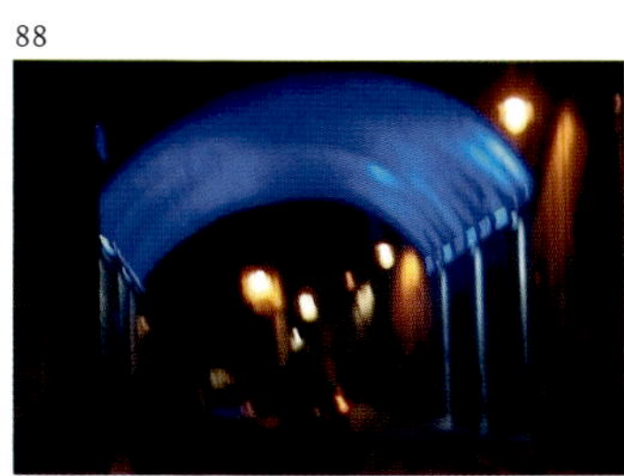

The blue-lit Stoney Street Rail Bridge, Borough Market
02/10/08, 8.23 p.m.
Nikon D200, lens 18–200
ISO 640, 1/5 sec, f5

89

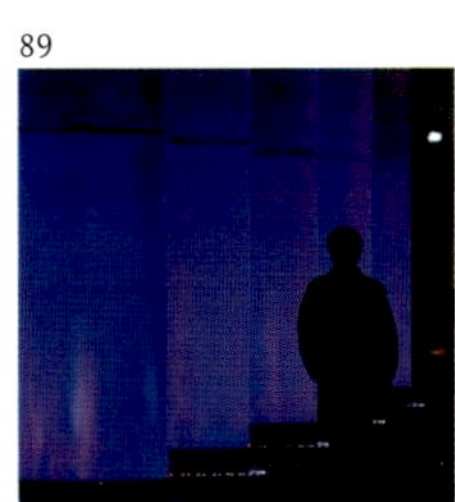

Park Plaza Hotel, County Hall
Nikon D200, lens 18–200
ISO 640, 1/5 sec, f5

90

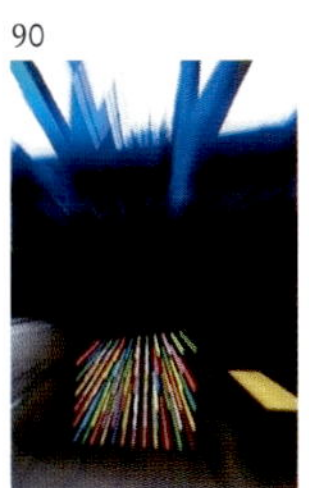

Southwark Street: 'Smarties' lighting installation
08/07/09, 1.29 p.m.
Nikon D200, lens 18–200
ISO 400, 1/8 sec, f11

91

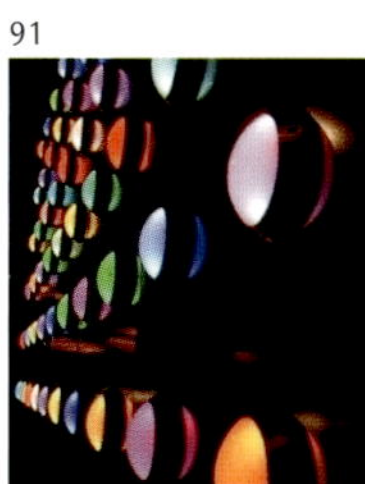

Southwark Street: 'Smarties' lighting installation
02/10/08, 8.13 p.m.
Nikon D200, lens 18–200
ISO 640, 1/160 sec, f7.1

92
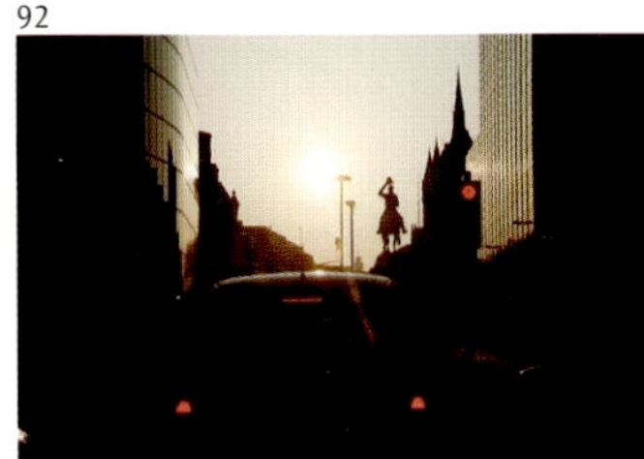
High Holborn, with Charles Bacon's statue of Prince Albert
22/04/08, 6.02 p.m.
Nikon D200, lens 18–200
ISO 100, 1/2000 sec, f4.5

93
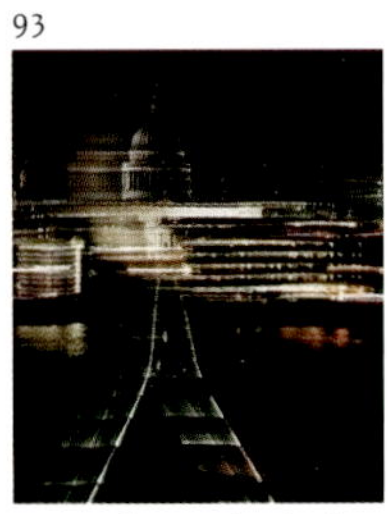
St Paul's Cathedral & the Millennium Bridge
18/01/08, 6.19 p.m.
Nikon D300, lens 18–200
ISO 1000, 1.6 sec, f4.5

94–95
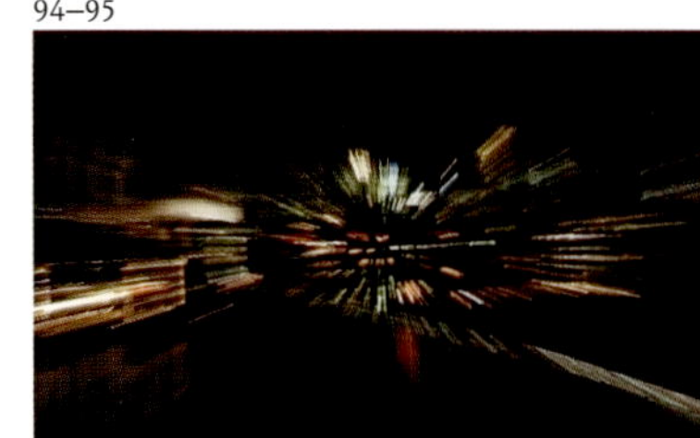
The Millennium Bridge & the City of London
18/01/08, 6.22 p.m.
Nikon D300, lens 18–200
ISO 1000, 1/4 sec, f7.1

96–97
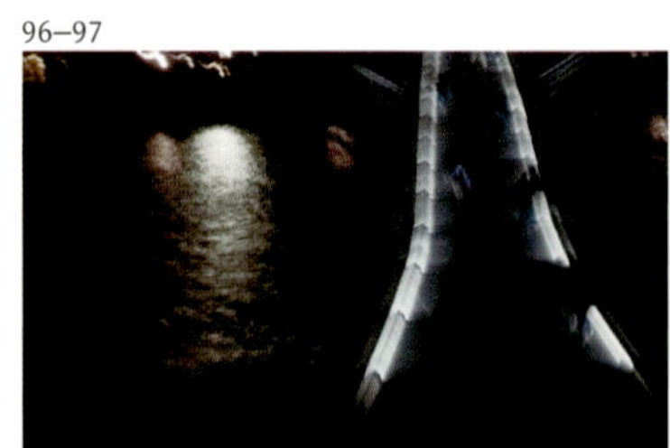
The Millennium Bridge
18/01/08
Nikon D300, lens 18–200
ISO 1000, 1.6 sec, f5.3

98–99
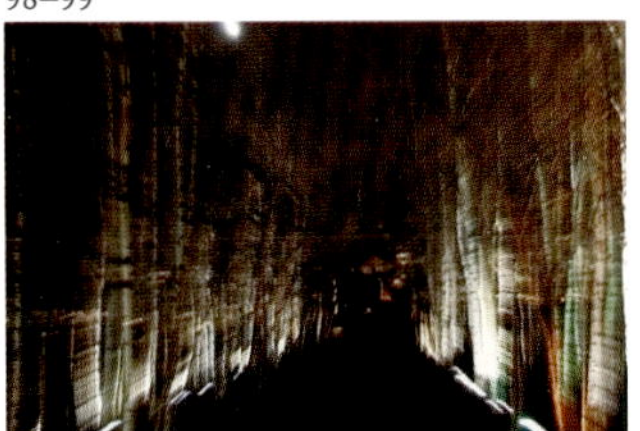
Silver birches at Tate Modern
18/01/08, 7.47 p.m.
Nikon D300, lens 18–200
ISO 1000, 1/8 sec, f3.8

100
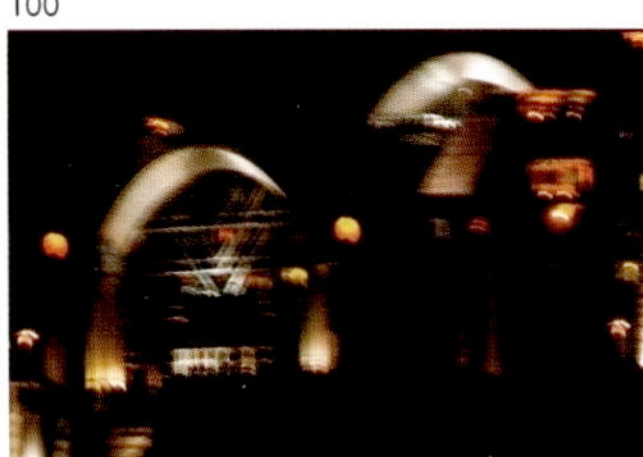
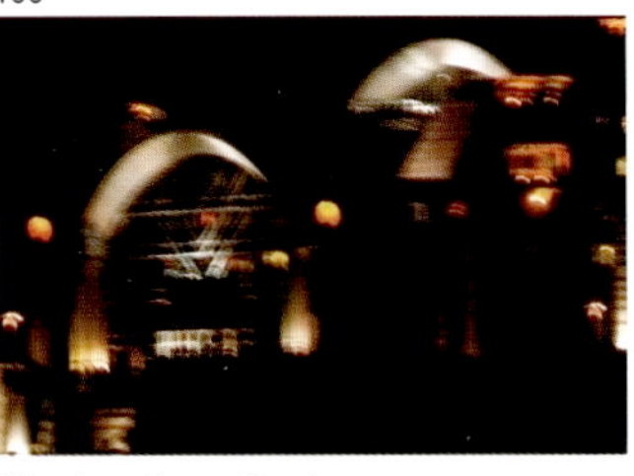
Charing Cross Station
10/05/08, 9.44 p.m.
Nikon D200, lens 18–200
ISO 1600, 1/13 sec, f4.5

101
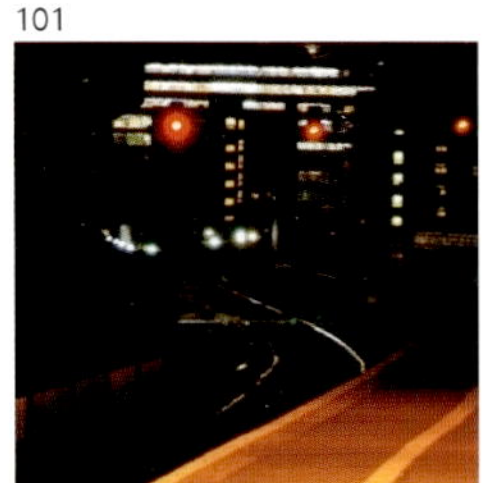
Blackfriars Station
10/05/08, 9.20 p.m.
Nikon D200, lens 18–200
ISO 1600, 1/6 sec, f5.3

102
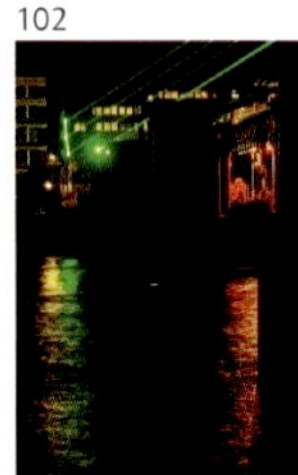
Green laser installation by Blackfriars Railway Bridge
03/10/08, 8.31 p.m.
Nikon D200, lens 70–300
ISO 640, 1/6 sec, f4.5

103
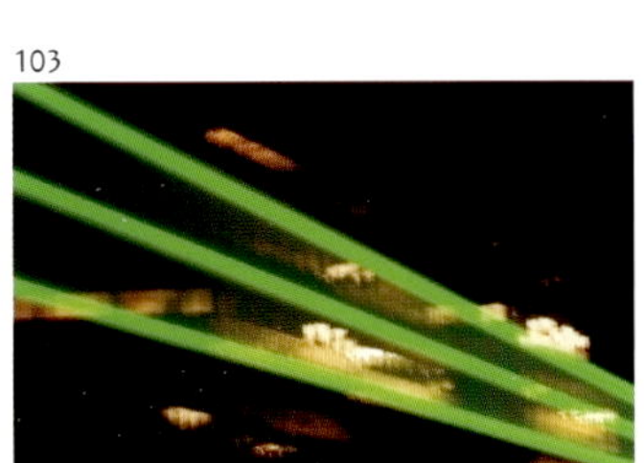
Green laser installation by Blackfriars Railway Bridge
03/10/08, 8.54 p.m.
Nikon D200, lens 70–300
ISO 640, 1.3 sec, f5.6

104–105
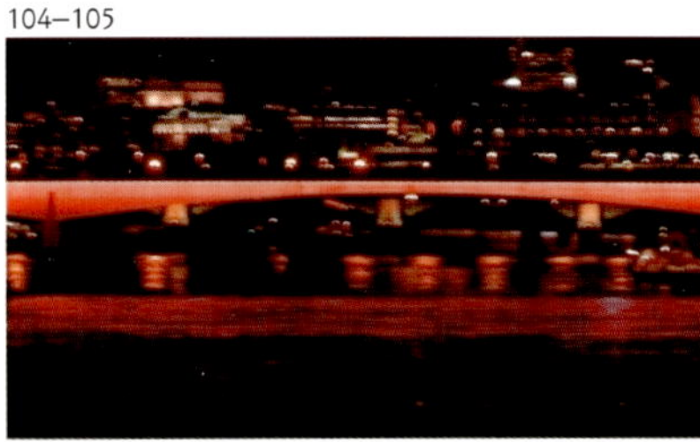
London Bridge
11/03/05, 8.40 p.m.
Nikon D70, lens 80–200
ISO 1600, 1/15 sec, f4.5

106

London Bridge & Telecom Tower
11/03/05, 8.38 p.m.
Nikon D70, lens 80–200
ISO 720, 1/3 sec, f4.5

107
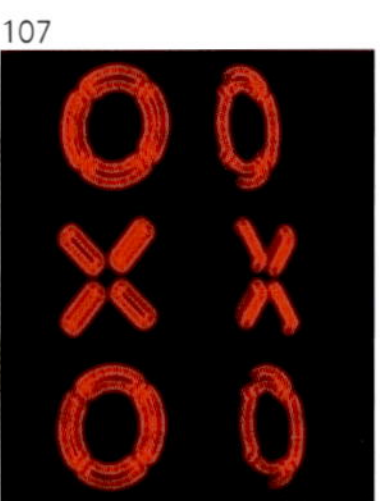

The Oxo Tower
10/05/08, 9.42 p.m.
Nikon D200, mirror lens 500
ISO1600, 1/50 sec, f8

108
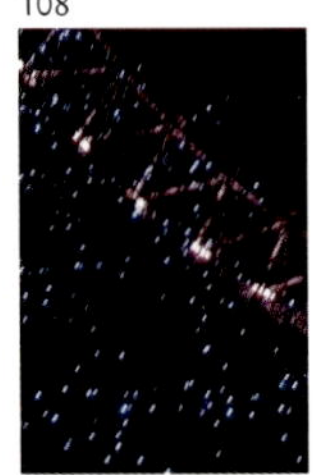
The London Eye
22/03/09, 8.14 p.m.
Nikon D200, lens 80–200
ISO 800, 1/13 sec, f5.6

109
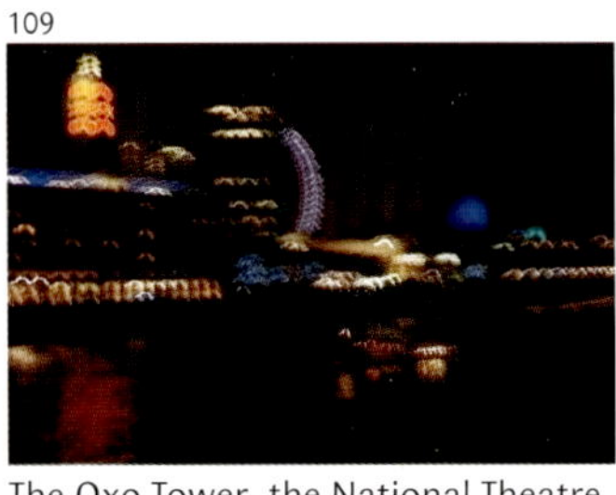
The Oxo Tower, the National Theatre & the London Eye
10/05/08, 9.50 p.m.
Nikon D200, lens 18–200
ISO 1600, 1.6 sec, f4.8

110
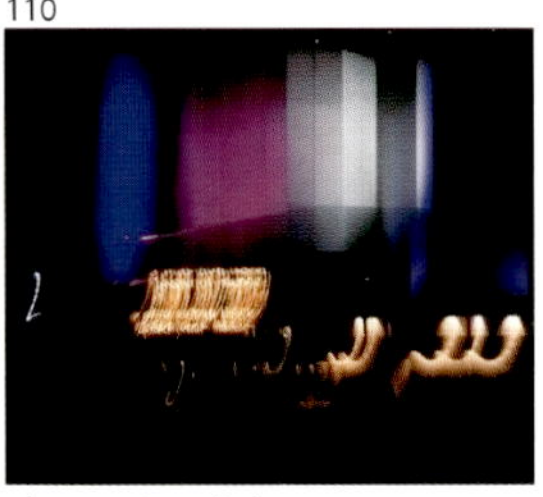
The National Theatre
30/05/08, 9.21 p.m.
Nikon D200, lens 18–200
ISO 800, 1/5 sec, f5.6

111
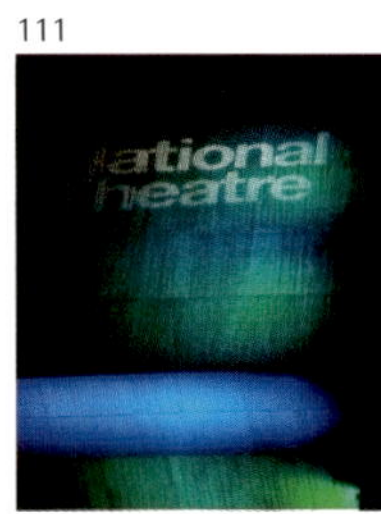
The National Theatre
10/05/08, 10.16 p.m.
Nikon D200, lens 18–200
ISO 1600, 1/25 sec, f9

112–113
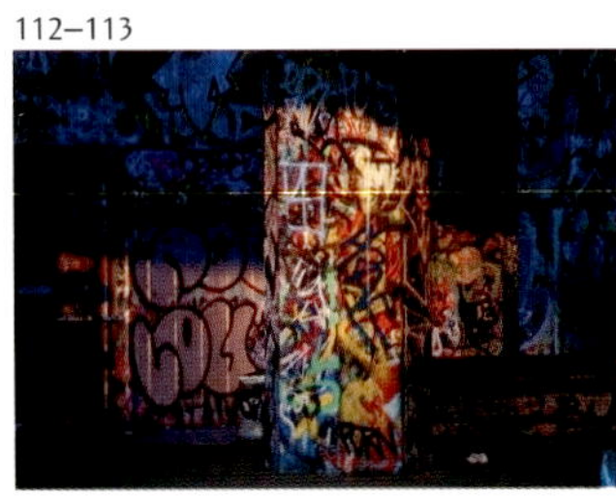
Graffiti on the South Bank
19/09/08, 7.33 p.m.
Nikon D300, lens 18–200
ISO 400, 1/50 sec, f6.3

114
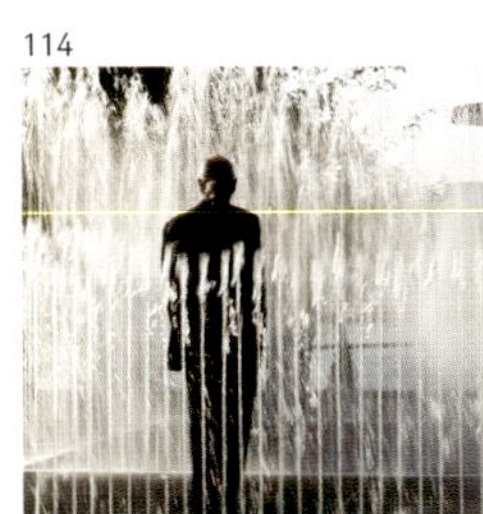
Fountain at the Festival Hall
13/09/07, 4.30 p.m.
Nikon D200, lens 28–105
ISO 100, 1/25 sec, f22

115
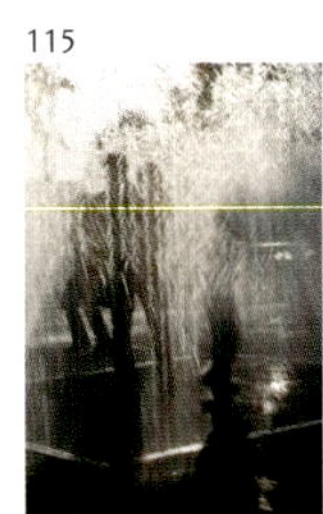
Scots football fans celebrating a win, in the Festival Hall fountains
13/09/07, 4.29 p.m.
Nikon D200, lens 28–105
ISO 100, 1/60 sec, f22

116
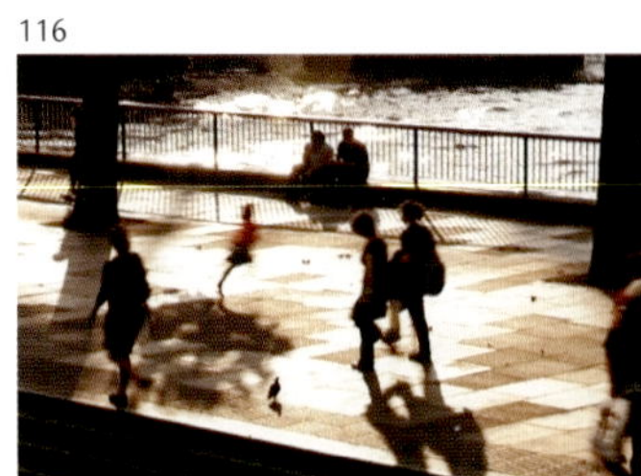
On the South Bank
13/09/07, 4.45 p.m.
Nikon D200, lens 28–105
ISO 100, 1/15sec, f22

117

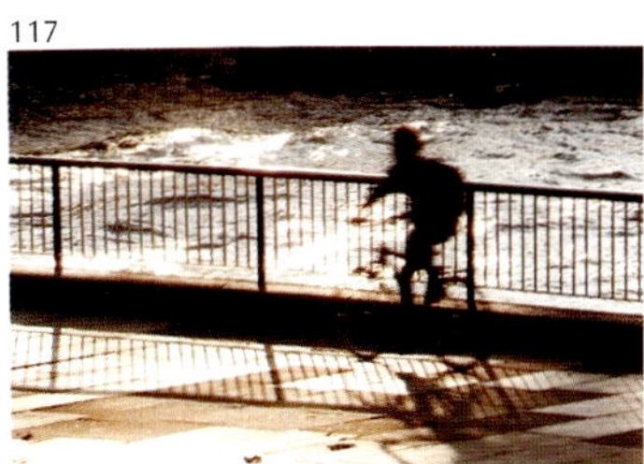

On the South Bank
13/09/07, 4.50 p.m.
Nikon D200, lens 70–300
ISO 100, 1/30 sec, f18

118

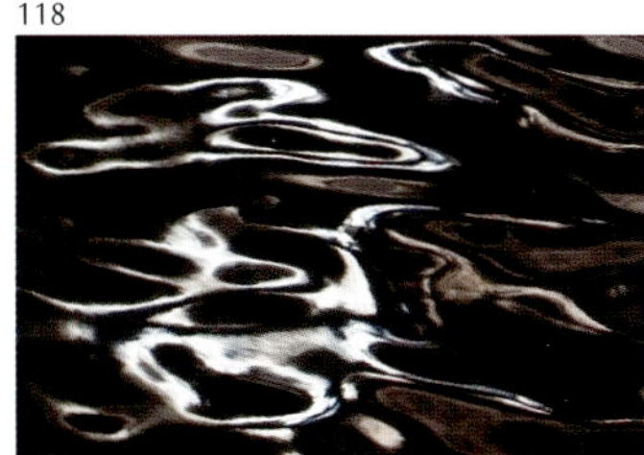

Satin-like reflections in the water
07/03/09, 2.49 p.m.
Nikon D300, lens 18–200
ISO 200, 1/500 sec, f11

119

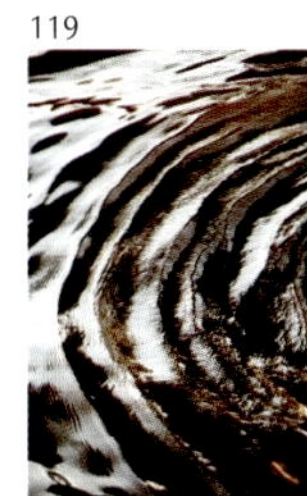

The Thames ebb tide
19/09/08, 7.22 p.m.
Nikon D300, lens 18–200
ISO 200, 1/50 sec, f5.6

120a

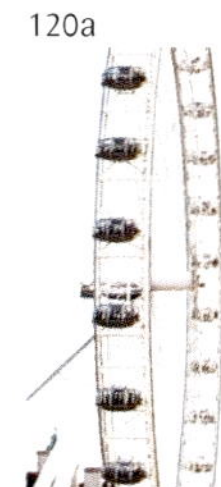

The London Eye
19/09/08, 7.08 p.m.
Nikon D300, lens 18–200
ISO 200, 1/60 sec, f5.6

120b

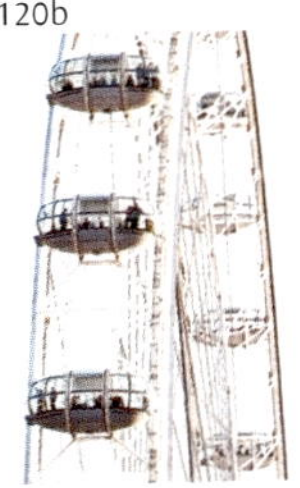

The London Eye
19/09/08, 6.59 p.m.
Nikon D300, lens 18–200
ISO 200, 1/30 sec, f9

121

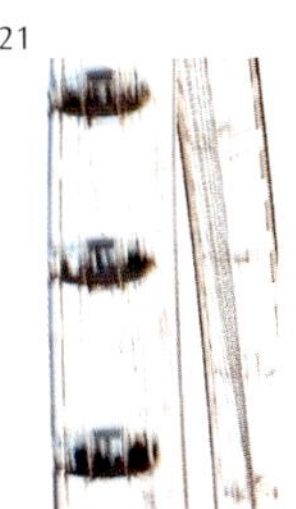

The London Eye
19/09/08, 6.57 p.m.
Nikon D300, lens 18–200
ISO 200, 1/25 sec, f11

122

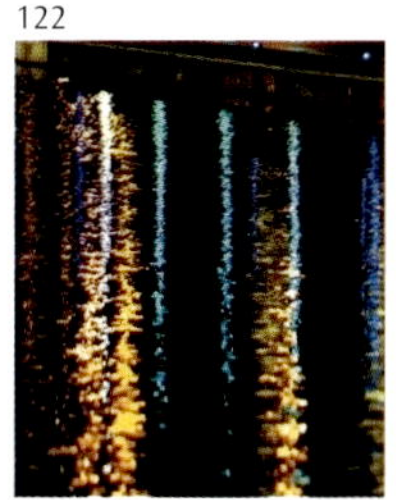

Reflections in the water
25/02/05 7.33 p.m.
Nikon D70, lens 80–200
ISO 1600, 1/20 sec, f2.8

123

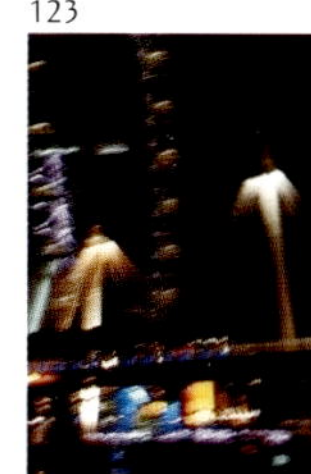

The London Eye &
Hungerford foot & rail bridges
02/10/08, 8.44 p.m.
Nikon D200, lens 70–300
ISO 640, 1.5 sec, f4.8

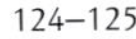

124–125

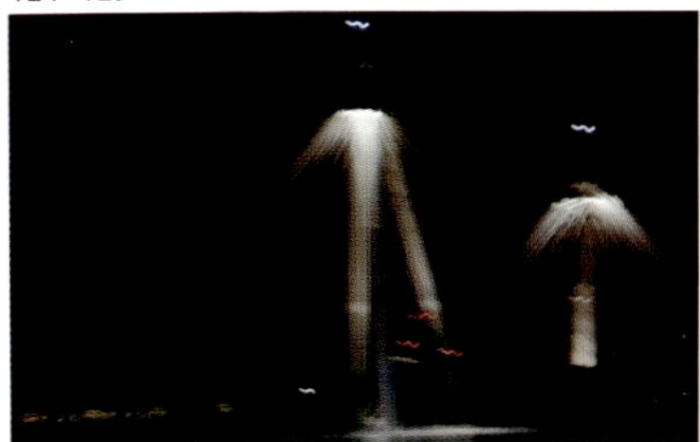

Hungerford foot and rail bridges
11/03/05, 9.51 p.m.
Nikon D300, lens 80–200
ISO 1600, 1/4 sec, f7.1

126

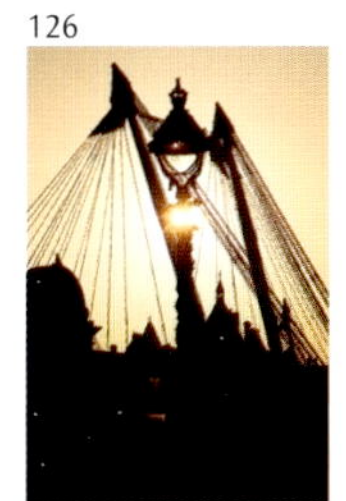

Hungerford foot & rail bridges
13/09/07, 5.11 p.m.
Nikon D200, lens 28 –105
ISO 100, 1/80 sec, f22

127

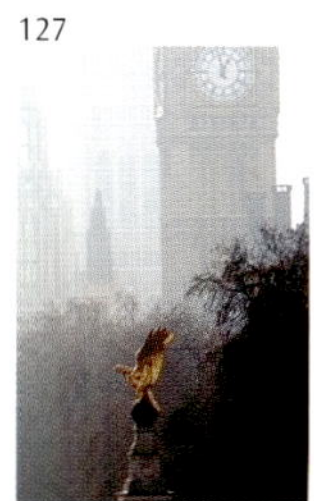

Golden Eagle
memorial sculpture
31/01/09, 2.57 p.m.
Nikon D300, lens 70–300
ISO 200, 1/500 sec, f10

128

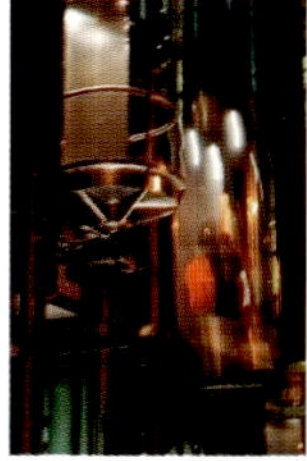

Exterior lifts of the
Channel 4 Building
09/03/05, 7.54 p.m.
Nikon D70, lens 28–105
ISO 1250, 1/3 sec, f6.3

129

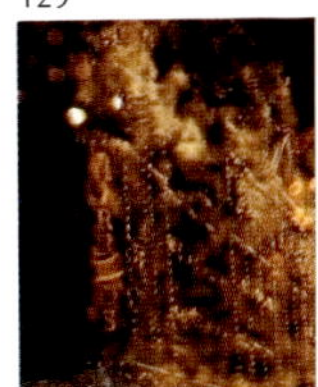

Harrods in the rain
11/03/05, 10.23 p.m.
Nikon D70, lens 28–105
ISO 1600, 1/6 sec, f22

130

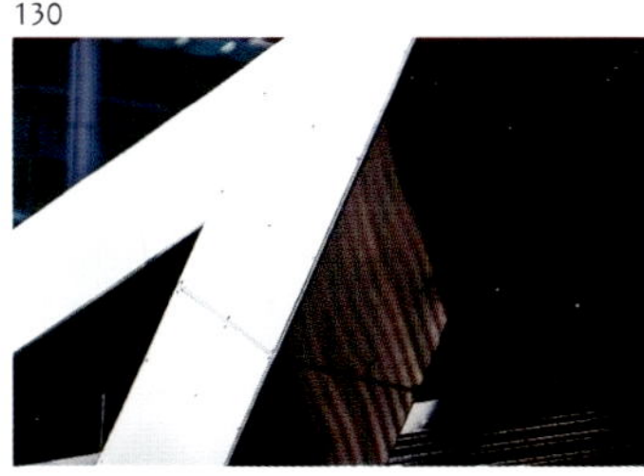

Vauxhall Bus Station
14/04/05, 6.09 p.m.
Nikon D70, lens 80–200
ISO 200, 1/400 sec, f5

131

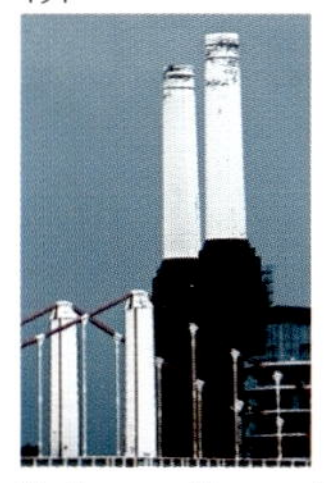

Battersea Power Station
15/04/05, 3.28 p.m.
Nikon D70, lens 80–200
ISO 200, 1/320 sec, f4.5

132

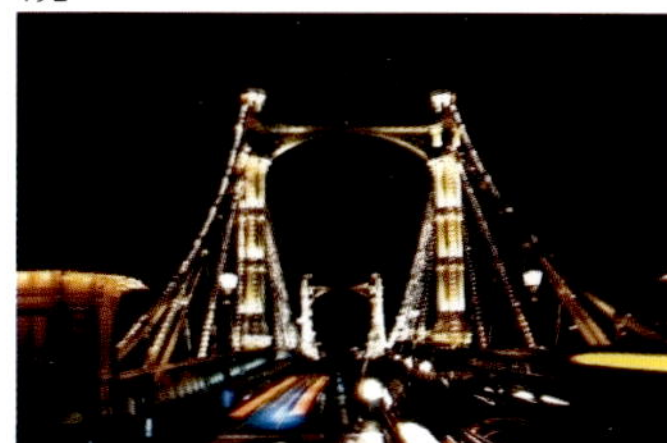

Albert Bridge
11/10/04, 9.48 p.m.
Nikon D70, lens 28–105
ISO 400, 1/60 sec, f8

133

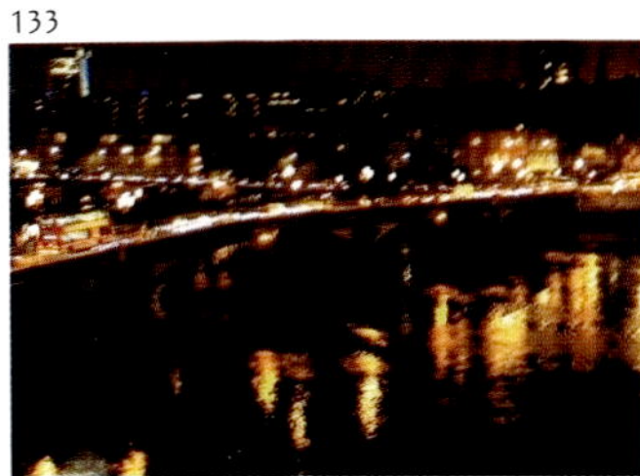

Battersea Bridge
29/10/04, 7.15 p.m.
Nikon D70, lens 28–105
ISO 800, 1.3 sec, f4.5

134

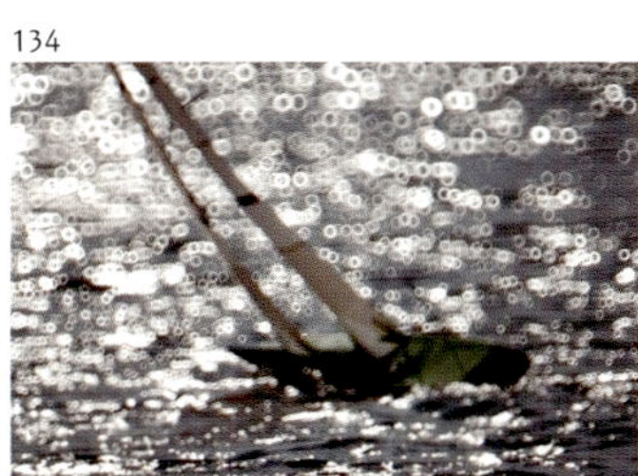

Model boats on the Round Pond,
Kensington Gardens
24/02/08, 12.03 p.m.
Nikon D200, mirror lens 500
ISO 100, 1/800 sec, f8

135

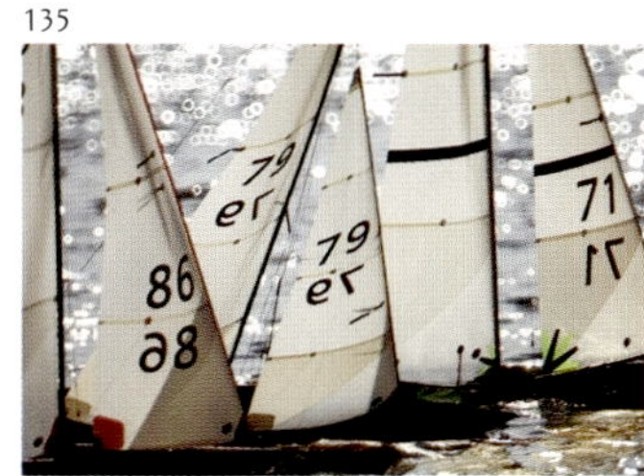

Model boats on the Round Pond,
Kensington Gardens
24/02/08, 12.12 p.m.
Nikon D200, mirror lens 500
ISO 100, 1/250 sec, f8

136–137

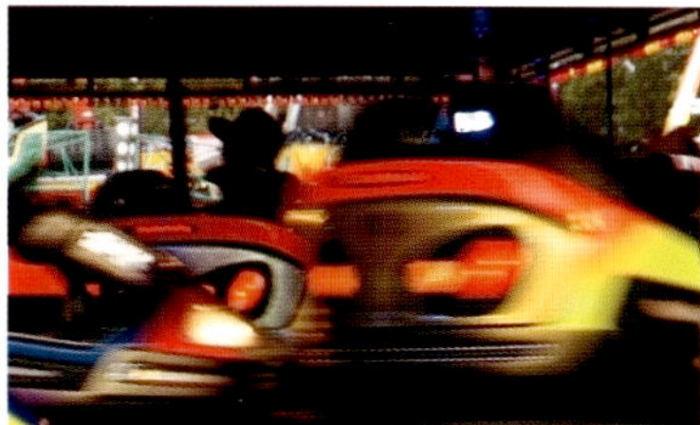

Bumper cars on Hampstead Heath
26/08/06, 5.10 p.m.
Nikon D70, lens 28–105
ISO 200, 1/30 sec, f9

144

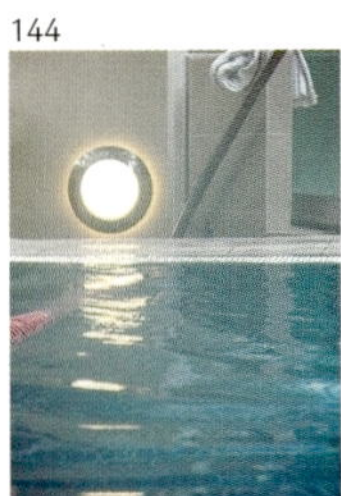

Brian's Light
28/05/09, 7.30 a.m.
Canon Powershot G7
ISO 200, 1/60 sec, f4

JACKET FRONT

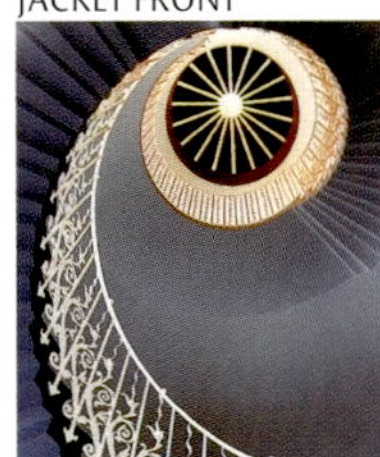

Tulip Staircase, Queen's House, Greenwich
28/02/06, 1.30 p.m.
Canon Powershot G7
ISO 200, 1/60 sec, f4

JACKET FRONT FLAP

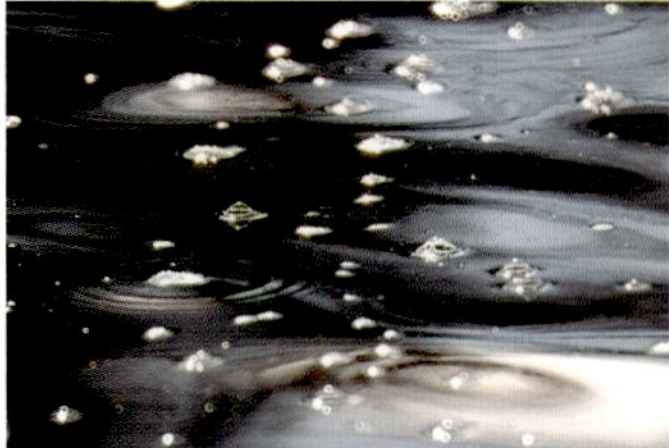

Fountains in the Italian Garden, Kensington Gardens
18/10/04, 10.50 a.m.
Nikon D70, mirror lens
ISO 200, 1/400 sec, f8

Acknowledgments

I owe enormous thanks to my agent, Bo Steer, who constantly pushes me to look deeper and go further. I shall always be grateful to Ian Hessenburg from the Photography Department at St Martin's School of Art, who steered me through the insecurity of being a student for almost the first time in my life.

Thanks also to my editor, Jo Christian of Frances Lincoln, who liked the pictures and has had the courage to publish them, and who keeps me from meandering too far off the track; and to my art director, Becky Clarke, also of Frances Lincoln, who is so very patient with my endless changes.

I don't know how I would have managed without Howard Woodruff of Flash Photodigital, who spent many hours helping and teaching me how to make the most of my digital pictures.

Lastly, thanks to my wonderful family, who are a continual support and full of love and encouragement.

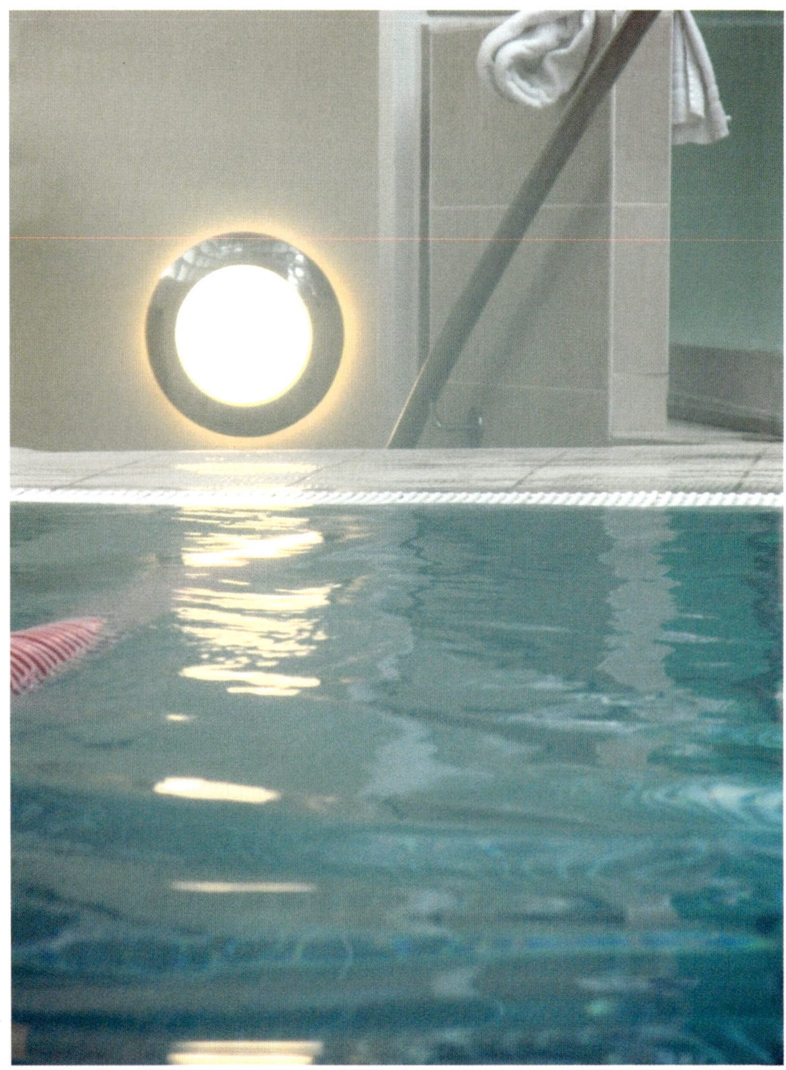

Brian's light